HE SHOT,
HE SCORED

The Official Biography

of Peter Ward

Matthew Horner

Sea View Media

First published in 2009 by Sea View Media,
6 Station Road, Bishopstone, East Sussex, BN25 2RB
www.seaviewmedia.com

ISBN 978-0-9562769-0-2

A CIP catalogue record for this book is
available from the British Library.

Typeset by: Rosamond Grupp (BookStudio@comcast.net)
Printed by: Cromwell Press Group

www.peterwardsoccer.com

To my beautiful wife, Jackie; my biggest fan.
Your passion for this book has always been as great
as mine and our dream has now come true.
I love you.

Peter

For Alex, Tony and Elizabeth Rachel.
Do whatever makes you happy
(and don't feel you have to read beyond this page).

Matt/'Dude'/Dad

CONTENTS

Acknowledgements

Peter Ward

Since I retired from football, I have wanted to write a book about my career. Last year, I was approached by Matt Horner and the rest is history. My very special thanks to Matt and Diana Horner for helping me to fulfil a dream that has been a long time coming.

To my Mum and Dad: Dad, if it weren't for you playing football with me in the garden, I might not have had this wonderful life.

To my three beautiful daughters, Rachael, Rebekah, and Louisa: I am so proud of you. Always keep dreaming big.

To my cousins, Bob and Dave: thanks for helping me through our younger years.

To Paul Camillin: thanks so much for always being my Brighton liaison.

To my heroes, Law, Best, and Charlton: thank you for inspiring me.

To the Ol' Scotland Yard Pub boys, the best mates a friend could ever have: George Clamp, Al Mcleod, Steve Deal, Mike Connell, Mark Lindsay, Bradley Chalmers, Refik Kozic, Jimmy Knowles, Paul Roe, Dougie Wark, Kevin Kiernan, Al Anderson, Steve Gogas, Mark Dillman and Ray Hales.

Special thanks to Eric and Eileen Cockayne, Jim Phelps, Ken Gutteridge, Peter Taylor, Alan Mullery, Mike Bamber, Harry Bloom, Brian Clough, Alan Hinton, Cornelia and Dick Corbett.

To my fans: thank you for always supporting me. My heart will always belong to Brighton. Up the Albion!

ACKNOWLEDGEMENTS

Matt Horner

If Sky Sports and the Internet had been around when Peter Ward was playing, it probably would have taken half the time that it has to research this book and I guess that I would have had only a fraction of the fun. So many people were asked to help and nearly all were willing to spare me some time. I hope that I don't miss anyone out in my thanks; but if I do, I'm sorry.

Thank you to Peter's family: Colin and Mavis, Rachael, Rebekah, Louisa, Sue, Gail and Mick, and cousin Dave.

Thank you to the managers: Alan Mullery, Alan Hinton, Rodney Marsh and Steve Gogas.

Thank you to Peter's ex-teammates: Ian Storey-Moore, Andy Rollings, Sammy Morgan, Brian Horton, Mark Lawrenson, Gary Williams, Ray Clarke, Jimmy Case, Ian Wallace, Viv Anderson, Gary Mills, Paul Hammond, Benny Dargle, Bernie James and Peter Millar.

Also, thank you to David Dresch at soccerfacts.org, Danny Hornby, Jan Reinertsen, the BigSoccer.com community, Mike Boult, David Falk at GOALSeattle.com, Gareth Glover from the Robert Eaton Memorial Fund, Dave Jenkins, Ian Morris, Paul Camillin and Ian Green at Brighton and Hove Albion, Fraser Nicholson at Nottingham Forest, Alan Webber and Paul Siegert at the BBC, Paul Hayward at the Guardian, Claire Huggins at Aston Villa FC, Terry Lawriw at the Cleveland City Stars, Lara Thorns and Jim Brown at Coventry City FC, Joanna Olszowska at EMG Sports, Julie Fort at North West Events, Kevin Hill, Rod Hadley at Tamworth FC, Steve Pearce at Ipswich Town FC, Tam Lever at West Ham United FC, Steve Powell at Houston Dynamo, and Tony Wainwright at the Evening Argus.

Apologies to all of the fans who sent me stories which I have not had the room to include.

Thanks to my editor, Diane Price, and to Kevin 'DJ Trevva' Browning for proofreading.

◇   ◇   ◇

Dad, thanks for taking me to my first game back in 1975 and so many since —it hasn't always been pleasing on the eye, but it has always been fun. Mum, thanks for not getting too cross when I made such a mess of the living room carpet practicing my Peter Ward skills. To Rachel and Dean, thanks for keeping the flag flying — I'm looking forward to sitting next to precious little Isabella at Falmer.

To my beautiful wife, Diana: thanks for your support, inspiration, ideas, feedback (honestly!) and for generally being there to make my life wonderful.

To my little Ellie Boo: thank you for being so patient over the past few months —you must have been bored of hearing me say 'sorry, not today— I need to finish my book'.

◇ ◇ ◇

Of course, thank you to Peter and Jacci Ward for trusting me with the project —I hope that I have done you justice.

UP THE ALBION.

CHAPTER 1

A Legend Returns

8th May, 2009
The Dripping Pan, Lewes, East Sussex

More than 28 years since he last played a competitive game for Brighton & Hove Albion, Peter Ward has returned to Sussex to appear in the eighth annual Robert Eaton Memorial Fund charity match.

An 8,000 mile round trip, a titanium knee and a little self-doubt ("I hope that they aren't too good") aren't enough to stop Brighton's all-time record scorer and Sussex's most popular sportsman from taking his place in the Brighton Supporters team. The presence of Ward, a few weeks short of his 54th birthday, has helped to draw a record crowd —double that of the previous year— and a healthy contribution to the REMF.

Many of the spectators and a few of his teammates are too young to have seen Ward's skills light up the Goldstone Ground pitch in the late 1970s. Others, including myself, are not, and have spent the last quarter of a century hoping that we might be lucky enough to see another player of Wardy's calibre don the blue and white stripes… we're still waiting.

Between 1976 and 1980, Peter Ward gave the Goldstone faithful the gift of expectation. If Ward had the ball, the anticipation levels in the crowd elevated beyond anything that I have experienced in thirty-five years of watching the Albion. For a seven-year-old boy living in Hollingdean, Brighton & Hove Albion made Saturdays special: Peter Ward made Brighton & Hove Albion special. Evening games were even more exciting — the smell of pipe smoke still evokes memories of the buzzing Goldstone floodlights transforming the pitch into the most wonderful bright green stage.

I was far from alone in my adoration for the Seagulls and their wispy, high-stepping number 8. Crowds of over 25,000 were commonplace and Ward was the main attraction.

His legacy continues and his popularity seems undiminished: a framed picture of Wardy overlooks the desk of Dean Harding, the owner of Hardings Catering based at Brighton Racecourse. A similar photo adorns the office of Paul Goldsmith, the boss of IT First fifteen miles or so up the road. There's even a poster of 'The Legend' hanging in my local fishmongers' store, twenty miles out of Brighton. Maybe it is, as my wife would say, that 'men of a certain age' don't want to lose touch with the days when the goals were flying in and everything else seemed so much simpler.

If any proof is required to confirm Ward's status, it is readily available: in 2005, viewers of BBC Football Focus voted Ward as Brighton's all-time cult-hero. Four years later, participants in a Sky Sports survey agreed: Peter Ward is Brighton's All-Time Great.

◇ ◇ ◇

Amongst the crowd at Lewes is Lisa Stevenson. Lisa and her husband John owned Albion Gifts on Brighton seafront. John, an avid Albion supporter, had become friends with Peter Ward during a family holiday in Florida in early 2001.

On one of Peter's trips to the UK, John presented him with a gift —a seat from the late Goldstone Ground. The gift — "the best that I've ever received from a fan"— is displayed alongside Peter's trophies and medals in the front room of his Tampa home. Sadly, John passed away suddenly in April of 2004, leaving two sons, Jack and Harvey Albion.

In 2001, Peter had sent a signed photograph to John's brother's brother-in-law in New York. The recipient of the photograph worked in the World Trade Centre —a gentleman by the name of Robert Eaton.

◇ ◇ ◇

Brighton's opponents in the REMF match are supporters of Crystal Palace, a team whose rivalry with Brighton helped make the glory days so much more exciting, and whose fans sang their own edited, less-than-complimentary version of 'He Shot, He Scored, it must be Peter Ward'.

Palace clearly haven't read the script and score two early goals. What's more, their left-back demonstrates that old habits die hard by twice flooring Ward with crunching challenges from behind. Maybe his tackles are a tribute to football in the 1970s?

Any motivational half-time talk for the Brighton team appears to have had little effect as Palace score again shortly thereafter. A ray of hope as Albion get a goal is quickly dimmed as Palace score a fourth. Game over? Well, not quite: a second Brighton goal is scored; then a third, by Ward's ex-Brighton team-mate Ricky Marlowe. Next, in true dramatic fashion, a late far-post header makes the score 4-4.

A penalty shoot-out begins to decide the outcome. First up for Brighton, Peter Ward…

CHAPTER 2

GEORGIE BEST BOOTS AND BROKEN WINDOWS

He would play with his mates and he would always make them look like fools, even if they were two or three years older. He always made people look daft with his skills: he was very small and people didn't believe that he could play football until they actually saw him play.

– Colin Ward, on his son Peter.

Peter David Ward was born on Wednesday, 27th July, 1955 at St. Michael's Hospital in Lichfield, Staffordshire. The first child of Colin and Mavis Ward, Peter's early months were spent in Tamworth, about 20 miles to the north east of Birmingham, where his father worked as a compositor for the Tamworth Herald.

Peter's parents, Mavis and Colin, were married in the May before his birth: they first met at the age of 15, as members of the Derby Serenaders Carnival band. The Serenaders were formed by Fred Ward —Peter's grandfather— and three of his friends shortly before the start of the Second World War; the band is still going strong. The band was very much the focal point for the Wards during the 50s, 60s and 70s; just one of a number of romances that blossomed to the beat of the Serenaders was that between drum major Colin and solo drummer Mavis. It wasn't long before baby Peter was encouraged to play the music that was in his blood, as one of Colin's earliest memories of his son illustrates: 'Peter was also a drummer and, although it is hard to believe, he was playing a miniature drum when he was sat in his pram —it was in his genes.'

With Colin working full-time, Mavis found life in Tamworth to be a little lonely; just two months after Peter's birth the family moved to Burton, within nine miles of Mavis' family and friends in Derby. For the next two years, the young family lived in Burton High Street, in a flat which had been provided by Colin's new employers, Tresises Printers.

Mavis remembers young Peter as a well-behaved youngster, who rarely provoked cross words from his parents: 'A real good little lad. You could take him anywhere: he was marvellous.' These sentiments are echoed by her husband: 'He was no trouble; always well behaved.'

By the time Peter could walk, the family had moved again: this time, to a new council house in Chaddesden, a suburb of Derby. This was home for Peter until he moved to Brighton two months before his twentieth birthday in 1975. Over 50 years after they first moved in, this remains the home of Colin and Mavis.

The new front garden provided the perfect venue for Ward junior to learn the skills that would see him become one of the hottest properties in British football. Although, as Colin recalls, the garden did need a little alteration:

> Peter kicked a ball around as soon as he could walk. From the time that he was two, we would play for hours. We used to play in front of the window: we had specifically laid slabs for that purpose.

> We had an archway with roses which was one goal; the end of the house was the other goal. I didn't let him have it all his own way. We played with a little plastic ball and he could instinctively kick it with either foot.

In addition to providing the improvised front garden training venue, the move to Chaddesden also situated the family within walking distance of the home of Colin's brother, Maurice, and his family. Colin had always been a keen footballer, and his older brother Maurice had been a very skilful player. Coveted by the then top division Preston North End, Maurice declined the chance to sign a professional contract as his wife thought that the £8 a week on offer was not sufficient to look after their family. Maurice's sons, Bob and Dave, were born within a couple of years of Peter, and proved to be ideal playmates.

Peter and his cousins were rarely separated, progressing from the front garden to the street and then to the local recreation field. As Peter explains, football was quickly becoming his focus:

> I was always playing football with my cousins in the street. Then we went up the green —a little field about 10 minutes walk from my house. From age 6 or 7 to 15, we picked two sides and we played, every night. Homework, what was that? I never did homework —I wasn't thick but I didn't care to do any. I did it when I got to school in the morning.

> I didn't do badly at tests and exams —I'd get A's and B's— but then I'd have E's and stuff in the class because, as the teachers said, I was a little pain in the arse.

> Every break time we just played football —we didn't do anything else.

As captain of the Cavendish Close Junior School football team, Peter decided that he was going to be a centre forward:

> I was always a forward —scoring goals. Dribble the ball and score goals, that's all I ever did —I was a greedy little so-and-so. My teammates would say "give him a ball and we'll have another one." I was hopeless at defending, though, and tried to avoid having to do too much of that!

12

In the winter, football would give way to rugby during physical education lessons, much to the young Ward's irritation:

I hated rugby. I used to go mad when we had to do rugby in PE because the idiot teacher would always get me, as the smallest, to tackle someone. I would always be the stupid hooker in the middle as well, getting punched and kicked —I hated it. I used to tell them, "I'm not playing bloody rugby!"

I didn't mind playing cricket in the summer months and I was alright, but I wouldn't say I was any good. I just wanted to play football.

In the Cavendish Close team, Ward was partnered in attack by Andy Rowland. Rowland also progressed to the professional game and went on play over 330 times for Swindon Town.

At the age of nine, with the birth of his sister, Gail, Peter lost his only-child status and with it the focus of his parents' attention. This may have been fortuitous for Peter, as the balance between school work and football was tipping very much toward the latter.

As Ward and his cousins grew and became quicker and stronger, wayward shots at goal and misplaced passes during their street soccer games became a concern for the neighbours:

I broke many windows at home and on the street. I remember one day when I was playing in the street: I'd hit this ball really hard and my shoe flew off. The ball went one way; my shoe went the other and hit and broke my next-door neighbour's window. If something like that happened we'd normally run off, but my shoe had been stuck in the window so I couldn't plead innocent to that one!

Another time, I was playing in a friend's back yard. I hit this volley straight through the next-door neighbour's window and the ball landed on their table as they were having Sunday dinner. I could hear the woman shrieking 'Peter Ward! We're going to tell your father!' I got a crack around the head and we had to pay for a new pane of glass.

◇　◇　◇

Peter enrolled at Darwin Senior School at the age of eleven, which meant the end of the prolific Ward/Rowland partnership. Andy attended a school on the other side of the city while Peter settled in to life at Darwin, affectionately known as Colditz by its students.

The big star of Derby schools football at the time was Steve Powell. Playing for Bemrose School, Powell caught the eye of legendary management duo, Brian Clough and Peter Taylor, who, at the time, were in charge of Derby County.

Steve made his debut in the Derby first team just 30 days after his 16th birthday and won the league championship in his first season with the Rams.

Ward was not given a chance to play for the Derby Schools representative team although Powell and Rowland were both regular members. Despite scoring goals by the hatful, Ward's slight frame meant that he was consistently overlooked for opportunities beyond his school team:

> I never played for Derby boys or the County representative team because they thought that I was too small. I didn't complain about it at that age because I assumed that they knew what they were talking about.

> I remember going to Derby County's camp for two or three weeks during one school holiday. One of the trainers was Jim Walker [Derby County midfielder], with whom I later played at Brighton.

> I won the Best Camper award in my Georgie Best boots, but they still weren't interested in giving me a trial for their boys' team.

Colin Ward agrees that his son's small stature made it easy for the scouts and coaches to fail to notice Peter:

> Peter was successful in both Junior and Senior school sides but it was the big lads who were chosen to represent the town team. He always made people look daft with his skills: he was very small and people couldn't believe that he could play football until they saw him play. All the kids at school would tell me that he should be in the Derby schools team.

Ignoring the knockbacks from the regional representative teams, Colin was still hopeful that his son had a chance to fulfil his dream of becoming a professional footballer and tried to encourage league teams to take a look at him:

> I wrote a letter to Matt Busby at Manchester United telling him about Peter. The club wrote back to me and they wanted to know in which fixtures they could come to see him play. Unfortunately, he was at the age where there were no set fixtures, so I couldn't send a useful reply.

Even within school, Ward's size led those in a position to motivate and inspire to do the exact opposite. In his final year of school, Peter had an appointment with one of the teachers, Mr Kelly, who had taken on the role of career advisor for the soon to be departing students. Asked what he wanted to do, Ward had only one answer: "Be a footballer". With no hesitation, Mr. Kelly offered his advice: "No chance. You are too small." With that, the meeting was over. Years later, Ward resisted the urge to say 'Up Yours' to Mr Kelly when he was invited back to the school as guest of honour at an awards ceremony.

◇ ◇ ◇

Like many boys, Peter's football allegiance was, and still is, firmly with Manchester United (even if he is a little embarrassed to give any indication of this when in the company of Brighton supporters). Much like the present day, it was a hugely exciting time for United; league titles, European success and the attacking trio of George Best, Denis Law and Bobby Charlton created a combination of excitement and skill that was irresistible to many young football fans.

Peter's bedroom was a shrine to United: 'MU' was written in huge red letters across his bedroom ceiling, "so that people in the street could see it." The tribute was somewhat tainted when little sister Gail decided that she wanted her half of the room to be decorated with pictures of the children's television puppets, singing piglet twins Pinky and Perky.

Occasionally, Peter travelled on his own to watch United play; one such trip occurred during a family holiday in Blackpool. With his parents' permission, Peter, who was only 10 or 11 years old at the time, caught the train from Blackpool to Manchester to see United take on Newcastle in an evening kick-off. On another occasion at about the same time, Peter travelled alone on a train to London to see United take on Tottenham Hotspur at White Hart Lane. Peter was kept out of trouble by an older Tottenham supporter whom he'd met in the capital and, having enjoyed the game, returned home safe and sound.

One United game against Tottenham remains clear in Peter's memory:

> I was at the game when Bestie [George Best] scored the lob against Tottenham. I was in the North Stand at Old Trafford. I'd gone on the train, changed at Stoke.

> George was my favourite player and I used to pretend to be him when we played in the streets as kids. Unfortunately, he finished playing in the States before I went over there and I didn't get to play against him.

> I've got one of Bestie's shirts, though —someone offered me five grand for it. I was tempted, but didn't sell it.

This game took place in February of 1971, when Peter was 15 years old. It was George Best's first game at Old Trafford, following the lifting of a ban imposed by his own club. Best had been punished for missing a training session: the result of an extended stay in the London flat of his latest girlfriend, actress Sinead Cusack. Back in time to face Tottenham, Best produced a glorious display in a 2-1 win for United.

Phil Beal, one of the Spurs players who were bested by George's precise, gentle lob in this game, eventually signed with Brighton in July of 1975; two months after Ward. Also part of the Tottenham team that day were two more of Peter's future team-mates, Joe Kinnear and Martin Chivers, and Peter's future manager, Alan Mullery. Coincidently, one of Mullery's first decisions after becoming Ward's Brighton manager was to terminate the contracts of both

Beal and Kinnear. Beal eventually joined the Los Angeles Aztecs, where his teammates included none other than George Best.

Ward was keen on seeing as many of United's matches as he could, but, closer to home, Clough and Taylor's revolution at Derby County was capturing the imagination of the locals. Colin Ward bought season tickets for himself and his son and these were renewed until Peter signed a professional contract with Burton Albion. By this time, Clough and Taylor had left Derby and taken over at Third Division Brighton. Whilst Clough had soon moved on, this time to an ill-fated 44-day reign at Leeds United, Taylor stayed on the south coast and was responsible for signing Ward for Brighton.

◇   ◇   ◇

During his final couple of years at school, on the rare occasions that Ward's focus veered away from football, his attentions moved to girls. His cousin Dave was a keen ally in this pursuit:

> *I would tell my parents that I was going to Pete's to play football and he would tell his parents that he was coming over to mine. Instead, we would go and meet a couple of girls at the local park. One of the girls was Julie, to whom I've now been married for 30 years.*

Young Ward's courting techniques sometimes scored more highly for initiative than for honesty…

> *When I was a kid, there was a girl whom I really liked at school; unfortunately, one of my friends, Steve Hendry, also liked her. He asked me to give her some chocolates that he had bought for her. I said that I would and I took them 'round to her, but I told her they were from me! I don't know if either of them ever found out.*

The Serenaders band was a popular meeting point for the local youth and it was here that Peter met his future wife, Suzanne (Sue) Shardlow:

> *I met Pete the day after he turned 14. On Sunday mornings, we would practice with the band; in the afternoons, the boys would play football and the girls would go to watch. Sometimes, we'd be invited to Sunday tea with them and sometimes, we wouldn't, so we'd just go home.*

> *Pete's total passion was football: Manchester United, playing football, every minute was football. I didn't mind because I liked football too. I was a Derby fan and Pete and his dad used to go. Me and my friends would go and stand on the terraces, the rowdy side, and we'd see Pete and his dad in the posh seats.*

◇   ◇   ◇

In addition to providing a social focus, the Serenaders —as an extended family— also provided Peter with the opportunity to expand his football horizons beyond the school team. Colin Ward explains:

> *The band led to Peter's involvement with the local football team. Once a year, the band would spend a weekend in Lowestoft to compete in a contest. There would be a challenge football match on the beach between the Serenaders and members of the other bands. Peter would play and always excelled.*

> *Charlie Simpson, who married Peter's cousin Sue, was a player with a local side. He recommended Peter to his club, Borrowash United. Many of the players thought Peter would be too small, but they soon realised how good a player he was.*

Peter continues the story:

> *Until I was 14 I only played at school —there weren't any organised leagues apart from school. When I was 14, I played for a men's team, Borrowash United.*

> *That was good: I had a couple of "uncles" playing. Well, they weren't uncles but cousin's husbands, so they were young. They were in their 20s and I was 14.*

Playing on Saturdays at Deans Drive recreation ground in sky blue and maroon striped shirts, Borrowash United was run by Eric and Eileen Cockayne. Eric managed the first team and his wife Eileen —being a very early trailblazer for women football managers— took charge of the reserves. Peter became good friends with Eric and Eileen's sons, Dave and Mick, and was a regular guest at the Cockayne's dinner table.

Having quickly broken into the first team, Ward was presented with the club's Most Improved Player award for the 1971-72 season. The following season, he was voted the club's Player of the Year as United were runners-up in the Derbyshire Football Association Junior Cup.

By now, Ward's talent for goal scoring was starting to attract attention and he was approached by one of the top local senior teams, Redfern Athletic. "I joined Redfern Athletic, who were a very good local team in Derby. I scored seven one day, and I'd only been there a few games."

Sixteen-year-old Ward followed the seven-goal haul with another five goals just two weeks later. With Ward's goals as a catalyst, Redfern went on to be crowned Derby and District Senior Football League Division One champions and Cup winners for 1972-73. They followed this with the Premier League double the following season.

◇ ◇ ◇

Peter left school at the age of 15 without any formal qualifications and started a three year apprenticeship at Rolls-Royce, one of the largest employers in the area. Life at 'Royces' didn't hold huge appeal for Ward and when he left, three years later, he vowed never to work in a factory again:

> *Everybody went from school to a job. I had a few interviews at different places and chose Rolls Royce for some reason, I don't know why —I was hopeless. I was an aero engine fitter and was there a couple of years— I passed my apprenticeship.*

> *It was near my Grandad's house and if I was on nightshift I would sneak out and go round to him to watch Sportsnight or Star Soccer on telly.*

> *I didn't want to work — I hated it. I remember thinking, is this it?*

◇ ◇ ◇

Ward's goals ensured that factory life certainly wasn't 'it' and playing two or three times every weekend didn't slow down his progress. Three hat-tricks in a matter of weeks, including one in a 9-0 win against Normanton Celtic, had put Ward in the local league spotlight even if, by today's standards, his pre-match preparation wasn't ideal:

> *I played for Redfern on a Saturday and Borrowash Athletic on a Sunday afternoon. I also used to play for GIC [General Industrial Cleaners] in the mornings on a Sunday and then Athletic in the afternoon. GIC was great: I'd get 7 or 8 goals a game. We used to play on a Saturday, go out on the piss, then play twice on a Sunday.*

Touted as 'outstanding' in the local paper after having scored 6 goals for Borrowash in an 11-2 win against Sinfin United, Ward couldn't stop scoring: 5 against Ley's and Ewart's, 4 against Challeston and 2 more in the title decider against British Celanese.

Jim Phelps, who scouted local talent in the Derby area for Burton Albion, was well aware of Ward's talent. Having worked with him at Borrowash United, Phelps recommended Ward to Albion manager Ken Gutteridge. Impressed with what he saw, Gutteridge offered Ward an amateur contract and Ward joined the Southern League club hot on the heels of their promotion to the Premier Division.

CHAPTER 3

A GEM UNCOVERED AT BURTON

He was sharp and bright and had an eye for goal.
Everybody, myself included, thought he had the potential to
go on and to further his career —which of course he did.

— Ian Storey-Moore

Burton Albion had just regained their place in the Southern League Premier Division by finishing second in the First Division in 1973-74. Managed by Ken Gutteridge, who had a reputation as a tough disciplinarian, the Brewers team consisted of a mixture of seasoned ex-pros, non-league journeymen and talented local players. A few of the players had professional contracts with the club and also worked separate full-time jobs, while many of the other players were amateurs, playing only for expenses.

The biggest name at the club was Ian Storey-Moore who, during 10 years with Nottingham Forest, had become one of the club's all-time greats. Financial problems at Forest in early 1972 precipitated the need to balance the books and selling 28 year-old Storey-Moore, who had been top scorer at the club for five seasons between 1966 and 1972, was seen as a quick way to raise much needed funds. A fee of £200,000 was agreed with Manchester United, but after only a season and a half at Old Trafford, Storey-Moore suffered an injury that forced him to retire from full-time professional football. Manchester United's loss was Burton's gain: Storey-Moore's became the highest profile signing in the club's history.

◇   ◇   ◇

The Southern League, a forerunner of today's Conference, was the highest level of semi-professional league in England. Thirty-five years on, 64-year-old Storey-Moore, who is now Chief Scout at Premier League Aston Villa, remembers the league as being very competitive:

The standard was pretty good — it was a tough old league, full of ex-pros. It was a very physical league and you had to have a tough mentality as well as good ability. As preparation for the professional game, it was ideal for young players.

Storey-Moore was very much the star of Burton's first team at the time that Ward started to make his mark in the Burton second string under the management of reserve team trainer Harold Bodle. Enjoying twice-weekly training sessions and benefitting from playing with a higher standard of teammates, Ward's talents impressed Bodle: the trainer had little hesitation in recommending him to first team manager Ken Gutteridge.

Ward's chance came a mere month into the 1974 season —Monday 2nd September— when Gutteridge picked him to play for the first team in the Birmingham Senior Cup game at Tamworth, Peter's place of birth.

As debuts go it was, as Peter says, 'the best': he played alongside Ian Storey-Moore and Frank Wignall, two ex-England internationals. Wignall had been Storey-Moore's team-mate at Forest and had also played for Everton, Wolves and Derby.

Debutant Ward grabbed the headlines with a spectacular hat-trick in a 4-1 win for Burton. With two ex-internationals and one future international in attack, it was little surprise that the Brewers so dramatically outplayed Tamworth.

> *I remember every goal. The first one was a smash from the top of the box, the second was a quick free-kick — Frankie Wignall put me through and I placed it in the corner. The third one was a throw-in from the left: I turned someone, cut inside and went past two or three players then stroked it in — brilliant.*
>
> *It was great: I was playing with two internationals, Wignall and Storey-Moore, and I couldn't believe how well it had gone.*

Gutteridge was delighted with Ward's display, calling it a 'dream debut', and while the 489 spectators present were no doubt impressed by the Burton newcomer, they probably would not have believed that just three years and five days later he would be scoring another debut hat-trick — this time for the England Under 21 team in front of a sell-out crowd of 18,500.

The following day, the headline in the Burton Mail read "Debut boy Pete hits hat-trick as Albion rip Tamworth apart". The next eight months would see many more headlines for Burton and their new star as they headed to their highest-ever league placing.

◇　◇　◇

Ward, not surprisingly, kept his place in the Burton side as they travelled to Plough Lane two days later to take on Wimbledon. The Dons were on their way to the first of three successive Southern League championships and proved a stiff test for the Brewers.

Ward's golden touch didn't take long to resurface as he scored the opening goal after just four minutes — a goal described as "a brilliant effort" in the

Burton Mail. Reporter Dave Fern compared the striker to Leeds' and England's supreme goal-poacher, Allan 'Sniffer' Clarke. Unfortunately, despite Ward's early goal, the hosts were too strong for Burton and won the match 3-2.

Gutteridge, sensing that they had discovered a potential gem in Ward, wanted to ensure that the Brewers were in a position to benefit from any potential future transfer. The day after the Wimbledon defeat, Ward was offered a professional contract which he signed readily. The contract rewarded Ward with a basic wage of £5 per week (assuming he was playing in the first team), which doubled after he had made 6 first team appearances. With a win bonus adding £2, and a draw £1, Ward, who was earning just £3 a week at Rolls-Royce, could earn £14 per week if the Brewers won on a Saturday as well as midweek.

Ward's productive introduction to the first team had not escaped the attention of teams from higher up the league pyramid and, by the end of September, scouts from Ipswich Town, Arsenal, Norwich City and Derby County had all made trips to watch him in action. Chelsea manager Dave Sexton travelled to Chelmsford to watch the young striker and Blackburn manager Gordon Lee witnessed Ward's debut hat-trick at Tamworth. Lee, who had recently taken over at Blackburn, had a keen eye for non-league talent and, as Port Vale manager, had signed Ward's future teammate Brian Horton from the little known West Midlands League part-timers Hednesford Town.

During the next month, Ward's form dipped —quite possibly as a result of pressure from the increased attention and publicity— and his goalscoring touch deserted him.

Gutteridge made the decision to drop young Ward for the trip to Cambridge City in early October, but he was retained as a substitute. An injury to one of his teammates early in the second half gave Ward an opportunity to prove that he was worthy of a place in the starting eleven. The young striker grabbed the chance, scoring the first of two late Burton goals to secure a 2-0 win. Ward's performance had ensured that his absence from the starting line-up did not extend beyond one game.

The Southern League was no place for the faint of heart, with its big, bruising, no-nonsense centre-backs: this provided a real test for lightweight Ward, who weighed in at a little over 10 stone. Regularly singled out by the opposing team's hatchet men, he was often given a rough ride and, in a bruising encounter at Stourbridge in early November, stud-marks visible above his right knee (courtesy of a high challenge from Stourbridge's ironically named full-back, Graham Saint), he was substituted part-way through the second half.

The return fixture with Cambridge on 16th November saw Ward back at his best: he scored two goals in a 4-2 victory. His display left the Burton manager raving that Ward had played 'one of the finest games I have ever seen by a player in non-league soccer.' Little did Gutteridge know that within four days the performance that he so enthusiastically eulogised would lead indirectly to his own departure from Burton.

◇　◇　◇

Burton received the first firm offer from a Football League team for Ward's transfer the day following the win over Cambridge. Third Division Brighton & Hove Albion made a combined bid of around £2,000 for Ward and team-mate Frank Corrigan. Under the management of ex-Burton boss Peter Taylor, Brighton were desperate to bring new players into the club, following a disappointing start to a season that Taylor had proclaimed would see his team win the Third Division championship.

Taylor's link with Burton and the semi-professional scene in the Midlands ensured that the impact of Ward's arrival had not gone unnoticed. Having just signed another non-leaguer, right-winger Gerry Fell from Long Eaton United of the Midland Counties League, Taylor turned his attention east and approached Ken Gutteridge about signing Corrigan and Ward, the latter of whom had already notched 10 goals.

Burton chairman Tom Bradbury's handling of the interest from Brighton enraged Gutteridge. Displaying little understanding of the protocol in dealing with potential transfers, Bradbury disclosed details of the offer to a local sports reporter: the headline, "Cash Offer," sat above the full story in Monday's Burton Mail.

Gutteridge felt that the premature and unprofessional release of information to the press had broken the code of confidence expected when the managers of two teams are in discussions about a potential transfer. The manager decided that his position had been undermined to such an extent that he resigned a day later, citing that the administrative side of the club had "a gross lack of professional expertise."

Burton rejected Brighton's offer on Tuesday, 19th November, and Ward remained a Burton player for the time being.

A little over a week after walking out on Burton, Gutteridge ventured south to join Brighton, becoming a trainer for Peter Taylor's side. Despite the fact that the catalyst behind Gutteridge's exit had been the handling of his potential transfer, Ward was not particularly troubled by the manager's departure:

> Me and Frankie (Corrigan) didn't know what was happening. We didn't know any more than anyone else and only found out what was happening from the paper or when we went in for training. It wasn't like now, when the players have power: we just did as we were told and got on with it.

◇　◇　◇

Back on the pitch, the team enjoyed a comfortable, if physical, 2-0 win at Barnet but followed that with a disappointing 3-1 defeat at Grantham. With the club chasing their highest ever league position and in the midst of a run in the Football Association Trophy, concerns that the proverbial wheels could fall off following Gutteridge's departure were not completely allayed when news of the his replacement were announced.

Harold Bodle had been an inside left for Birmingham, Bury and Stockport during the 1940s and '50s and was briefly Accrington Stanley manager before being sacked in 1960. Following his time at Accrington, Bodle spent the next fourteen years away from football, running a grocery shop. He had only returned to football a few months earlier when he was appointed reserve team boss at Burton. When news broke that 54 year-old Bodle was Gutteridge's successor, his long absence from the game was a concern for the Brewers' supporters.

However, under Bodle, Albion maintained their strong start to the season and the players found the managerial change to be an easy transition. Ward remembers his new manager, who died in 2005, as 'a nice guy, a really nice guy', and Peter's first wife Sue shared his sentiments:

> I didn't have a car, so when Pete was at Burton I'd go with the manager, Harold, and his wife, Audrey, to watch the games. I'd go to their house after work and get a lift to the games. Harold and Audrey were both really nice people.

At the turn of the year, Burton were still favourably positioned in the top half of the table and had reached the third round of the FA Trophy (the top knockout competition for non-league clubs) with victories over Yorkshire side Mexborough, Southern League rivals Atherstone Town and South Bank of the Northern League.

The good results continued but inconsistency started to creep into Ward's own performances; he was dropped for the second time in the season for a game against Atherstone. Playing instead for the reserve team, Ward trained hard and performed well, taking the disappointment on the chin. He regained his place in the first team for the FA Trophy tie against Mossley AFC. An impressive 2-1 win for the Brewers against the strong Manchester-based club from the Northern Premier League put them through to the quarter finals and a trip to Isthmian Leaguers Dagenham.

The trip to Essex in early March and Ward's performance in that game still linger in Ian Story-Moore's memory:

> I remember playing with Peter in the quarter-final of the Trophy at Dagenham. It was a tough game and Dagenham was a difficult place to play.
>
> We played really well, winning 3-1. Peter was very impressive that day and scored two goals.

The confidence from the cup run transferred to league performances and Ward scored the first goal in a superb 2-1 victory at title chasing Kettering.

By the time the Trophy semi-final draw was made in April, pairing Burton with another Derbyshire team, Matlock Town, Ward was hitting the net regularly and had scored over 20 goals. The victors of the two-legged semi-final would win a trip to Wembley to play on the same pitch that had seen England win the World Cup just nine years earlier.

Following a 1-0 win in the first leg at Matlock, courtesy of a Frank Corrigan penalty, confidence was high in the Burton camp as they headed into the home leg. However, Burton suffered massive disappointment as Matlock won 2-0 at Eton Park to end the Wembley dreams of Ward and his teammates. After the game, as the opportunity of playing at the world's most famous football stadium vanished, Ward broke down in tears.

◇ ◇ ◇

With the Trophy run over, Albion saw out their remaining league games to finish fifth in Premier Division. A tally of 25 goals gave 19-year-old Ward an impressive return from his first season at Burton and it was no surprise when Brighton renewed their interest in signing him.

On 3rd May, 1975, Ken Gutteridge travelled to Burton for their season-ending fixture. Most football fans were engrossed in watching West Ham beat Fulham 2-0 in the FA Cup Final at Wembley: Gutteridge's focus, however, was a long way from west London. Immediately after watching the 3-1 Burton victory, Gutteridge approached his successor, Harold Bodle, and made an offer on behalf of Brighton to buy Ward.

Gutteridge's presence at the game and the timing of Brighton's approach proved to be vital in securing Ward's signature for the Sussex side. Bodle had promised several other clubs, including Nottingham Forest, Peterborough and Mansfield, that he would contact them should there be any transfer developments regarding Ward. The fact that negotiation between the two Albions started on Saturday night meant that by the time any other clubs could be alerted on Monday morning, Ward had already agreed to sign for Peter Taylor's Brighton.

That Brighton made a new offer at all was down to Gutteridge's persistence and conviction that Ward was a player with huge potential. Interviewed in 1999 for a video entitled Wardy - An Albion Legend, Gutteridge explained that he had told Peter Taylor that he would only join the Brighton coaching staff if Taylor promised to sign Ward. Six months later, Taylor held true to his word although, having watched Ward twice himself and having also sent his assistant manager Brian Dakin to watch the Burton youngster, Taylor was not completely sure that Ward was as good as Gutteridge believed. The first time

24

that Taylor watched Ward, the striker played well but failed to score; the second time, he hardly had a kick. Luckily for Ward and a generation of Brighton supporters, Taylor decided that he'd seen enough promise in the first game to gamble on the striker. In 1977, reflecting on his decision to buy Ward for Brighton, Taylor referred to the striker's quickness and turning ability plus the fact that, despite his lightweight frame, he was quick to get back to his feet every time a defender knocked him down.

This time, Burton Chairman Tom Bradbury delayed announcing the details of the deal until it had been finalised. Bradbury told those attending the club's end of season dinner (at the Stanhope Arms in Bretby) that a staggered fee of £5,000 had been agreed between the clubs for Ward's signature.

Bradbury wished him well and expressed his hope that he would soon break into the Brighton first team (thereby triggering additional transfer payments), and Ward happily bid farewell to his teammates and headed south.

◇ ◇ ◇

With the season over and Ward officially a Brighton player, he still had one big match appearance to make in May of 1975: his wedding to long-term girlfriend, Sue Shardlow, was quickly arranged following the completion of the transfer from Burton. The couple, both only 19 years old, saw marriage as the perfect way to add a little stability to what had been a whirlwind few months.

As Sue remembers, the prospect of setting up a new home on the south coast was a very exciting one:

> When Brighton signed him we thought, 'let's get married and go!' We were young and foolish. So, we arranged the wedding for later that month and went to Brighton for a week for our honeymoon. I was really excited. We were both thinking 'you only live once; let's go to Brighton and see what happens.' It seemed like a long way from Derby at the time but I loved Brighton.

The move to Brighton also met with the approval of Peter's father. Even though Brighton had finished the season just outside the relegation places in the Third Division, Colin Ward was confident that the opportunity was ideal for his son:

> When Brighton came in I was thrilled for Pete. It was better than going to a First Division club, where he wouldn't get a chance. Arsenal were interested, but when they learned of his age they thought that he was too old.

> We knew that Peter Taylor, who had been at Derby, was at Brighton and we were confident that he and they would look after our Pete.

25

For Peter, the prospect of being a full-time professional was appealing but, at the same time, a little daunting:

> *I didn't have to work for a living but I was scared, going to Brighton. You second guess yourself - can I do it?*

History shows that Ward, despite a ten-month wait for his first team debut, had little to worry about in regards to his own abilities.

CHAPTER 4

BREAKING THROUGH AT BRIGHTON

It was my debut, Match of the Day, I scored after 50-something seconds and everybody knew who I was from then on. Sometimes things just come together and you get lucky.
— Peter Ward

Brighton & Hove Albion fans had just endured a miserable 1974-75 league campaign which ended with their team's narrow escape of relegation to the Fourth Division. A second consecutive nineteenth place finish in Division Three gave little indication that the club was on the verge of what supporters now refer to as 'the golden years'.

For many outside observers, Brighton was a typical, unremarkable lower league team. Historically, the Sussex club had spent forty-eight of its fifty-three league seasons in the bottom two divisions. Two short spells in the lofty heights of the Second Division had been the pinnacle of the club's achievements since joining the Football League in 1920. The team's last promotion, in 1972, had resulted in a disastrous single season of Division Two football: home crowds dropped to approximately 5,000.

A little less than two years before Peter Ward left one Albion for another, Brighton chairman Mike Bamber made a move that instantly transformed the club from a run-of-the-mill Division Three outfit to the most talked-about club in the country.

In November 1973, Bamber announced that Brian Clough and Peter Taylor were to take over management of the team from Pat Saward (who had been sacked three days earlier). Clough, with an appetite for success and a penchant for controversy, and Taylor, very much more reflective and private, were convinced by Bamber that Brighton was an ideal place for them re-embark on their managerial journey.

Just two weeks earlier, Clough and Taylor had left Derby County following a highly publicised dispute with the club's board of directors. Aggravated by the fact that the club he had led from the Second Division to a European Cup semi-final felt that they could survive without him, Clough was revelling in a vociferous campaign that supporters at Derby were waging to get him re-instated. Unperturbed, Bamber first convinced Taylor, who in turn persuaded

Clough, that their careers would benefit from making the drop from the First to Third Division.

Albion supporter David Dresch had been following the team since 1964 and was shocked by the news of Clough's appointment:

> *I couldn't believe it: it was unreal. It would be like Sir Alex Ferguson leaving Manchester United and going to manage a Third Division team now — I was totally amazed. We had had a good season a couple of years before and been promoted, but we came straight back down and Saward got the sack. It was always my belief that Mike Bamber wanted a big name manager who would have the presence to bring big name players to the club because he, Bamber, was willing to put big money into the team.*

> *Clough was too big a manager for the club and everyone knew that. Nobody expected him to stay too long. To give him his credit, he cleared the club out and brought in some much better players.*

Andy Rollings, one of Clough's first signings at Brighton, remembers the manager making no attempt to hide his plans to make wholesale changes at the club:

> *Cloughie and Peter Taylor came up to Norwich and convinced Ian Mellor, Steve Govier and me to drop down a division and join Brighton.*

> *We signed in the final week of the season and then travelled down to Bristol to watch Brighton play Rovers. We sat in the directors' box and when the game was finished, Ian Mellor stood up and said to Cloughie, 'right, Boss; shall we go down and meet the players?' In typical fashion, Cloughie responded, 'there's no point in meeting that lot, they won't be here next year.'*

> *A week later, we flew off with the club to Majorca. Out of the eleven players who had played at Bristol, only four were on the plane. There were more new players on that trip than there were existing Brighton players.*

◇ ◇ ◇

In his autobiography Cloughie - Walking on Water, Clough referred to Bamber as 'the pleasantest and finest chairman who ever employed me', but, despite the chairman's full support, life at the Goldstone Ground lasted less than a full season for the charismatic and unpredictable Clough.

A chain of managerial changes, starting with the sacking of England's World Cup winning manager, Sir Alf Ramsey, was the catalyst for Clough's premature, if not completely surprising, exit from Brighton. Fresh from guiding Leeds United to the First Division championship, Don Revie was chosen as Ramsey's successor as England manager. In turn, Leeds made the surprising decision to offer Revie's position to Clough. As manager of First Division rivals

Derby County, Clough had been openly critical of Leeds' 'cynical and dirty' approach and took over the Elland Road hot seat facing resentment from both players and fans. Unable to win over either his team or their fervid supporters Clough's reign at Leeds lasted for just 44 days.

With Clough gone, Peter Taylor decided to stay with Brighton to continue rebuilding the Third Division club. Continuing what Clough had started, a massive clear-out of players was undertaken and a number of new signings made. Taylor was confident that the changes in personnel would bring success and, on the eve of the 1974-75 season, announced with Clough-like hubris that not only would Brighton gain promotion but that they would be crowned Third Division champions come the end of the season.

Taylor's publicly declared expectations only served as a millstone around the neck of the team. With eight players, including Fred Binney, Ian Mellor and Andy Rollings, making their debuts in the first three months of the season, the team struggled to find consistency. Recording just two wins in the first sixteen games of the season, the club, surprisingly, languished near the bottom of the table.

Rollings remembers a lack of motivation as one of the key reasons behind the poor run of results:

> Peter Taylor would never get involved with training and would always be behind his desk. Before games, he would try to motivate us but he just couldn't do it. He was a deep person and would talk about all sorts of things in team talks but he didn't know how to get the best out of us.

Looking to improve the club's fortunes, Taylor turned to Burton Albion, a club he knew very well, and made his unsuccessful first attempt to sign Ward and Frank Corrigan from Burton Albion.

Over the course of the season, Albion's home form (only two defeats all season) was in sharp contrast with fortunes away from home, where just two games were won. Fortunately, the points picked up at the Goldstone Ground proved to be enough to keep Albion in the division as Bournemouth, Tranmere, Watford and Huddersfield were relegated.

◇   ◇   ◇

Following the signing of Peter Ward at the end of the 1974-75 season, Taylor made further moves to strengthen his squad in preparation for the new campaign. Adding some much needed know-how to the team, he signed four players with significant First Division experience: Republic of Ireland international Joe Kinnear and Phil Beal joined from Tottenham, striker Neil Martin joined on a free transfer from Nottingham Forest (who were now managed by

Brian Clough), and former West Ham defender Dennis Burnett joined from Hull.

One player whom Taylor expected to sign for the club during the summer of 1975 was striker Peter Withe. Withe was a Wolverhampton Wanderers player at the time but was one of a number of English players who spent the summer months playing in the NASL in North America. Having agreed on a £40,000 fee with Wolves manager Bill McGarry, Taylor was confident that Withe would become the big target man that Albion needed. However, Birmingham City manager Freddie Goodwin flew to Portland to watch Withe play and signed him for £50,000 whilst in the States. This move left Taylor bitterly disappointed, especially as Goodwin had been manager at Brighton before taking over at Birmingham. Taylor had to wait another 14 months before he could finally sign Withe (for Nottingham Forest at a cost of £43,000). The big striker went on to score the winning goal for Aston Villa in the 1982 European Cup Final and won eleven England caps.

With the Brighton board financing the influx of new players, chairman Mike Bamber was keen to ensure that his team were well looked after and the club's welcoming treatment of the newly-married Wards was no exception:

> *I met with Peter Taylor after Sue and I had been on honeymoon. It was just me and him in his office — no agents, no lawyers. Pete said 'this is the offer' — it was £50 a week — and I said 'magic, thank you — where do I sign?' and that was it.*

> *A few weeks later, Sue and I moved down to Sussex to live in a club-owned house at Rottingdean. It was a lovely, big detached house overlooking the sea. We shared it with two other new signings, Phil Beal and Neil Martin — they were great guys. We were only there three weeks and because I couldn't drive I would get a lift in with Phil or Neil and sometimes get the bus back.*

> *After that, we moved to another house owned by the club. It was a nice three-bedroom semi in Hangleton. We were there for seven or eight months — until I got into the first team. Then, we bought our own place.*

Ward, who turned twenty a week before the opening pre-season friendly of the season, soon adjusted to the physical demands of being a full-time professional and training every day. The camaraderie between the players was good and the new signings were given a friendly welcome. In training, Ward much preferred ball work to stamina building exercises:

> *I hated pre-season training. I hated the long-distance running but I enjoyed the normal day-to-day training. There wasn't much individual training; it was mainly group things. We would work on pattern of play, free kicks and corners, but it wasn't as specialised as it is now.*

Ward started the season as a regular in the reserve team under the watchful eye of assistant manager Brian Daykin. Ward's memories of his early reserve team games include a victory in the final of the Sussex County Senior Cup —a competition where all of the previous rounds had taken place in the preceding season— and winning a game held inside the security-walled grounds of Lewes Prison. However, a poor start in the London Midweek Football League saw Albion's second string fail to win any of their first eight games. Ward found it difficult to score in the under-performing side.

The first team was also making a slow start to their Third Division campaign and the prospects of another disappointing season started to increase. These worries were soon eased by a 6-0 home win over Chester, which started a run of 14 consecutive home wins stretching from September to March. A 1-0 win at previously unbeaten Crystal Palace was followed by three more victories that lifted the Albion up to third place in the table by the middle of October.

First team strikers Fred Binney and Neil Martin were finding the net regularly and this meant that there was little opportunity for Ward to make the step up from the reserves. However, the reserve team's results did show a striking improvement: 11 wins from the next 12 games following the initial 8 game winless run. The team started to hit the back of the net with ease: the highlight was an 8-1 win against Northampton on January 6th. Ward's form improved and his goal touch returned but the performances of the first team did not show any signs of slipping.

In December, Taylor looked to further strengthen his team. Despite the excellent run of reserve team results, rather than promoting one of his squad players he turned to the transfer market. Six-foot-one Northern Ireland international Sammy Morgan, weighing in at thirteen and a half stone, was signed for £30,000 from First Division Aston Villa and immediately replaced Martin in the starting eleven. Taylor hoped that Morgan, who at school had been a teammate of George Best, was the type of player who could keep possession of the ball, especially when away from home; the poor form from the previous season was continuing. Recalling his decision to drop two divisions to sign for Brighton, Morgan remembers the manager and chairman with great affection:

> Peter Taylor, god rest his soul, had wanted to sign me when he was at Derby and I was at Port Vale. He must have remembered me because when I wasn't getting a chance at Villa he came in for me again. I could have gone to Cardiff, but Peter and Mr. Bamber convinced me to join Brighton. I can't say enough about how nice Mr. Bamber was. He was a wonderful man and the club was very generous.

> They were starting to get a good team together and it felt like an honour to be asked to join because Peter Taylor was a very good judge of players. There was good experience, good young players and good spirit.

As 1975 drew to a close, opportunities for Ward to break into the first team still seemed to be in short supply. Fred Binney had already notched 15 goals; newly-signed Morgan was settling in; and Brighton were sitting second in the league.

Luckily for Ward, Morgan's arrival did not sit well with Neil Martin who, having just celebrated his 35th birthday, felt that the new signing would limit his own chances in the first team. Making his grievances known to Peter Taylor, Martin unwittingly closed the door on his own Brighton career and in doing so moved Ward a step closer to the first team.

◇ ◇ ◇

Morgan was now first choice to partner top scorer Fred Binney, and Brighton continued to move up the table. A resounding 6-0 win over Colchester in mid-January maintained the team's second position. An injury to Morgan gave Martin an unexpected recall to the team and he took his place in the side alongside Binney, who scored the only goal in a 1-0 win against promotion rivals Millwall at the Goldstone. This game proved to be Martin's last for the Albion and he was eventually transferred to Crystal Palace. Interestingly, the Goldstone crowd of 15,000 was reported in The Times as having been larger than that which had watched Arsenal at Highbury the previous Saturday. This was an indication that the Sussex fans were starting to believe that their side had a real chance of promotion.

The following game, on Saturday, 7th February, Albion travelled to mid-table Bury and for the first time Ward was called up to travel with the first team. With Martin no longer in contention, Morgan still injured and Binney dropped, manager Peter Taylor turned to the reserve team for reinforcements. With the second string still in fine form, winger Tony Towner was called up for his first appearance since November and Ward was named as substitute. At this time, teams were only allowed to name one substitute and more often than not this player would only be called upon if one of their teammates sustained an injury. Unfortunately for Ward, his services were not called upon and a 1-1 draw dropped the Albion down to third in the table.

A week later, Albion entertained Ipswich Town in a friendly match at the Goldstone Ground. The game was arranged in the wake of both teams being knocked out of the FA Cup. In front of a crowd of 5,000, Ward took his place in the starting lineup alongside many of the first team regulars. Ipswich, under the guidance of future England manager Bobby Robson, would go on to finish sixth in the First Division; on this occasion, however, they were soundly beaten by Albion. A 3-1 victory, including two goals from Ian Mellor and one from Andy Rollings, had been well deserved. It was Ward, though, who caught the eye of Evening Argus reporter John Vinicombe: he noted that, even though he had been marked by Ipswich's Northern Ireland defender Allan Hunter, the young striker's performance had given further proof that he would fit into the league side.

Despite the impressive performance three days earlier, Ward was replaced by Joe Kinnear as substitute for the next game at Southend United. This ended in a 4-0 defeat for the Albion. The following Saturday, Ward was restored to the bench for the home fixture against Halifax Town. Both Binney and Morgan returned to the team and a 1-0 victory maintained the promotion push although, once again, Ward did not make the action.

For the next seven games, Ward did not even make the bench as the Binney-Morgan partnership continued to reap dividends. As Ward returned to the reserve team, Peter Taylor signed another player who would help to form the foundation of the club's successes over the next five years. Twenty-seven-year-old midfielder Brian Horton joined the Albion from Port Vale on transfer deadline day, March 1976, for £27,000. Seeing Horton as a natural captain, in his 1980 book With Clough, Taylor reflected that the "determination and influence" that Horton exuded should have seen him playing in the top division from the start of his career rather than taking the unglamorous route through non-league and lower league competition. Horton's departure from Vale caused uproar among that team's supporters, but, despite having made over 200 appearances for Vale, the decision to move south was an easy one for Horton:

> I'd played at Palace for Port Vale on the Tuesday night and we'd drawn 1-1. I'd scored a penalty and we were right up there with Palace and Brighton in the promotion race. I didn't know until after the game that Peter Taylor was in the crowd and that he had already made an offer to buy me.
>
> I spoke to Taylor that night and signed on the Thursday. It wasn't a hard decision — I'd played at Brighton many times and they were always getting great crowds. It was a nice place to play and a lovely place to live. Peter Taylor made me captain almost straightaway and I settled in quickly.

By the time Ward made his next appearance as unused substitute on 20th March, the Albion were still sitting handsomely in second place in the table. A 2-0 win over Swindon, courtesy of two Morgan goals, ensured that the Albion went into their next game, on Saturday, 27th March, —away at league leaders Hereford United— confident that they could achieve a rare away victory.

◇   ◇   ◇

As Third Division games go, this was the biggest of the season so far; top of the table against second, only one month left of the season: the winners gave themselves a fantastic opportunity of achieving promotion. Added to this was a rare chance for the players to perform in front of the BBC's Match of the Day cameras and an estimated twelve million Saturday night viewers.

With 25 goals to his name already, four in the last five games, Albion striker Fred Binney must have been more than a little shocked with the way that the pre-match preparation unfurled. Peter Ward takes up the story:

> *I travelled up with the team but was really only hoping to be substitute. I had a cold so Glen Wilson (Albion's Trainer) was filling me with whiskey the night before. On the Saturday morning the whole team went for a walk, and then we sat down and watched the football at the start of Grandstand. After that we got together for a team meeting at the hotel and Pete Taylor just says 'Fred, you're not playing. Peter, you are in'. I thought 'Jesus Christ' but my nerves disappeared once the game had kicked off.*

> *Fred Binney was nice, a great fella: there was no friction between us and I didn't really have time to think about how he was feeling.*

It was a brave, and what proved to be a successful, attempt by Taylor to halt a run of four successive away defeats. The Albion manager also dropped Ian Mellor, who took over Ward's place on the bench, and Ward took to the field for his league debut wearing Binney's green number nine shirt.

Partnering big Sammy Morgan up front, it took Ward less than a minute to score his first league goal and ensure that he grabbed the headlines on both Match of the Day and in the Sunday papers. Using a single touch to control a Tony Towner pass and spin away from a Hereford defender, Ward hit a left foot cross-cum-shot that eluded the lunging Morgan at the near post and was fumbled by United goalkeeper Kevin Charlton into his own net. The thousand or so Albion fans standing behind Charlton's goal went crazy and celebrated the spectacular entrance of Ward onto the League scene.

Although Hereford equalised eight minutes into the second half, a 1-1 draw at the league leaders was a good result for Taylor's re-organised team.

If the game had not been televised it is quite likely that the Ward goal would have been awarded to Morgan, whose claims to it were rejected following slow motion replays on Match of the Day. Asked about the goal in 2009, Morgan, who is now head of Ipswich Town's youth academy, remembers that there was some confusion about who had scored and adds with a mischievous laugh that 'Peter always said that I had scored his first goal!'

For Ward, confirmation that the goal was his rounded off a truly memorable day:

> *It was on Match of the Day — that's luck, isn't it? There were only two games on Match of the Day in those days and to see a Division Three game*

was really unusual. It was my debut, Match of the Day, I scored after 50-something seconds and everybody knew who I was from then on. Sometimes things just come together and you get lucky.

Coming back from Hereford, we stopped in London to watch the game on TV. I didn't know that I'd scored until we watched the match. Sammy Morgan said he'd got a touch, but the pictures on the TV showed that he hadn't.

As well as proving that the goal belonged to Peter, the Match of the Day cameras gave his very proud parents the opportunity to see their son's dream start. Colin Ward, who at the time didn't hold a driving licence, remembers:

Because it was a last minute thing, I had no way of getting transport to the game. It was someone around here who heard on the radio that Peter was playing and told me about it. In the evening we watched it on Match of the Day — it was quite exhilarating — the fastest goal in a debut ever on Match of the Day. That must have given him a lot of confidence.

Ward's confidence was no doubt further boosted by a headline of Ward Wonder Start Wins a Point and a Man of the Match rating in the Evening Argus. Ward had completed another dream debut and his manager agreed, telling The Guardian that he would not sell Ward for £40,000 which was ten times the amount he had bought him for.

◇ ◇ ◇

The following Saturday, Albion were on the road again, this time travelling to Yorkshire to face relegation-threatened Rotherham United. Even though there were no Match of the Day cameras and the crowd numbered only 4,300, Ward had no trouble in motivating himself. His early goal gave Albion hope of an away victory. For the second consecutive game, an equaliser for the home team early in the second half meant that the game finished 1-1. With a goal in each of his first two games, the start of Ward's Brighton career was remarkably similar to his early Burton Albion days, when he had made a goal-scoring debut, scoring four minutes into his second game.

Brighton fans had yet to have the opportunity to see Ward play a competitive game at the Goldstone. His third appearance was a midweek visit to Chesterfield: in a game which included three penalties, Chesterfield were first to score after a foul by Steve Piper and led 1-0 at half-time. Early in the second half, Ward was fouled inside the box and Joe Kinnear levelled the score. Unfortunately for the Albion, a controversial hand ball decision against Andy Rollings granted the hosts their second penalty of the night and sent Brighton to defeat.

The loss to Chesterfield dropped Brighton out of the promotion places and, despite only picking up 2 points from the previous six games, Peter Taylor made only one change for the home game with Port Vale, recalling Fred Binney at the expense of Sammy Morgan.

Still hoping that their team would earn promotion, more than 19,000 fans packed into the Goldstone for this game. Compared to the 3,000 who had witnessed the return fixture at Port Vale in September, this was a striking example of the growing support for Taylor's team in Sussex.

Binney gave the Albion a 1-0 half-time lead and Ian Mellor doubled the score midway through the second half. With 10 minutes to go, Ward capped a fine performance by scoring his first home league goal: he hit a brilliant half-volley into the far corner of the net from a Horton pass to earn Brighton a convincing 3-0 victory.

While his third goal in four appearances has become a faded memory, Ward does recall one lighter moment from the win over Port Vale:

> My home debut was great: I remember that during the game my shorts ripped. I didn't have time to go off and get changed so they threw a new pair on for me and I had to put them on in front of the West Stand. I gave my bum a bit of a wiggle, which amused the fans no end.

The victory lifted Brighton back into the top three places but it proved to be the last win of the season. Albion's promotion hopes vanished.

A 3-1 defeat by promotion rivals Millwall on Good Friday, 16th April, in front of 23,000 passionate south-east Londoners was a hammer-blow to Peter Taylor's team and saw the Lions leapfrog the Albion into third place. Later, Taylor would pick out this particular defeat as the one that cost the club promotion. Despite scoring with a late consolation goal, Fred Binney's day was made worse when Taylor, already fuming after the defeat, told the coach driver to leave without Binney after the game. Ward recounts one of the few occasions when Taylor let his frustration get the better of him:

> Pete Taylor had just had a real go at us in the changing rooms and we were all sitting in silence on the coach, wanting to get home as soon as we could. Fred was the only one still not on the bus because he was standing around talking to someone. Pete wouldn't wait and said to the bus driver, 'F*** him. Leave him, let's go'. It wasn't the sort of place at which you'd want to be left but, luckily for Fred, he got a lift from some fans and managed to get back to Brighton before the coach.

Brighton ended the season with three consecutive one-all draws and, although the results were not good enough to secure promotion, the fact that Ward scored the equalising goal in each game meant that his run of eight first team starts had produced six goals: a very impressive return. Sharing the points at relegated Aldershot and then at home to Gillingham, where Ward scored in the 88th minute, meant that the final game of the season at home to Sheffield Wednesday was meaningless in terms of league position.

8,000 fewer fans turned up than for the previous home game and the match was very much an anti-climax. Despite receiving a warm reception from the fans on a pre-game lap of honour, Brighton started slowly and fell behind after just two minutes, when Eric Potts (who would be signed to Albion in the future) scored. Ward scored his sixth goal of the season in the final minute of the match, but many of the spectators had left the ground. Ward remembers thinking "God, the ground is empty" as he celebrated his goal.

A fifth place league finish was a vast improvement on the previous two years but still a disappointing end to a season that had promised much. With the season over, many Brighton fans were eagerly awaiting the 1976-77 campaign to see whether Peter Taylor and Ward, to whom he was now referring as "the hottest property in English football", could guide the team to Division Two and fulfil the manager's prophecy of two years earlier.

CHAPTER 5

36 GOALS AND A STAR IS BORN

This kid was like Roy of the Rovers: he was beating
people and smashing the ball into the net and he
weighed about 9 stone dripping wet.

– Alan Mullery, MBE

As the Brighton players started to enjoy their summer break, Taylor jetted off for a six week holiday in Majorca. Peter Ward, fresh from his auspicious first team breakthrough, had little time to relax as eight days into May, his wife gave birth to the couple's first child, daughter Rachael. Present at the birth, Peter recalls:

> Rachael was born in the Sussex County hospital. It was May 8th, she weighed 8lbs, she was born in room number 8 and I had just made 8 appearances for Brighton — I took that all as being a good sign!

The good news continued for Ward with Taylor's return to the UK. One of the manager's first tasks was to sit down with his young striker and to offer him an improved contract:

> Pete (Taylor) got me in the office in the summer and gave me a new contract. I was on £50 a week before that, and he gave me a new deal with a signing bonus and everything — it was unbelievable. So now I was maybe earning £150/£200 per week, which is twenty times as much as I was on when I left Burton just twelve months before!

In an attempt to improve the team's disappointing away form from the previous four seasons, Ward's new contract included a £15 bonus for each away point won. The £30 win bonus for an away fixture was six times the amount on offer for a home win. Two other clauses in Ward's new deal proved to be very lucrative over the course of the season — the 'League Position Clause' and the 'Attendance Clause'. A £50 bonus was paid for every week that the team was in the top three in the table, and for attendances over 8,000, £2 was paid for each additional thousand spectators up to 15,000 and £5 for each additional thousand over 15,000. With the team only slipping out of the top three for 3 or 4 weeks during the season and home crowds averaging over 20,000, Ward's bonuses alone were worth more than his previous contract.

Unbeknownst to Ward, the motive behind his new contract was not that Taylor wanted to ensure that Ward remain a Brighton player for years to come. Instead, as the deal was being signed, Taylor knew that it would be his last transaction as Brighton manager: he hoped that Ward would follow him back up to the East Midlands.

◇ ◇ ◇

On 16th July, 1976, a week before pre-season training was due to start, Peter Taylor handed in his resignation. Telling Mike Bamber that he regarded himself as a failure for not having achieved promotion within two years, and ignoring Bamber's offer of more players, higher wages and a new car, Taylor walked away from the club. He denied the inevitable speculation that he would join up with Brian Clough again at Nottingham Forest, saying that his only plans were to walk his dog. Despite Taylor's reluctance to admit to it, a meeting with Clough had already taken place: Clough had flown to Majorca to meet with Taylor. This was a journey that Clough, in his 2002 autobiography Cloughie — Walking on Water, referred to as "the most productive flight I ever made".

Two days later, dog walking appearing to have lost its appeal, Taylor's move to Forest was officially confirmed and the Clough-Taylor alliance was once again heading for incredible success. This time, Clough and Taylor guided Forest, eighth in Division Two in 19'75-76, to become double European champions in just four seasons.

◇ ◇ ◇

Taylor's chair at Brighton did not remain empty for long. Although admitting that he was 'dazed, shattered and depressed' by Taylor's resignation, Mike Bamber acted with astounding speed to appoint a successor. By the time that the day's Evening Argus had hit the presses, the headlines announcing Taylor's departure were appended with the news that Alan Mullery was appointed as his replacement.

Thirty-four-year-old Mullery, a confident and straight-talking Londoner, had brought his playing career with Fulham to a close a few weeks before Bamber called. The departing Taylor called the Brighton job "a manager's utopia," due to the unremitting backing of the board that he had experienced. It was little surprise that it took Bamber fewer than ten minutes to convince Mullery to take over.

Interviewed 33 years later, Mullery, who was awarded an MBE in 1975, clearly remembers Bamber's reasons for offering him the position:

Mike Bamber and I got on very easily. He said to me that he offered me the job because of my will to win. He'd seen me play twice against Brighton and in one of the games, when I was playing for Fulham, I struck one of my own players because he was arguing with me on the pitch and wouldn't do what he was told. Bamber said that if anybody wanted to win so badly that he would hit one of their own players, he, Bamber, should give me the job. We'd beaten Brighton 5-2 or something that day. Why he was impressed with that I don't know because I regretted it afterwards, but he was.

Bamber convinced me that the directors wanted success and they were willing to pay for it; and that is what they did.

Brighton had an excellent squad. They had just missed out on promotion in the Third Division and had a lot of experienced players. I looked at it and thought, 'what a great opportunity to take over.'

For the players, Taylor's departure was totally unexpected and Ward, despite his new contract, was now faced with the prospect of having to prove himself all over again:

Peter Taylor's leaving was a shock. He'd given me the new contract and then all of a sudden he was gone and Mullery came in. I thought, 'I've just made a name for myself and now that manager has left. Jesus Christ, I'm not getting in the team now.'

Brian Horton, the team captain, saw Mullery's arrival with even more trepidation. Rumours amongst the players hinted that the new manager would take on the dual role of player-manager and that he would provide a direct threat to Horton's own place in the team:

I had only played twelve games for Peter Taylor and then he left to go back to Cloughie. It was a dramatic change when Alan Mullery came in. He changed quite a few things but, luckily, retained my position as captain. We had good players and Mullery didn't need to play. He signed some great players and we got on really well.

Reflecting on Taylor's departure, Sammy Morgan agrees with a commonly held view on the reason behind the change:

Peter Taylor really missed Brian Clough. They were so good together but so lost apart.

I felt that Peter wasn't equipped to manage by himself. He was first and foremost a finder of players. He would find them, trainer Jimmy Gordon would get them fit and Cloughie would motivate them.

At Brighton, Taylor could find the players but he couldn't motivate them to play. He would never put his tracksuit on and come to training — that was one big difference between him and Alan Mullery.

◇   ◇   ◇

Pre-season training started the Monday after Mullery's appointment and the new boss wasn't slow to make an impression. Ward recounts Mullery's initial introduction to the players:

> *Mullery came in and addressed all of the players. He told us that he was a winner and showed everyone his medals to prove it. He pointed at Joe Kinnear and Phil Beal, who he had played with at Spurs, and told Kinnear that he was out of shape and that everyone needed to be fit. He slaughtered them a bit, which I thought was wrong — it seemed that Mullery and Kinnear didn't get on very well — but I guess that he was showing the rest of the squad that he wouldn't have any favourites; not even those who had been his teammates.*

Following the introductions, the players and their new manager took to the training pitch. Before the players had started any drills, Mullery took a ball and from thirty yards out smashed it against one of the goal posts. To dispel any doubts that the first shot was a fluke, he took another ball and hit the other post from the same spot. With his own credentials clearly displayed, Mullery ran the rule over the players that he had inherited. His first impressions of the Brighton squad were positive:

> *There were some very experienced players at Brighton: Peter Grummitt, the goalie, had been a marvellous goalkeeper; Chris Cattlin had played at Coventry; Brian Horton was an excellent captain; Fred Binney was up front; Ian Mellor had been at Manchester City; Dennis Burnett, Joe Kinnear, Philip Beal. There was a very nice balance of experienced players and young players.*

Although many of the players were familiar, Mullery had little prior knowledge of Ward and tells the story of the first time he witnessed Peter's talents first hand:

> *I had never heard of Peter Ward: I didn't have a clue about him. My first experience of seeing him was when I arrived, which was just as pre-season training was starting. I went to training up at Sussex University and I said to Ken Gutteridge that I wanted a full-scale practice match and that he should organise the team that finished last season, if that was possible, and that they would play against the reserves.*

> *I said that we'd play for half an hour and see how that went; if I needed to make any changes I would. There was a little skinny fellow, weighing about 9½ stone, whom Ken had put in the reserve team. He scored a hat-trick in the first half-hour against the first team. I said to Ken 'who's that?' He told me that it was Peter Ward and that Ward had played a few games at the end of the last season and scored some goals. I told Ken to put him in the first team and take the place of Fred Binney.*

I didn't know Fred Binney personally but I knew of him; I think he'd scored 28 goals or something the season before. But this kid was like Roy of the Rovers, he was beating people and smashing the ball into the net and, as I say, he was about 9 stone dripping wet.

In the second period I changed Ian Mellor from being a wide midfield player to playing up front with Ward at centre forward; I brought Stevie Piper, who was a big centre half in the reserves, to sit in front of the back four. Wardy scored two more goals against the reserves in the next half-hour. He'd scored five goals in an hour, which was quite impressive — and this was the first time that I'd ever seen him.

So, in that first training session I had made a few positional changes which we stuck to for the rest of the season, but the rest of the side were very good - Big Andy Rollings at centre half, Brian Horton in the middle of the park, Peter O'Sullivan and Pete Grummitt.

When Ward caught his new manager's eye, Fred Binney, the previous season's leading scorer, decided to give Mullery his own thoughts on the best way forward for the Albion. Mullery remembers Binney's visit to his office:

Fred Binney came to see me and told me that Wardy would get me the sack. He said that Ward was too skinny for the Third Division and that he wouldn't last the season. He told me that he (Binney) had scored 28 goals last season and that he, not Ward, was the goalscorer in the club. I said, 'thanks very much for your advice, Fred' and inside of two months I'd sold him to Exeter.

◇ ◇ ◇

For Mullery's players, pre-season training meant running up and down the steep hills of Waterhall on the outskirts of the town. Although he was keen to impress his new manager, Ward found it impossible to hide his dislike of the running drills, as Mullery remembers:

I don't think Peter enjoyed the cross country over the Dyke and things like that. He was a bit browned off when I used to run them up the hill at Waterhall - I think he was sick the first time I made them do that. I could see in his face that he didn't enjoy it but he got through it. I found out about him and Joe Kinnear hiding in the café and soon put a stop to that.

Kinnear's card was marked from day one of Mullery's reign, but it was Ward's idea to attempt to sidestep the running workout. This led the pair to feel the wrath of the new boss:

Pre-season, I used to walk Rachael around in her pram, a ten- to fifteen-minute walk to the pub or the grocery shop, so I got to know the area pretty well. I hated long distance running and Joe Kinnear just couldn't run.

Our cross country training run used to take us by one of the shops that I would walk Rachael past so I told Joe that I knew the people in the shop. We would hang back from the rest of the team when they were running and then dive into the shop and have a sit-down and a drink.

We would wait for the other players to come back around on their way back and then join up with them again looking as fresh as a daisy!

We didn't feel quite as clever when Mullery found out, though…

To the relief of the players, pre-season was brought to an end with two low-key friendlies, away to Torquay United and at home to Luton Town. Both games ended in 1-1 draws; the Torquay match was most notable for an injury to Sammy Morgan which sidelined the striker for three and a half months.

◇   ◇   ◇

For the league opener at home to Oxford United, Mullery opted for a forward combination of Ward and Binney, although many observers thought the pair too similar in stature and style to be effective. Binney's two goals and another from Horton saw Brighton scrape a 3-2 win.

The next game at Chester City saw Ward grab his first goal of the season as Albion's 1-0 win maintained their unbeaten season start. Another Ward goal gave Albion a 1-1 draw at Preston in a match that he remembers more for the journey than for the game itself:

We went up to Preston on the train; it was still summer but it wasn't very warm, so Ken Gutteridge decided to wear a sheepskin coat. We were changing trains at Euston, and as we were getting off one train he couldn't find his coat.

*We were in a bit of a rush because we had to get on the next train; Ken thought that we'd hidden it but we hadn't. So he started to go mad — "Where's my f***** coat? Who's got my coat? You'd better give it back right now!" All the players cracked up and he really started to lose his temper.*

Anyway, we had to get the next train to go up to Preston and we couldn't wait around for Ken to look for his coat. So we all got on the train, including Ken; then, this fella got on the train, sat next to Gutteridge and he had Ken's coat on!

So when Ken realised that this guy had nicked his coat all hell broke loose - "That's mine! Give me my coat!" and he was wrestling with this guy. He got it back eventually and we were all in hysterics.

We used to call Ken 'the ferret' or 'Martini' after Danny Devito's character in One Flew over The Cuckoo's Nest — I think Sully (Peter O'Sullivan) started that one.

Ken was a nice guy — a really nice fella but don't touch his coat!

The match at Deepdale was the first time that Ward's future teammate, Mark Lawrenson, had played against the Brighton striker:

Wardy had already scored a few goals and I know that I was eventually bought by Brighton because I played well against Peter when I was playing for Preston.

He was gaining a reputation throughout the division and he was quick, left- and right-footed and had great balance.

Playing Ian Mellor alongside Ward was the masterstroke really — Mellor was an out-and-out footballer and a perfect partner for Wardy.

The point at Preston was followed by a trip to face First Division Ipswich Town in the second round of the League Cup.

A very creditable nil-nil draw in East Anglia earned Albion a home replay a week later and Mullery's team scored a memorable victory. A last-minute goal from defender Graham Cross secured a surprise 2-1 win for Brighton in front of 26,000 jubilant fans. Ipswich, under the management of Bobby Robson, finished the season third in Division One.

Brighton's first defeat of the season, 2-0 at Grimsby Town, brought the team down to earth but they later bounced back in style with five second-half goals, securing a 7-2 win over York City and giving the visiting Match of the Day cameras a game to savour. Ward scored twice, the first time that he had done so in League Football, but, more significantly, the game was Fred Binney's last for the club.

One of the best goalscorers in the lower divisions and popular with the Albion supporters, Binney was perhaps the biggest victim of Ward's stunning introduction to league football. As Mullery made the tactical changes that would see his team never fall lower than third place in the league throughout the entire campaign, Binney was seen as surplus. In the fifteen games that Binney and Ward played together, including those from the previous season, there was only one game where both players scored. Having given the pair a chance to work together and having, in his mind, seen it fail, Mullery decided to replace Binney with Ian Mellor. Mellor had made most of his previous appearances for the club as a wide midfield player and his long legs and gangly style had earned him the nickname 'Spider'.

44

Asked about his decision to partner Ward with Mellor, Mullery explains:

Ian Mellor had the ability: he was a big tall lad and he had super pace and a great left foot. I thought that they would form a terrific partnership.

In my opinion, Mellor was wasted in midfield. He could hold on to the ball and he'd learnt his skills from Malcolm Allison and Joe Mercer at Manchester City, who were both great coaches. He shouldn't really have been playing at the level we were at —he was too good— but he was and that was great for us.

Peter would be ready for anything from 25 yards out. Spider would get the ball to him and Peter would go on these mazy runs and, 9 times out of 10, would knock the ball into the back of the net — in the lower divisions especially.

The partnership is history now, but they were absolutely fantastic together.

Mullery's captain, Brian Horton, has similar views on the Ward/Mellor combination:

In the first year, Ward and Spider were unbelievable. We didn't have a big target man but the movement with those two was fantastic. They got about fifty goals between them and I chipped in with about a dozen more.

The first outing for the new partnership was the League Cup third round game at top division West Bromwich Albion, Brighton's reward for knocking out Ipswich in the previous round. In what Mullery called a 'magnificent performance', Brighton pulled off their second consecutive giant-killing with a 2-0 win. Ward was the star, scoring both goals in front of a collection of scouts from higher division clubs. Mullery used his post-match press conference to warn off any potential bidders, saying that Ward was not for sale and that they would be wasting their time in trying to sign him.

Following the game, the West Brom player/manager Johnny Giles applauded the Brighton players off the pitch and, some years later, reminded Ward that he was lucky to have made it to the end of the game in one piece. As Ward remembers:

Johnny Giles was my manager at the Vancouver Whitecaps, when I first went there. At one of the first training sessions he reminded me and everyone else how he nearly broke my leg when he was playing for West Brom.

We beat then two-nil and I was holding the ball near the corner and he 'did me'. He said I was lucky that he didn't break my leg, I said 'Thanks very much!' He was a good coach, very good and I enjoyed playing for him despite his attempts to kill me!

Following the West Brom victory, Mike Bamber awarded Mullery a new four-year contract. Just one defeat in his first dozen games and a series of impressive performances had confirmed Bamber's initial hope that Mullery was the perfect man to take the club forward.

A 3-1 win at Tranmere, with Ward scoring his seventh goal of the season, saw Brighton heading into October at the top of Division Three and looking forward to a League Cup fourth-round tie at home to another First Division side, Derby County.

◇ ◇ ◇

In October, Peter Taylor phoned Brighton's offices, wanting to speak to Mike Bamber. Taylor was calling to recommend that Bamber sign a young striker who Forest were keen to sell. The player in question had failed to make any significant inroads into the Forest first team during his three years at the club and, despite wanting to play as a forward, had been used primarily as left back or midfielder for the Forest reserves. The player's name was Tony Woodcock. As Bamber was unavailable to take the call, Taylor left a message suggesting that Brighton make a £14,000 bid.

Possibly thinking that Brighton's excellent early season form made any new signings unnecessary, Bamber failed to act upon his ex-manager's tip. Within a month, Woodcock had broken into the Forest first team and he went on to star in Forest's incredible run of success in the late seventies. A regular in the England side, winning 42 caps, Woodcock was transferred to West German side FC Köln for a German record £650,000 in 1979.

◇ ◇ ◇

A home draw with Crystal Palace was followed by a match which remains firmly in the memory of many Brighton fans; this was also the most memorable game for Alan Mullery during his time at the Goldstone:

> *One game stands out: an evening match against Walsall. It was a snowy day and I had a phone call at about one o'clock from Frankie Howard, who was the groundsman at the Goldstone Ground. He said 'Guv'nor, we've got a big problem — there's snow on the pitch.' I didn't really see that as being too big of a problem and I told him to sweep it away. He said, 'there's another problem. Glenn Wilson [the Brighton kitman] has told me we haven't got any orange footballs.' So I asked him to just go and buy some. He told me, 'we've been everywhere and nobody has got any.'*

> *So I drove in to Sutton —I was living in Cheam at the time— and bought three orange match balls. I drove down to Brighton and we painted the lines on the pitch blue and got the apprentices and anyone else we could find to sweep the snow off the terraces.*

46

The game went ahead but it was like a practice match, with both teams giving the ball away all the time. It had started to pour with rain and at half-time it was 0-0. When the players came in to the dressing room I tore into them.

I told them that the people who had come to watch were getting soaked and had paid good money to get in to the grounds but that they, the team, were playing like a bunch of prats.

The players were cold and wet and wanted to put on dry kit and have a cup of tea but I was so mad that I threw them out of the changing room after one minute and told them to go and wait on the pitch in the rain. I went up to sit in the stand and all the fans and directors didn't know what was happening.

Inside twenty five minutes we had scored seven goals and we won the game 7-0! Peter Ward got four goals and I think that Ian Mellor got the other three. That was the most memorable game we had at the Goldstone and I'll never forget it.

The deluge of second half goals was too much for the Walsall goalkeeper Mick Kearns: at one point, he turned to the press photographers gathered behind his goal to ask how many goals he had conceded. As Mellor completed his hat-trick, scoring the opening, third and fifth goals, Ward was not to be outdone and scored the games' final two goals within 90 seconds of each other. He remembers the final goal with a laugh: "Spider took a shot and it hit both posts and rolled out to me and I tapped it in from about two yards. So he ended up with three and I got four!"

Ward's four goals, his first senior hat-trick, took his season tally to eleven and once again prompted Mullery to attempt to deter any potential suitors from making a bid for his free-scoring forward. Mullery told the national press that he was the only manager in his division who could turn down a bid of £200,000, and said that he was not surprised that teams such as Queens Park Rangers, Spurs, West Ham and Arsenal had all watched Ward: he wasn't for sale, though, and there was no pressure from his board to cash in on the youngster.

◇ ◇ ◇

A growing reputation and national interest in his quick rise from non-league anonymity meant that Ward's young family was also suddenly brought into the spotlight. Photographs of Peter, his wife Sue and baby daughter Rachael appeared in both The Sun and Daily Mirror, and while Peter seemed to take the publicity in his stride, for Sue it was strange to see herself and her family in the media:

I think that it was easier for Pete because he was used to people watching him when he played. I found it weird when we were in the paper. John Vinicombe, from the Evening Argus, was really nice to us: he was always very kind and gave us advice on what to say and what not to say. The strangest thing for me was seeing Pete on Match of the Day. We'd be sitting there, in our home, watching TV and there he was, on the telly!

◇   ◇   ◇

The League Cup clash with Derby County was an opportunity for Ward to show the club who had ignored him as a youngster what they had missed.

Under the Goldstone Ground floodlights and in front of a sell-out 33,500 crowd, Ward did not have to wait long to send a clear message to the Rams. With only 37 seconds on the stopwatch, he reacted quickest as County keeper Graham Moseley parried a Mellor shot and smashed the rebound into the goal in front of an ecstatic North Stand.

Midway through the half, Derby equalised to take the game to a replay. For Ward, this meant an opportunity to play at the ground that he used to visit as a young fan:

Evening games at the Goldstone were the best. If the pitch was a little wet you could slide around and the crowd used to love it. Playing Derby was brilliant. Steve Powell, who I had played against at school, was on their team and Roy McFarland, who was captain when I used to watch them and was still in the England team, was marking me.

After the game we were disappointed that we hadn't won, but I was thrilled to have had a chance to play at Derby in the replay.

Dad Colin, who used to take Peter to watch the Rams, remembers the tie clearly:

Derby had won the league a couple of years before and still had a really good team. Of course I would have liked to have seen Peter play for Derby, but he didn't even have a trial with them. I always thought that he would have more chances if he went to a Third Division team and this proved to be the case.

He scored really early in the first game and in the replay it was a real thrill to see him play at the Baseball Ground.

The pre-match media spotlight again focused on Ward. Albion chairman Mike Bamber told the press that his exciting, young goalscorer could become the hottest property in football if he continued to improve at such a rate. Unfortunately, the replay proved to be the end of Albion's cup run as Derby held on for a 2-1 victory and a place in the quarter-finals.

◇ ◇ ◇

The two cup games against Derby did not affect the team's focus on promotion and three consecutive wins in the space of eight days maintained Albion's position at the top of the table. Ward scored in each of the victories, at Northampton and Reading and at home to Swindon, and his season total stood at fifteen by the middle of November.

The striker's goals and the high level of media coverage he was receiving had seen Ward become a focus for what The Sun referred to as 'the Third Division bully boys'. Alan Mullery, no stranger to dishing out a few welcoming tackles as a player, regarded Ward's bravery as one of his key strengths:

Peter would get more than his fair share of kicks but there was no cowardice about him at all — he would always come back for more.

After he had scored a few goals, and especially after he had been on TV a couple of times, the other team would generally save the first bad tackle of the game for Peter. But, like a lot of great players, he wouldn't retaliate and he had a great temperament. More often than not he would get the final word with a goal.

The rough treatment dished out to Ward proved futile and his resilience was demonstrated by the fact that he played every single minute of all fifty-six first team games during the season.

Further goals in consecutive 2-2 draws, against Port Vale and in the FA Cup against Crystal Palace, put Ward second (with 17 goals) in the race to be the top goalscorer in the entire Football League. Second Division Charlton Athletic's Derek Hayles (with 18 goals) was heading the list and Aston Villa's young Scottish striker Andy Gray, now a pundit for Sky Sports, was leading the way in Division One (with 16 goals).

On 22nd November, two days after the draw with Palace, the Derby Evening Telegraph reported that First Division strugglers West Ham United had bid £200,000 for Ward. Mullery denied the reports, saying that he had not had any contact with Hammers' boss John Lyall.

◇ ◇ ◇

A second draw against Crystal Palace in the FA Cup replay was followed by three consecutive losses as the previously high-scoring Albion attack suddenly ran out of goals.

A 2-0 defeat at home to promotion rivals Wrexham was Brighton's first home defeat for over fourteen months; it was also the first time that Ward had experienced a league loss at the Goldstone Ground. Another defeat to a promotion contender, this time 1-0 at Shrewsbury, saw Albion drop to third in the table.

A miserable two weeks concluded with a 1-0 loss to Crystal Palace in a bad-tempered second FA Cup first round replay at Chelsea's Stamford Bridge ground. The Palace defeat ended Brighton's cup interests for the season and left Mullery wondering how his team "could lose to rubbish like that."

Despite the run of disappointing results, Ward's excellent form had caught the eye of Don Revie, the England manager. Writing in his regular newspaper column, Revie commended Ward for his "pace, tight control and cool, clinical finishing" and, drawing comparison with Leeds and England striker Allan Clarke, wrote that Ward had captured his attention more than any other striker that season.

A come-from-behind home victory over Chesterfield ended both the bad run and Ward's four match goalless streak. His second-half equaliser and sub Sammy Morgan's first goal of the season ensured a 2-1 victory and put the Albion back at the top of the table, albeit briefly.

A surprise loss at Portsmouth the day after Boxing Day was followed by a 2-0 win over Gillingham at the Goldstone as Albion went into the New Year second in the table.

◇ ◇ ◇

New Years Day, 1977, and the name of referee Alan Robinson will forever be etched in the minds of Brighton supporters and players.

Despite persistent sleet and a sodden County Ground pitch, Robinson decided that the game between hosts Swindon and their Sussex opponents should go ahead.

Peter Ward takes up the story of the thrashing that never was:

> It was a really horrible day; we didn't want to play because we knew we were the better team and the conditions made it more like a mud wrestling contest than a football match. Swindon couldn't believe their luck when the referee said the match would go ahead and they completely hammered us.
>
> At half-time we were two-nil down and it could have been even worse. It soon was, as Swindon scored two more after half-time and the rain and snow just kept falling.
>
> With about twenty minutes to go, the referee blew his whistle and we didn't know what he was doing. He signalled for everyone to leave the pitch and said that the game was abandoned! Now it was us who couldn't believe our luck and the Swindon players and fans were going mad.

50

Mullery told us to run to the changing rooms. I can't remember if we even bothered to get changed, we just got on the coach and got out as soon as we could, in case the referee changed his mind. It was a miracle!

The Swindon score was wiped from the records, if not the memory, and two days later Albion beat Northampton 2-0 at the Goldstone: Ward scored his nineteenth goal of the campaign. A goalless draw at Sheffield Wednesday was followed by two more Ward goals in a 3-0 win over Chester City.

Ward's brace against Chester put him on 21 goals for the season. In the race to be the top scorer in the country, Ward was now one goal behind Andy Gray but three ahead of Derek Hayles, who had moved from Charlton to Derby County.

February saw the promotion challenge maintained with home wins over Preston (2-0) and Grimsby (3-0), and a win and a draw on the road. Scoring once against Preston, twice against Grimsby —including his first penalty as a professional— and getting the only goal of the game at York, Ward had now had 25 goals: this made him the leading scoring in country. Interviewed by the Derby Evening Telegraph about his teammate, Brighton winger Peter O'Sullivan said that Ward had "outstanding technical skills, fantastic close control and tremendous pace." O'Sullivan tipped Ward to beat Andy Gray in the top scorer race.

In March the promotion challenge faltered with Albion defeats at Crystal Palace and Peterborough and disappointing one-all draws at home to both Tranmere Rovers and Bury — a game that Mike Bamber referred to as the worst performance for three or four years. The only win of the month, and Ward's only two goals, came against Shrewsbury Town in a 4-0 victory.

The Peterborough game was a day short of marking the first anniversary of Peter Ward's League debut. In the space of 12 months he had made 53 consecutive appearances and scored a staggering 33 goals - a phenomenal strike rate.

◇ ◇ ◇

The phrase 'natural goal-scorer' is often used to describe Ward and other players who enjoy extraordinary success in hitting the back of the net but, while there is little doubt that some players have the knack of scoring, Mullery knew that Ward would only produce his best form if he worked hard at improving specific facets of his game.

I used to work with Peter a lot after training. I'd get him to work on spinning defenders in the box. I would ping the ball to him with his back to the goal and put two or three defenders on him and get him to beat them and score.

51

We would work him really hard and he became extremely good at it. I taught him how to feel the defender behind him and work on turning both ways to win a penalty or score a goal.

There was a lot of work that went into it. He wasn't big enough or strong enough to hold people off, but over 10 yards he was electric and in the box he was magic.

Peter's great strengths were pace over 10-15 yards and an eye for a goal. He could score goals at any time. At times, he was a greedy little bugger like a lot of great strikers. I used to see that in Jimmy Greaves in his heyday. Jim wouldn't pick out anyone else if he had a chance to score a goal and that was the same with Peter.

Peter was really keen to work at his game and it was nice to see him learning. He'd only been at a club for a year or so and had very little experience. He was starting from scratch and in many ways I was starting from scratch too, but we seemed to work together really well. Having somebody with his ability to score goals in our side certainly made my job a lot easier.

The hard work clearly paid off for Ward and Mullery. In late March, the striker, along with teammates Brian Horton and Graham Cross, was named in the Professional Footballers Association Division Three Team of Season at the annual awards dinner in London.

◇　◇　◇

Going into the final six weeks of the 1976-77 season, third in the table, the expectation that Brighton would achieve promotion was high and the Sussex public headed to the Goldstone Ground in droves. The average attendance for the final five home games was just short of 26,000 and the team responded with a run of vital wins.

The first victory, 3-1 over league leaders Mansfield Town, helped Albion to leapfrog their rivals and to regain the top spot. Mansfield took an early lead and it looked to be an uphill struggle for Brighton but, when Ward converted a penalty that he himself had won, the tide turned. Gerry Fell put the home side in front before half-time and constant Albion pressure in the second half was finally rewarded when Ward scored his second goal of the game with 25 minutes remaining.

With 29 goals, Ward remained at the top of the nation's scoring table — although Rotherham winger Alan Crawford was only one goal behind, with 28. Andy Gray, with only two goals since January, was still the leading scorer in the top flight but his total of 25 left him well behind Ward.

Four days later, another Ward double helped Albion to a revenge 4-0 success over Portsmouth and put them two points clear at the top of the table. Before the game, Pompey defender Paul Cahill had boasted to a local TV reporter that he would play Ward out of the game. Peter recalls that the defenders predictions didn't quite come true:

> His comments fired me up and I ran him silly. I scored two goals and he couldn't really get near me. At one point in the first half I put the ball through his legs and as I ran around him I tapped the top of his head just to wind him up.

With 31 goals, 27 of which had come in league action, Ward was now rapidly closing in on the club scoring record. The previous best, for league goals, stood at 30: these had been scored by Hugh Vallance during the 1929-30 season when he notched 32 goals in total. The club record for overall goals (league and cup) belonged to Arthur Attwood, who had scored 35 goals during the 1932-33 campaign. At the time of Ward's record-breaking season, Attwood's achievement was generally ignored as eleven of his goals had been scored in the FA Cup qualifying rounds.

A hard-fought win at Gillingham, during which Ian Mellor scored the only goal of the game, and a 2-0 home victory over Reading —both goals to Ward— saw Brighton sitting at the top of the table with just seven games remaining. Ward's brace, his 32nd and 33rd of the season, saw him overtake Vallance's total figure of thirty-two goals: the Evening Argus proudly proclaimed that Ward was the new owner of the record that had lasted for forty-seven years.

A trip to the Midlands to face Walsall gave Ward an opportunity to score the one goal that he needed to equal Vallance's league record. However, the 1-0 defeat left Ward a goal shy of that particular landmark and only Mansfield's surprise loss at Reading kept Albion at the top of the table. In the wake of the defeat, Mullery announced confidently that his team needed just six more points from their final half a dozen games to guarantee promotion.

Four days later, another tricky away game at Lincoln City, who themselves still had an outside chance of promotion, allowed Albion to gain a vital point with a 2-2 draw. Again, Peter Ward failed to score, and Albion were grateful for two cracking goals from Steve Piper and Brian Horton.

On the day of the next game, at home against Port Vale, England manager Don Revie's newspaper column again trumpeted the virtues of the country's leading goalscorer. Revie mentioned that he had hoped to pick Ward for the England Under-21 team to play in a recent international against Wales, only to discover that he was too old to play by just six days.

As the England manager sang his praises and an expectant Goldstone Ground crowd packed the terraces, the scene was set for Ward to break the league goalscoring record and to take the recently christened Seagulls a step closer to the Second Division. Although Ward was presented with an impressive cup before the match to celebrate his goalscoring exploits, his teammates looked to have run out of luck as they hit the woodwork four times before

Gerry Fell's headed goal finally gave them the breakthrough—and vital victory— that they needed.

With just four games left, the Seagulls were now six points clear of the teams just outside the promotion places and needed four more points to be mathematically certain of going up.

The long trip to second-placed Wrexham appeared to be the toughest match of Albion's run-in. A goalless draw was a point well earned and it kept them at the top of the table. With three games remaining, the Albion now knew that a win in the next game, at home to Sheffield Wednesday, would guarantee promotion.

◇ ◇ ◇

Twelve months earlier, Wednesday's visit to the Goldstone signalled the end of a failed promotion bid for the Albion. By contrast, the evening of 3rd May, 1977, presented Brighton with an opportunity to wrap up their home fixtures with a glorious achievement. 30,756 fans came through the turnstiles with high hopes that they would witness a promotion-clinching victory.

Wednesday, which no longer had a chance of promotion, silenced the home crowd with an early goal for the second year in a row. This time, it took the visitors just 33 seconds to take the lead. Feeling the heavy weight of expectation on their collective shoulders, the Albion players struggled to get into the game during the first half. It took a calming half-time team talk from Mullery to re-focus his players.

Six minutes into the second half, Albion were awarded a penalty and Ward, who had not scored for four games, stepped up to take the spot kick. Looking to place his shot into the corner of the net, Ward screwed the kick wide of the goal and covered his head in despair. Sensing the increasing desperation of the situation, the Albion crowd roared encouragement. Within six minutes, Ward had made amends and had, at last, matched Hugh Vallance's league scoring record when he raced on to Ian Mellor's chest flick to level the score.

Fourteen minutes later, the Seagulls were awarded another penalty when Ward's header was handled. This time, Brian Horton, sensing that Ward was nervous about taking another penalty, placed the ball on the spot and scored to put the Albion in front. Steve Piper made the score 3-1 with four minutes left and the game was safe. Despite Wednesday's late second goal, the final whistle started a pitch invasion and thousands of jubilant fans joined their heroes to celebrate promotion.

◇ ◇ ◇

With promotion secured, the final two games of the season saw Albion travel to Swindon, rearranged after being abandoned earlier in the season, and to Chesterfield for the season finale.

Going into the Swindon game with 30 League goals, it took Ward eleven minutes to break the deadlock and to overtake Vallance's club individual League scoring record. The record-breaking goal was the lone high point of the game for Brighton. Two goals from Swindon midfielder Ray McHale condemned Mullery's men to defeat. To win the championship, the Seagulls were now reliant on winning their final game of the season and hoping that leaders Mansfield would lose at Wrexham.

Unfortunately for Mullery and his team, neither game ended with the necessary result and a physical 1-1 draw at Chesterfield let the Albion to a runner-up finish, second to champions Mansfield. Ward's late equaliser goal for the Seagulls brought his final season total to 36 goals, 32 of those being in the league.

Wrexham, who had been in the promotion places for most of the season, fell away over the last three weeks of the campaign and were pipped to the third and final promotion place by Crystal Palace, who beat the Welsh team twice during the final ten days of the season.

Having claimed the Brighton club scoring record for both League and total goals in a single season, Ward's achievements also put him clear of any other player in the English League. With 25 goals, Andy Gray shared the Division One League scoring title with Arsenal's Malcolm Macdonald.

Ward's incredible goalscoring exploits led to his nomination as the Third Division Player of the Year by managers of the other teams in the division. However, despite Ward's goals, Brighton's supporters voted inspirational captain Brian Horton as the club's Player of the Season.

Reflecting on the success of his first season in charge, Mullery has no hesitation in picking out his team's greatest strength:

> Goalscorers win you games. Everyone else can play well but if you haven't got a goalscorer you can't get anywhere. Goalscorers are like gold dust and we had two in that first season: Mellor and Ward got 50 or so between them. Brian Horton also chipped in with 14 or 15.

> When your strikers are scoring and you get that sort of support from midfield, you've got a chance.

> When I played with Jimmy Greaves, who was probably the greatest goalscorer I've ever seen, it didn't matter how much hard work I did as long as Jimmy was scoring goals.

◇ ◇ ◇

No doubt also taking a little pride from the fact that the Brighton team that he had assembled had finally achieved promotion, Peter Taylor, along with Brian Clough, was celebrating a promotion of his own. Nottingham Forest had finished third in Division Two and were heading to the top league. Much of Forest's success stemmed from the goals of Peter Withe and Tony Woodcock - two players who could easily have been competing with Ward and Mellor for places in the Brighton side.

◇ ◇ ◇

Ward's Brighton records still stand some thirty-two years later, a fact of which he is understandably very proud.

> *At the time, I didn't know that I was going to get close to the goalscoring record, which probably helped. If I had known, I would have wanted to take the penalties as well. I only took four because for most of the season Nobby (Horton) or Graham Cross took them. I may have scored 40 if I had been taking the penalties from the start of the season, but 36 is a pretty good number.*
>
> *When Bobby Zamora was almost breaking the record a few years ago [Zamora twice hit 28 League goals for Brighton] I was getting calls from the Argus and other papers and they were asking me what I thought about Zamora having a chance to break my record.*
>
> *I would tell them that I hoped he did it but, to be honest, I was really hoping that he would miss every chance he got! I think he had something like five games left one season and only needed three or four goals to get the record, but he only got one more. I would have put money on him breaking it but it didn't happen.*
>
> *I have spoken to him a few times and he seems like a nice guy — I hope he breaks a record... but somewhere else!*

◇ ◇ ◇

As reward for gaining promotion, the club awarded the first team squad a joint £20,000 bonus. The players' contracts specified that the money would be "shared between the players based on the number of matches in which they played or were named substitute" although "the final allocation [would] be made at the manager's discretion."

Ward, never slow to put his view forward, argued that the money should be divided amongst the players based on their appearances as stated in the contracts. Not all of the players agreed. Sammy Morgan takes up the story:

At the end of the promotion season we had a pot of bonus money. Alan Mullery asked us how we would like to split the money and a lot of the lads said that we should split it evenly amongst the players.

I had been in and out of the team because I had suffered a really bad facial injury and players like Graham Winstanley had only played a few times.

Young Peter, who had played in every single game, suggested that it should be split based on appearances. I took him aside and said 'Hey Peter, just you think about it, son. The reason I've only played a few games is because I was injured. I got injured because I put my head in where it hurts so that players like you can score goals. So if we get rewarded by appearances it will be a little unfair and people like me will stop getting hurt for people like you.'

He went away and thought about it for a little while and came back and said 'Sammy, you're absolutely right. We should all get the same.' He was a young lad and didn't quite understand, but in the end he made the right decision.

◇ ◇ ◇

Promotion was celebrated with a club-organised buffet dance at Hove Town Hall. With approximately 400 supporters joining the players and club staff, it was an ideal way to round off a wholly successful season. As Ward recalls, the evening cost Sammy Morgan a little more of his bonus money than it should have:

When we were promoted to Division Two, we had a do at the Town Hall in Hove. There were loads of fans there too and we all mingled together — it was great.

The players had our own room with a separate bar and we ended up in there, all sitting around: just having a laugh. It was Sammy Morgan's turn to get the drinks, so he got up and headed to the bar.

After about five minutes he still hadn't come back, so one of the other players decided to go to the bar and came back another round. We waited another fifteen minutes or so and eventually Sammy came back with a big tray of booze.

We drank quite quickly in those days, and we had soon finished the drinks so I said to Sammy, who was big and could carry more, 'It's your turn to get 'em again'.

Sammy said 'I've just got up: it must be someone else's turn. And anyway, those last drinks cost me a fortune.'

I said 'What? The drinks are free — you don't have to pay for them!' He looked at me and said 'What are you talking about? Where are the drinks free?' I pointed to the bar in our private room and his face dropped. He hadn't realised that we had our own complimentary bar and had spent twenty minutes queuing with all the fans. He had ended up paying for his round!

That was pretty typical of Sammy: he was a great guy and a very good player too.

CHAPTER 6

ENGLAND'S NUMBER 8

I told Ron Greenwood that an Under-21 game at the
Goldstone would probably get a crowd of between
8,000 and 10,000... but if Peter Ward played, you'd
probably get nearer to 20,000.

— Alan Mullery, MBE

Alan Mullery and Mike Bamber moved quickly to keep hold of their record-breaking striker once the season was over and, for the third consecutive summer, Ward agreed to a new contract. The new four-year deal provided improved terms plus the added comfort of a long term commitment from the club.

The next move for the Albion manager was to meet with the club directors to discuss strengthening the squad for the upcoming Division Two season. Mullery remembers the meeting very clearly:

> Keith Wickenden, who was MP for Dorking, was the vice-chairman — he was a nice man and very, very wealthy. We had a board meeting a week after we had sealed promotion and Keith asked me 'If I give you £250,000 where will that get us in the Second Division?'
>
> I told him that that would probably buy the players to keep us there.
>
> 'If I give you £500,000 where will that get us?'
>
> I said that would give us a shout of getting promotion again.
>
> So he said 'Right, you've got half a million pounds.'
>
> I knew what the next question was going to be and immediately he asked me who I wanted to buy. I had already spoken to Nobby Stiles, who was assistant manager at Preston, about two defenders: Mark Lawrenson and Gary Williams.
>
> Keith said that he didn't remember either player but, luckily, Preston were playing that night at Crystal Palace and I told the directors that we should go and watch.
>
> Lawrenson had a great game and he was still only nineteen years old. The directors told me to go and buy him there and then, but by the time I got down to the changing rooms the Preston management had already left to go home.

The next morning, I spoke to Nobby again and he told me that Liverpool had already bid £75,000 for Lawrenson. I called Mike Bamber and told him that we'd have no chance of signing him now that Liverpool were interested. But Bamber wasn't going to give up and told me to offer Preston £100,000 for him.

I spoke to the Preston manager, Harry Carrick, and told him that we would pay £50,000 now and the rest over the next year. Harry told me that he would need to speak to the Liverpool manager Bob Paisley. He phoned me back and told me that Liverpool weren't willing to match our offer, so Mark signed for Brighton, which was fantastic.

When he had played against Wardy, he had looked like a very good player. Wardy was the King in the Third Division but Lawrenson played him very well. He was intelligent and quick, and turned out to be the best player I ever signed.

Lawrenson's signature cost Brighton a club record £111,000 and within a couple of weeks Mullery again turned to Preston to sign 23-year-old full-back Williams. Graham Cross, who had been so impressive throughout the previous season, headed in the opposite direction, joining Preston along with Harry Wilson. With Lawrenson and Williams teaming up with Andy Rollings and Chris Cattlin, Mullery had now assembled the defensive combination that would provide the foundation of the Seagulls' rise to the First Division.

Coming to Brighton was a straightforward decision for both Lawrenson and Williams. Lawrenson was keen to further his career and saw Brighton as an ideal opportunity:

Preston were having semi-hard times and needed the money. It was an easy choice to move to Brighton — Brighton were on an upward curve and Preston on a downward curve.

When I arrived it was easy to fit in because, with just a couple of exceptions, all of the players were from out of the area and everyone knew that a new member of the squad needed looking after. Of course, it helped me that Gary Williams came down too.

When asked about joining Lawrenson at Brighton, Williams tells a similar story:

When I signed for Brighton it was an easy decision. They brought me down in the summer and put me up in the Metropole Hotel. I woke up in the morning and went out onto my balcony overlooking the sea and thought 'wow'.

There was a fantastic buzz around the town. When I was at Preston we would look forward to the Brighton away game because of the size of the crowds. We would treat it like a Wembley trip because we knew we'd be running out in front of 25,000 to 30,000 people — it was fantastic.

Wardy already had a reputation when I arrived — he was a top man. I remember when we played Brighton at the Goldstone when I was at Preston. We all knew about this 'wonder kid,' Peter Ward, and he took us to the cleaners that day: they beat us 2-0. We had a good team and were going for promotion but Brighton were awesome.

I remember that I was marking Tony Towner on the wing and Brian Horton kept shouting to him, 'take him on, he's shit. He's absolutely shit.' Brian was brilliant at motivating his teammates. I think Wardy and Towner both scored that day too.

◇　◇　◇

For the opening competitive game of the season Albion travelled to Cambridge; this was the first leg of their first round League Cup tie. Cambridge, under the management of Ron Atkinson, had won the Fourth Division the previous season and proved to be a tough test for Mullery's team. A goalless draw was followed by a similar result in the return leg at the Goldstone, with Ward missing a penalty and creating the need for a replay in Brighton a week later.

Before the Cambridge replay, Brighton, along with 5,000 of their supporters, travelled along the south coast to Southampton for their opening Division Two fixture. The Saints viewed Ward's goalscoring talents as the biggest threat that Brighton offered and they responded by sending two or three defenders to surround him whenever he had the ball. With Ward shackled, Southampton captain Alan Ball put the home side in front just before half-time; a late goal from substitute John Ruggiero earned Albion a well-deserved point.

The game was twice interrupted as fighting in the crowd spilled onto the pitch and what became known as 'the English disease' was, unfortunately, a regular occurrence at games during the next few years.

Asked whether 'aggro' on the terraces was ever a worry to the players, Ward says:

As a player it normally wasn't that frightening. The only time it was a little scary was when we played Millwall at the Goldstone before they had put the fences around the pitch. We came out of the tunnel and all I could see were these men in balaclavas shouting that they wanted to kill me. Jesus Christ, I was frightened to death! Luckily, after that game they put the fences up and caged the away fans in.

Another time, when we went on the coach to play at Millwall, we all had to sit on one side of the coach because the Millwall fans were throwing anything they could find at the other side.

Most of the time, though, we would just get on with playing and it was only when some idiot came onto the pitch that we'd pay much attention to it.

◇ ◇ ◇

Ward's first goal of the season came in the replay against Cambridge. Two Brian Horton goals had allowed Albion to take a 2-1 lead and Ward scored a rare headed goal in the 85th minute to seal a 3-1 victory. A familiar face in the Cambridge side was Sammy Morgan, who had switched clubs a few days earlier for a fee of £15,000.

Morgan remembers the game and his battle with Brighton defender Andy Rollings:

Andy Rollings and I knocked ten lumps out of each other — I think Andy lost a tooth. John Vinicombe wrote in The Argus that my disciplinary problems were no longer a concern for Brighton, which I thought was a bit harsh. Little did he know that Andy and I were the first in the bar after the game — the best of friends. It was always like that.

◇ ◇ ◇

On Friday, 26th August, the Daily Express reported that Ward was emerging as 'the people's choice' to become the first player for five years to score 30 league goals in either of the top two divisions. The newspaper was offering a £10,000 prize to the player who achieved the feat and bookmakers Corals had shortened Ward's odds from 50-1 to 25-1.

A day later, before the first home league game of the season against Millwall, Ward was presented with the Third Division Player of the Season award from the previous season. On a rain-soaked Goldstone pitch, the Seagulls found themselves two goals down at half-time and looked to be heading to defeat. A half-time blast from Alan Mullery rejuvenated his players and, five minutes into the second half, Ward scored his very first Second Division goal, bringing the Albion back into the game. Two late goals from Eric Potts and Steve Piper capped a fine comeback and gave Albion a 3-2 win.

Oldham Athletic visited the Goldstone Ground for a second round League Cup game on 30th August but, despite an impressive performance from Ward, the game finished nil-nil.

◇ ◇ ◇

The following day, Ron Greenwood performed the first task in his new role as England manager by announcing the Under-21 squad to face Norway in a European Championship qualifier. To the delight of 22-year-old Ward, he was named as one of the two permitted over-age players in the eighteen-man squad. Even more exciting for the striker was that the game was scheduled to take place in Brighton.

Greenwood, appointed in the wake of Don Revie's surprise departure to become coach of the United Arab Emirate's national team, lived in Hove and, as Alan Mullery explains, was a frequent visitor to the Goldstone Ground:

> Ron lived nearby and came to most of the home games. He would come into the boardroom after the games and we'd talk about various players.
>
> He told me that he wished that Brian Horton was younger because he was impressed by his competiveness; he thought that Brian could have been an international player if he had been playing at a higher standard when he was younger.
>
> Ron would also talk about Wardy. He liked Peter's skill and ability and it was very obvious that at the time Peter was a top class goalscorer and in great form.
>
> He spoke about putting on an England Under-21 game at the Goldstone and asked what sort of crowd I thought he'd get. I told him an Under-21 game would probably get a crowd of between 8,000 and 10,000 but if Peter Ward played you'd probably get nearer to 20,000. He said 'Are you sure?' and I told him how much everybody loved Peter in Brighton.
>
> Ron did pick him and played him, and it was a sell-out. Ron was delighted — the night was a great success.

◇   ◇   ◇

Before the England game, Ward and his teammates travelled to Mansfield for a Division Two fixture. A 2-1 victory for the Albion, ending an unbeaten run of 38 home matches for the Stags, continued their unbeaten start to the season. However, for the first time in his Brighton career, Ward was substituted. Complaining of a heavy cold, he came off after 55 minutes and, with the England Under-21 game only 3 days away, there were concerns as to whether he would be fit enough to participate:

> At Mansfield, I was coughing and spluttering and just couldn't get rid of this cold. At half-time I'd had enough, really, and was finding it hard to breathe; I lasted about another ten minutes. I think I still got Man of the Match in some of the Sunday papers though.
>
> I was grateful that Mullery took me off because I wanted to be fit for the England game. We got back to Brighton on Saturday night and I just rested on Sunday.

We (the England team) trained at the Goldstone Ground on the Monday and I felt ok, so Dave Sexton, who was in charge of the team, said that I could play - which was a massive relief.

After the game, once the excitement had worn off, I was ill again and ended up spending a week in a nursing home. I had to have blood tests and everything and eventually they decided that I had a chest virus.

◇   ◇   ◇

As kick-off approached on Tuesday, 6th September, 1977, the order was given to close the Goldstone turnstiles. A miscalculation meant that the club's matchday staff were under the impression that the ground had reached 33,500 capacity even though the actual attendance was 18,500. Thousands of disappointed fans were turned away and denied the chance to see Peter Ward complete a memorable international debut.

As Ward prepared to become the first Brighton player to represent an England team since Tommy Cook some fifty-two years earlier, little did he know that events a few yards away almost literally turned the lights out on his big occasion before it had even started.

The club had invested £40,000 in installing new floodlights that were powerful enough to allow television coverage of evening games. Work on the lights had only been completed the week before the England game and they had yet to be used for a full match. With a little over an hour to go before kick-off, the lights were switched on. The main fuses were immediately blown, and the lights went out. Club Secretary Ron Pavey summoned the local electricity supplier, Seeboard, to investigate the problem and, after another failed attempt, a temporary solution was finally patched together and new electrical transformers installed. These, fortunately, lasted for the duration of the game.

With the floodlights illuminating the bright Goldstone pitch, Ward lined up for the national anthems, standing between Southampton's Steve Williams and Manchester City's Gary Owen. Even in his wildest dreams, Ward could not have imagined what the next 90 minutes would hold.

Fourteen minutes into the game, Ward scored the first goal in front of a jubilant South Stand crowd. Ward's strike partner, Aston Villa's John Deehan, aimed a powerful header towards goal that the Norway keeper Jan Eric Olsen could only palm away. The ball fell to Ward and, in his typical relaxed style, England's number 8 calmly placed the ball into the goal.

Six minutes later, Manchester City winger Peter Barnes increased the lead and, in the 35th minute, Ward got his second and England's third goal. Following up a fierce free-kick from Southampton's David Peach, he demonstrated his uncanny knack of being in the right place at the right time with another simple finish from the edge of the six yard box.

Five minutes into the second half, England scored 4-0 with a header from Deehan, and Ward's incredible evening climaxed with his hat-trick goal after 67 minutes. Chasing a lobbed pass from West Brom's Laurie Cunningham, Ward headed the ball into the top left corner of the net to the delight of the fans massed in the North Stand.

There was still time for Deehan to get a sixth goal as he rifled home a left-footed shot following a headed pass from Ward.

It is little wonder that Ward still harbours fond memories of a very special night:

It was fantastic. I was nervous before the start and I knew that there would be loads of fans there; I didn't want to let them down because they were always so good to me. Alan Mullery had really been talking me up to the press before the game and I didn't want to let him down either.

My mum and dad had come down for the game and my wife was in the stand, so I was just hoping that it would go well.

Dave Sexton was managing the team and at the time he was manager at Manchester United. He was really good and calmed everyone down before kick-off. Once the game got underway I just felt relaxed — everything seemed to go right.

I hit it off with John Deehan straight away and we really seemed to gel, and Steve Williams and Gary Owen in midfield completely ran the game.

I scored with my right foot, and then my left foot and finally with a header — they call that a perfect hat-trick — fantastic. The crowd gave me a standing ovation after the game: it was an incredible moment and one I'll never forget.

◇   ◇   ◇

The day after the game, the back pages of the national papers were emblazoned with headlines trumpeting the dream debut; "Wow! Ward is Sheer Magic," "Super Ward!," "Ward looks a Wizard," "It's Wonder Boy Ward."

Dave Sexton expressed his delight at the performance, saying that Ward played "tremendously well and was mustard in the box". Ron Greenwood was also impressed and admitted to being "delighted with the performance"; Mullery commented that Ward "was superb."

Never shy to trumpet Ward's talents, Peter Taylor told the Daily Express that Ward should be an automatic selection for the full England team and likened the striker's goalscoring aptitude to that of a certain Brian Clough.

⬦ ⬦ ⬦

As Ward became the hot topic in the sport sections of newspapers across the country, a recurrence of his breathing problems sent the striker to spend the next ten days under medical supervision in a nursing home in Hove.

Ward's run of 71 consecutive games since breaking into the first team was broken as he missed both a home win against Hull City and the League Cup replay at Oldham, which ended in a 2-2 draw.

Ward returned to the team for a goalless draw at Burnley — a result which lifted the Seagulls to fifth in the table, the highest position the club had held in 76 years of existence. The goal touch returned as he scored in a 2-1 defeat in the second replay against Oldham, and then twice more in a 2-1 win at home to Sheffield United — a win which lifted the Seagulls to fourth place.

Further goals, as Albion defeated Luton Town 3-2 at the Goldstone and won 2-0 at Sunderland, saw Brighton sitting proudly at the top of the Second Division and still unbeaten in the league as September gave way to October.

⬦ ⬦ ⬦

In anticipation of Ron Greenwood's announcement of his full England squad to would take on Luxembourg in a vital European Championship qualifier, a number of pundits suggested that either Ward or his Under-21 strike partner John Deehan would be selected.

When the squad was announced, the news that Greenwood had opted for Ward came as a welcome surprise for the Brighton striker:

> I didn't even know that the squad was being announced and at first I thought it was a joke. Then at training, Alan Mullery confirmed that I had been included and all of the players gave me a round of applause.
>
> I had been playing well and was scoring plenty of goals but it was still less than two years since I had made my league debut. It was like a dream

Ward's inclusion in the squad, alongside established stars such as Kevin Keegan, Peter Shilton, Emlyn Hughes and Trevor Brooking, was greeted with excitement and approval by the nation's football writers. Justifying his choice, Greenwood joined the ever-growing list of people in the game to compare Ward to Jimmy Greaves and, as England expected a goal-feast against Luxembourg, Ward was hopeful of getting a chance to play.

Before the day of the England match, Brighton faced two more league games.

⬦ ⬦ ⬦

A midweek trip to Charlton provided a number of talking points but ultimately signalled the end of the unbeaten run. The team travelled by train to the game but delays to the rail service meant that the players, who at one stage had to walk down the train line, arrived at The Valley with only twenty minutes to go before kick-off. Sensing that their opponents were ill-prepared, Charlton made a positive start and within 30 minutes were 2 goals up. Ward reduced the deficit just before half-time with a landmark goal - the 50th of his Brighton career. Reaching this milestone and having played only 77 first team games was a fantastic achievement.

Given new impetus by Ward's goal, Brighton started the second half looking like a top of the table team. They were awarded a penalty when Ward was fouled. Brian Horton had been handed responsibility for penalties after Ward missed his second spot-kick of the season against Luton Town a week earlier. However, Horton's first attempt was saved by Charlton keeper Jeff Wood and he was relieved when the referee ordered the kick to be retaken; the keeper had moved too early. Horton's second try sailed wide but once again the kick was ordered to be retaken. By now, Mullery had seen enough and shouted to Horton to let Ward take the third attempt. Ward sent Wood the wrong way and his ninth goal of the season tied the scores.

A rare Graham Winstanley goal put the Seagulls 3-2 up but two late goals from Charlton swung the game back to the home side and left a spirited Albion with nothing to show for their efforts.

◇   ◇   ◇

The next game, at home to new league leaders Bolton Wanderers, resulted in the second successive Albion defeat; the Seagulls dropped to third place.

With the Luxembourg match approaching, attention switched to whether or not Ward would have the opportunity to win a full England cap. Manchester City coach Malcolm Allison suggested that Ward should play as the central striker and Jimmy Greaves himself wrote a newspaper column saying that "Peter Ward must play."

Despite support from many sources for Ward's inclusion in the team and much to Peter's disappointment, Greenwood decided against picking him.

We all flew to Luxembourg the day before the game and trained when we got there. At first it was a little intimidating, training with all of these great players, but I felt that I could fit in. I was used to playing with some great players at Brighton and this wasn't that much different.

Some of the players stayed in their little groups -like all the Liverpool lads- but everyone was friendly.

When Ron announced the team I was really disappointed that he hadn't picked me and that I wasn't even a sub.

We only won the game 2-0, and one of those goals game in the last minute. Everyone had been saying beforehand that we should be getting a hatful of goals because Luxembourg were a really poor side.

After the match, quite a few of the lads went out for a drink. I got drunk with Brian Greenhoff, who was at Manchester United. When I got back to the hotel I was a bit of a mess and I don't think that Trevor Brooking, who was my roommate, was too impressed with me. Maybe Brooking had a word with Greenwood and told him that I was a lunatic —I don't know— but I didn't get another chance with England for a long time after that.

For lifelong Albion fan Rod Clark, the Luxembourg trip was a series of disappointments:

I organised a coach party to go from Sussex to Luxembourg in the hope of watching Wardy make his England debut. It was really disappointing when he didn't play and the game was rubbish. On the way home we decided to stop at a beer festival to drown our sorrows. Unfortunately, we drowned them a little too much and got thrown out.

◇ ◇ ◇

The disappointment of the Luxembourg adventure behind him, Ward returned to Brighton intent on helping the team to rediscover the winning touch. However, a 1-0 defeat at Stoke was the third loss in a row.

A week later, 28,000 fans headed to the Goldstone Ground to see Albion once again lock horns with rivals Crystal Palace. Ian Mellor's goal, only his third of the season, gave Albion a 1-1 draw and stopped the run of defeats.

The next game saw Albion return to their winning ways with a convincing 4-0 victory over Cardiff City. Ward hit his tenth goal of the season and Albion jumped back up to third in the table. The game was marred by a red card for Cardiff's enigmatic and self-destructive forward, Robin Friday. Making his first appearance of the season, Friday was sent off for kicking Mark Lawrenson in the face 10 minutes into the second half. Storming out of the ground before the game finished, Friday disappeared and failed to report for training in Cardiff the following week. In fact, the game proved to be Friday's last ever and he walked away from professional football.

◇ ◇ ◇

Although the team was struggling to maintain their promising start to the season, Ward's popularity amongst fans and local businesses continued to grow. The day before the next game, at home to Orient, Ward took ownership of a brand new Rover car, sponsored by local car dealers Caffyns. A smiling Ward was pictured in the Argus receiving the keys for his new car. Not everyone at the club, however, was quite as happy:

> I was the first player at the club to get a sponsored car and Alan Mullery went nuts. It was a silver Rover, a really nice car but Mullery was livid — he didn't think that any of the players should have a sponsored car if he didn't. He got someone to sort one out for him the next season.

Ward's teammate Gary Williams remembers the incident well:

> Wardy still really had his feet on the ground although he was such a star at the time and he would get loads of attention. He didn't cause any problems intentionally but he was the first of the players to get a company car and this didn't go down too well.

> There were a few raised eyebrows among the other players because it wasn't like now: footballers weren't paid so much that they could buy a new car every week! I think that Mullery was jealous, though, and it wasn't long before the club had arranged for him to have one too.

> Eventually, a few of the other players also got them, but it ended up with half the team having a car and half not which wasn't great for those who didn't — it didn't feel right.

Mark Lawrenson remembers Ward arriving in his new perk:

> He pulled up in this great big Rover, 2.6 litre, automatic. Everyone else was driving around in all-sorts — Toyotas and Fiats — and when he turned up in this car it was 'whoa!'

> I think that everyone understood that he was the main man so there wasn't too much fuss - I got one a couple of months later and so did Brian Horton.

◇ ◇ ◇

Brian Horton's penalty proved enough to beat Orient, but the match brought an end to Steve Piper's Brighton career. Mullery signed 18-year-old midfielder Paul 'Tank' Clark from Southend United as a replacement for Piper and the youngster went straight into the team for the next game, away at Mullery's old team Tottenham.

A couple of days before the Spurs match, Manchester United manager Dave Sexton made an official approach to Brighton about the possibility of signing Ward. An offer reported to be in the region of £250,000 was rejected and, with rumours circulating that Nottingham Forest had also made a bid for the player, chairman Mike Bamber announced that "Ward is not for sale at any price, not even one million pounds!" At this time, the British record transfer fee was the £500,000 that Liverpool had received from Hamburg for Kevin Keegan in June of 1977. It wasn't until Clough's Forest signed Trevor Francis from Birmingham during the following season that the million pound barrier was breached.

48,613 fans crammed into White Hart Lane to see the second placed Spurs take on the Brighton team, which was sitting just one place below them in the table. Unfortunately for ITV's Big Match cameras, the game failed to meet the expectations of the fans and the nil-nil result provided little excitement for the Sunday afternoon national television audience.

Mullery was delighted by the Spurs result, but sensed that there was still a need to improve his team. Paying another of his old teams, Fulham, a club record £200,000 for striker Teddy Maybank, Mullery sent out a clear message to Brighton's rivals that the club was intent on maintaining their promotion challenge.

Maybank's arrival ended the Ward and Mellor partnership that had been so successful the previous season. The new striker replaced Mellor for the next game - Blackburn's visit to the Goldstone Ground. It only took seven minutes for the new strike partnership to produce a goal and Maybank's shot from Ward's cross looked to have set the Albion on the way to victory. An equalizer from Blackburn, followed by Towner's first goal of the season, saw Albion lead 2-1 at half-time but a mix-up between Albion keeper Eric Steele and Graham Winstanley let Blackburn take a share of the points.

Maybank scored again in a 1-0 win at Blackpool and the remaining five games in December resulted in one win, two draws and two defeats.

For Ward, the Blackpool game evokes memories of two embarrassing situations:

> *Although we won the game it wasn't the best couple of days I ever had. I managed to do quite a few stupid things during my career and this particular weekend included a couple of the best examples. It got off to a pretty bad start...*
>
> *At Blackpool, they had a little white kerb that went all the way around the pitch. It was only an inch or so high but as we ran out onto the pitch I managed to trip over it and went flying. You can imagine how amusing the Blackpool fans found that.*
>
> *For some reason, I had driven up to the match — maybe I was going to stop off to see my mum and dad afterwards, I can't remember. Anyway, after the game I was driving back and something went wrong with my car. I had to pull over and eventually the car rescue people came. They told me that it would cost £500 for them to tow the car back to Brighton.*

I didn't usually carry much money around with me, but on this occasion I had £600 in my pocket because I was hoping to stop somewhere and buy a video recorder — a Phillips one, which was pretty expensive. I didn't know what to do because I was really set on getting a video player, but I was stuck in the middle of nowhere and didn't have any way of getting home. So I decided to give them pretty much all of my money so that they would drive me home to Brighton.

Anyway, the following day I had a call from Caffyns, which was the car dealership that had supplied me with the sponsored car. They asked how I'd got the car back to Brighton and I told them that it had cost me £500 to have it towed. At this point, the guy from Caffyns asked if I had ever looked in the glove compartment of the car. I asked him why and he said that the AA membership details were in there and that I could have had it towed or fixed for free! I was such a prat — what a waste of money!

The final ten games of 1977 had not produced a single goal for Ward and his new strike partner Maybank had failed to win the affections of the Brighton supporters.

Mullery was quick to support his record signing and felt that the abuse that the player received from the crowd was unjustified:

We had let Ian Mellor go because we felt that he had reached a certain age and had probably peaked. When Teddy Maybank became available we thought that he was a better option.

He got a lot of stick from the fans but he worked extremely hard. He was a battering ram and was very good at making goals for other people.

He also got some vital goals himself, especially in the second season that he was with us.

Ward does not attribute his goal-less spell to the end of his partnership with Mellor nor to Maybank's introduction:

I didn't really care who I played with — I just got on with my own game. Teddy was a good player and Mullery loved him. I was struggling to score when Teddy came into the side but I was playing OK.

We were only scoring a goal a game, whereas we had been used to getting two, three or four goals every time that we played at the Goldstone. The defenders were better and we weren't getting as many chances, but I didn't doubt that I would start scoring again.

Off the pitch Teddy was terrible — a real tart.

If any of the boys were going around his house he would always tell them not to knock on his door. Instead he would leave his curtains open a little

71

bit and tell to them look into his front room so that they could see if he was
busy 'entertaining' any lady friends....

◇ ◇ ◇

1978 started with Albion sitting fifth in the table and welcoming third - placed Southampton to the Goldstone Ground. Just under 33,000 fans watched a 1-1 draw and Mark Lawrenson scored the equalizing goal for Brighton.

Ward finally broke his 11-game, two-month scoring drought against non-league Scarborough in the FA Cup third round on 7th January. He headed Albion's first goal ten minutes before half-time and further goals from the re-called Eric Potts and Horton sealed a comfortable 3-0 win.

Albion returned to league action the following Saturday and Ward scored the only goal in a 1-0 victory at Millwall. The goal, his twelfth of the season, followed a quick one-two with Maybank and was just reward for a game that the Seagulls dominated.

Scoring in successive games lifted Ward's confidence and old Division Three foes Mansfield Town were the next unfortunate victims of the rejuvenated striker. A Ward hat-trick, a goal for Maybank and another for Horton helped Albion to their biggest win of the season, 5-1.

Five goals in three games seemed to indicate that Ward was back in top form but, once again, the goals stopped. With Maybank out injured and Ward misfiring, newly-signed Malcolm Poskett picked up the scoring slack with goals in his first two games.

When Maybank returned to fitness, Alan Mullery was faced with a dilemma over which of his strikers he should leave out:

Malcolm Poskett did a terrific job when we signed him. He was one of the most under-rated goalscorers — absolutely brilliant.

He was really similar to Wardy, very sharp and very quick but a bit taller and a bit stronger. He was a good pro and quite willing to play second fiddle to Peter. On two or three occasions after Malcolm had done really well I dropped him in favour of the Peter and Teddy partnership, which, looking back, was maybe not fair to Malcolm.

The trip to second-placed Bolton at the start of March was one such occasion and fit-again Maybank joined Ward in the starting eleven. A one-all draw was a point well earned but it was an unhappy afternoon for Ward. Struggling to shake the attention of Bolton defender Sam Allardyce, he failed to make an impact on the game and was substituted midway through the second half.

◇ ◇ ◇

When Mullery signed Welsh international Peter Sayer from Cardiff City, the skilful midfielder changed the appearance of the Brighton team in more ways than one. Sayer was the first player at the club to sport what is now disparagingly called the 70s footballer perm. Before long, other members of the team followed suit and Ward was one of the first to succumb to the curse of the hairdresser's curlers.

Long-time Albion fan and close friend of Ward, Danny Hornby, takes up the story:

> Peter Sayer came in from Wales and he was sporting an impressive 'afro'. Mark Lawrenson was in digs with a chap called 'Dinky' Doo and his wife Kay. Kay was a hairdresser and Mark took the plunge and had a perm.
>
> At the time I thought that it looked great, so I had one done too. The next time I saw Wardy he really made fun of my new look, so imagine my surprise when a few days later he drove past me in his sponsored car tooting his horn. He wound down his window and showed off his very own afro!
>
> The first time he went into training the players all made the most of it and instead of calling him Wizz (after cartoon character Billy the Wizz) they started to call him Doris! I've greeted him with that name ever since.

Ward's recollection is fairly similar:

> I first had it permed in Derby at the same place that I always had my hair cut. I felt a little self-conscious sitting with all the girls with curlers in my hair and when my wife saw it she couldn't stop laughing.
>
> The first time I went into training after I'd had it done, Mullery said 'what does she look like?' and all the lads cracked up — I couldn't help but join in.
>
> It wasn't even the worst hair cut I had — a couple of years later I had highlights put in and they were supposed to be blond but they turned my hair pink! It was a nightmare and took me ages to get rid of them. Obviously I got hammered by the lads at training about that too....

◇　◇　◇

Newly-permed Ward again lined up alongside Maybank —Poskett was confined to the bench— for Stoke's visit to the Goldstone. Two goals inside the first five minutes from Potts and Sayer gave Albion a 2-0 half-time lead but, again, Ward was struggling to get involved in the game. Looking tired and lacking his usual sharpness, he was substituted for the second consecutive game midway through the second half.

After the game, which Albion won 2-1, Mullery told the press that he was baffled as to what was causing Ward's lack of form and the player himself told the Argus that a spell in the reserve team may do him good.

Ward got his wish and, two days later, played a full 90 minutes for the second string at Brentford. Again he looked sluggish and Mullery gave him another 90 minute run-out the following night as the reserves took on Watford. A much better performance and two goals from the out-of-form striker gave some hope that Ward would rediscover his goal touch.

The day after the Watford game, The Sun newspaper printed its own theory as to why Ward was looking tired on Saturday afternoons. On page 3, under the headline "I'm Not Out Chasing All the Birds!" the article quoted Ward rejecting claims that rather than chasing goals he was chasing girls. Citing rumours of a split with his wife as "unpleasant nonsense," Ward confirmed his desire to remain married and put his drop in form down to purely football reasons.

Unconvinced that his star striker was mentally or physically ready to make a positive contribution to the team, Mullery dropped Ward from the team for the short trip to Selhurst Park to take on Terry Venables' Crystal Palace. It was Ward's first experience with being dropped since making his Albion debut two years earlier; Mullery decided against even naming him as substitute.

Ironically, just 24 hours before Ward was dropped, he was named as Albion's sole representative in the Professional Footballers Association Division Two team of the season.

While his teammates headed to south London, Ward stayed at home and listened to Nottingham Forest draw 0-0 with Liverpool in the League Cup Final at Wembley. Four days later, a John Robertson penalty gave Forest a 1-0 victory in the replay at Old Trafford and the Clough and Taylor partnership had another trophy to add to their growing list of achievements.

Brighton's nil-nil draw with Palace did little to indicate whether or not Mullery had made the right decision in dropping Ward, but Peter was recalled for the following game, the long trip to Cardiff on Good Friday.

Losing 1-0 to a relegation threatened side was not how Ward had hoped to mark his return to the team. This was the first time that Mullery had played all three of his main strikers at the same time, to no avail.

Easter Saturday saw a straightforward 2-0 victory over Fulham with goals from O'Sullivan and Clark. Showing signs of rediscovering his best form, Ward received the Man of the Match award and the win ensured that Albion went into the final month of the season just one place outside the promotion places and still standing a chance of gaining promotion to Division One for the first time in the history of the club.

On the day following the Fulham win, the Sunday Express announced that Ward had finished third in a long-running poll to find the nation's favourite footballer. Manchester United and England winger Steve Coppell won the award, with Ward's England room-mate, Trevor Brooking as runner-up. Tottenham's Glen Hoddle finished fourth in the voting.

◇ ◇ ◇

April Fools' Day saw Albion have the last laugh on Notts County with a come-from-behind 2-1 victory. The Brighton scorers were Horton and O'Sullivan; a knee injury sustained by Teddy Maybank put a premature end to his season.

◇ ◇ ◇

With only six games to go, two crucial fixtures loomed: a trip to Lancashire to take on the team one place below them, Blackburn Rovers; and a game against league leaders Tottenham at the Goldstone.

A solitary Eric Potts goal five minutes from full-time gave Albion a priceless victory at Blackburn and, with Southampton drawing against Fulham, the gap between the Seagulls and third place was now just three points.

The game had all of the ingredients to be a classic encounter: two in-form teams battling for promotion; two of the country's most promising young stars, Ward and Glenn Hoddle, going up against each other; and a first-ever visit to the Goldstone Ground for Brighton manager Alan Mullery's old team Tottenham Hotspur.

Unfortunately, a number of the 32,647 who packed into the ground on a fine April afternoon were more intent on causing trouble than watching a game of football and their actions created as many headlines as Albion's excellent 3-1 victory. Fighting on the terraces twice spilled onto the playing surface and caused the referee to take the teams off the pitch. In total, the game was held up for 15 minutes as the police attempted to restore order and a number of injured supporters were moved from one end of the ground to the other. The menacing atmosphere in the stands failed to intimidate the Brighton players, however: the goalscorers were Clark, Winstanley and Potts.

After the game, Ward discovered that the crowd disorder had not been confined to the terraces:

> The notorious game against Spurs is one of the few times that I can re-member there being any trouble at Brighton. Before the game, I had parked around the corner from the ground and loads of Tottenham fans had seen me get out of my car. I thought that I was going to get some stick but they didn't give me any hassle apart from a few comments.

> After the game, though, I went back to my car and they had made a real mess of it — it was dented all over the place! It was my sponsored car and it was really nice, so I was pretty annoyed.

The victory maintained Albion's fourth position but left the top three, Spurs, Southampton and Bolton, all level on 53 points, four more than Brighton.

◇ ◇ ◇

A 4-0 midweek victory at Bristol Rovers followed the win over Spurs. For once, the Brighton striker taking the plaudits was not Ward, and Malcolm Poskett was the hero of the day with a fine hat-trick. Ward did score the other Brighton goal, which raised his season tally to sixteen, and it was his first success since his hat-trick against Mansfield some three months earlier. With three games remaining, the Seagulls were now only two points behind both Southampton and Tottenham.

The final away game of the season was the long trip to Oldham. A tense game ended in a 1-1 draw; Tony Towner scored for the Albion.

◇ ◇ ◇

100 miles south of Oldham, Clough and Taylor were celebrating again: a goalless draw at Coventry had confirmed Forest as First Division Champions less than 12 months after they had been promoted from Division Two. With strikers Peter Withe and Tony Woodcock again leading the way, Forest finished the season seven points clear of second-placed Liverpool.

◇ ◇ ◇

Brighton's final two games were both at home: a visit from Charlton was followed by a last day showdown against Blackpool.

A Goldstone crowd of 31,000 witnessed a nervy Brighton performance against an inspired display from Charlton goalie Jeff Wood. Brighton dominated the game but Ward and his teammates missed a number of opportunities which would normally have ended in the back of the net. Ward's frustration eventually got the better of him and, when the referee failed to award Brighton what Ward thought was a clear-cut penalty, the striker pushed the official and was booked for dissent.

The pressure paid off in the 69th minute, when Poskett scored with a header. The two points temporarily moved Brighton above Spurs and into the promotion places.

The following night, a dubious late Tottenham goal in a 1-0 win over Hull City pushed Brighton back into fourth place and meant that results on the final day of the season would determine which teams would be promoted to the heady heights of Division One.

Brighton's final game was a visit from mid-table Blackpool, while the two teams that Brighton could overtake, third placed Tottenham and second placed Southampton, played each other at Southampton's Dell ground. What could have been a day of great achievement and celebration for Brighton ultimately ended with a feeling of being the victim of an unsporting conspiracy. The memory still rankles with many of those involved with Brighton football club, including Peter Ward:

> We knew what was going to happen before we even started. It didn't matter what result we got because if Southampton and Tottenham drew then they would both be promoted even if we won. They were cheats — pure and simple.
>
> We beat Blackpool 2-1 and I got the first goal - it was a great goal too, one of the rare ones that I remember. I chipped it into the far corner of the net as the goalie came out.
>
> That was just after half-time. A few minutes later, I was fouled and the ref gave a penalty. I should have taken it but Nobby asked me if I wanted him to take it instead, so I said yes. He scored and although Blackpool got one back we were never going to lose that game.
>
> We heard the crowd going wild a few times towards the end of the game and we thought that maybe Southampton or Spurs had scored, but of course they hadn't.
>
> When they announced the final score as being 0-0, it was all over: we had missed out on goal difference, and there were a few tears in the dressing room. We had had a great season, though, and although we were bitterly disappointed we decided that we would open the champagne that the club had put in the changing rooms because we felt that we had achieved a lot that year.
>
> Mullery went out and told the fans that we would go one better next year and while at the time we all had our doubts, he was true to his word.

The actions of Mullery's counterparts still irritate him:

> Before the game started at Southampton, the two managers, Saints' Laurie McMenemy and Spurs' Keith Burtenshaw, walked around the pitch arm-in-arm holding their hands up in the air - unbelievable.
>
> Southampton had scored in every home game that season and Spurs had let a goal in every time they played away, yet this game finished nil-nil.
>
> We'd played Tottenham twice that season — drawn nil-nil up there in front of 50,000 and beaten them at the Goldstone. Southampton couldn't beat us either, yet they finished second. It was very disappointing.
>
> I promised the fans that we would get promoted the following season and we did, which was great. I was confident that we could. I had the backing of the board and the players who could do it.

The disappointment of missing out on promotion was equally bitter for Albion players, staff and fans. Dave Jenkins, however, who was 17 years old at the time, lost more than the prospect of seeing his team in the First Division:

> *During the Blackpool game, a few of my 17-year-old mates and I were once again worshipping Wardy in the North Stand.*
>
> *Yet again, in a desperately tense game, Wardy came to the rescue with a piece of typical fleet-footed magic. As the ball sped into the net, the North Stand erupted with even more thunder than had been usual in those fabulous years under Taylor and then Mullers. The surge from the back of the stand lifted us fully 10 steps down that crumbling terrace.*
>
> *As I was being carried down towards the pitch in a state of delirium, I can remember the feeling of my new, and very expensive, Ravel of Western Road moccasins being ripped from my feet by thousands of equally out-of-control Brightonians.*
>
> *Needless to say, I never saw those shoes again: I had to walk back to central Brighton barefoot.*
>
> *Not really feeling up to much, we decided to have a beer of commiseration in Shades (now the Pavilion Tavern). Unlike today, a bloke taking to the pubs and clubs without any shoes was a bit unusual in 1978.*
>
> *It turned out to be a hugely successful evening with some of the town's best-looking girls, and even the bouncers in the Queen Anne pub let me in shoeless and shod in Wranglers (very unusual) - all because of my response to the obvious question 'What happened to your shoes?' My answer was, 'I lost my shoes because of Peter Ward.'*

Albion's total of 56 points would have been enough for them to gain promotion in any of the previous 10 years and was 4 more than Forest had achieved when they were promoted the previous season.

While 17 goals was less than half of his total the previous season, Ward finished as Brighton's top scorer for the second year in a row and his 14 league goals made him the only Albion player to reach double figures in the league.

CHAPTER 7

RIDING THE CHAMPAGNE EXPRESS TO DIVISION ONE

*We went through every carriage, sang with everybody,
danced with everybody. If we could have got on top of the
train, we would have done. It was unbelievable — what a day!*
— Gary Williams, Brighton defender

Newly promoted Tottenham prepared for life back in the First Division by signing Argentine's 1978 World Cup winning pair Ossie Ardiles and Ricky Villa. The blockbuster £750,000 deal was made in sharp contrast to the lack of transfer activity in or out of the Goldstone Ground. Alan Mullery was confident that his team were strong enough to live up to the promise that he had made at the end of the previous season — that Brighton would achieve promotion to the First Division for the first time in their history.

Peter Ward and his teammates were keen to go one better and to achieve the promotion which they felt had been unfairly denied them two months earlier:

I couldn't wait to come back for pre-season, even if it did mean that we would be doing loads of running up and done those bloody hills at Waterhall for a couple of weeks. After missing out the previous season, we were all thinking 'surely we can't do that well again'... but we did.

Mullery hadn't made any new signings — not because the club was short of money but because he knew that the squad was good enough. We were all a year older and some of us were a year wiser!

We didn't feel any additional pressure because of the promise Mullery had made: maybe he did, though. We just wanted to prove that we were good enough to play in the Premiership (First Division).

Albion were offered a chance to host AFC Ajax of Amsterdam in a high-profile pre-season friendly but, as the Dutch champions demanded a £10,000 appearance fee, the invitation was declined. Instead, Albion took on First Division Queens Park Rangers at the Goldstone Ground in their final warm-up game.

Rangers, with five England internationals in their team, were soundly beaten and the 2-1 scoreline did not really reflect Albion's dominance. A crowd of

11,359 included one familiar, if somewhat unexpected, face. Nottingham Forest assistant manager Peter Taylor decided to miss watching his own team take on Ipswich Town in the Charity Shield at Wembley; instead, he chose to return to the Goldstone Ground to watch the striker that he had brought to the club three years earlier.

The following day, the Sunday Express reported that Forest were preparing a British record £500,000 bid for Ward. In response to the rumour, Brighton chairman Mike Bamber told the paper that they "would never dream of selling Ward"; Mullery chipped in that "Forest don't have a cat's chance in hell of signing him."

◇ ◇ ◇

The opening league game at Wrexham coincided with the hottest day of the year and, by kick-off, the temperature had risen to a stifling 85 degrees. Neither team could muster a goal in the searing heat, so the Seagulls returned home with a point.

A surprise two-nil defeat at home to newly-promoted Cambridge was followed by the visit of Sunderland, one of the favourites to challenge for promotion. A goal from Man of the Match Ward in each half gave Albion a promising 2-0 victory. However, Mullery's post-match comments to the press gave an early indication that the relationship between the two-goal hero and his manager was not as unfaltering as it had been during Mullery's first two seasons at the club. Mullery told the reporters that Ward was not as sharp as he could have been and that he "should have scored a hat-trick". Asked about the £500,000 price tag being suggested in the papers as Ward's potential transfer fee, Mullery replied that if Ward was worth half a million then Mark Lawrenson must be worth "at least three-quarters of a million."

A crushing defeat at Leicester —many of the Albion squad were suffering from a flu bug— was followed in midweek by a 2-2 draw at top of the table Stoke. A spectacular Ward goal and a late equaliser from Maybank gave Albion their share of the points and it was only the second time in twenty-two starts together that both players had scored. Gerry Ryan made his debut for Albion in the Stoke match following an £80,000 move from Derby; his wing-play gave fresh impetus to the Seagulls' attack.

Ryan's impressive home debut made a big contribution to Albion, rounding off September with an impressive 5-1 destruction of Preston. Ward scored after 29 minutes as Albion raced to an insurmountable 4-0 half-time advantage. The win lifted Albion to third in the Division Two table, behind Stoke and Crystal Palace.

Ward with two, and Maybank both scored in a 3-1 League Cup win at Burnley. Ward's double brought his season total to six goals from nine games and, between them, Ward and Maybank had hit the target an impressive ten times in the first ten matches of the season. The early season form suggested that Mullery's preferred strike-force was at last fulfiling his expectations.

◇ ◇ ◇

The early flow of goals proved to be a false dawn and a 3-1 defeat at Palace was the first of a run of twelve games in which both strikers would fail to score.

A 3-0 win over Fulham, with two goals from Ryan, preceded consecutive defeats at Burnley and at home to West Ham, which dropped Albion to mid-table. Mullery reacted by dropping Ward and Paul Clark for the trip to Yorkshire to play Sheffield United.

With Ward banished to the reserves, his replacement, Malcolm Poskett, scored the only goal in a much-needed Seagulls victory. In the following day's papers, Ward was quoted as saying that he was prepared to work his way back into the team and aimed a barb at his manager saying that he was "not the only one who [had] been playing below form."

Named as substitute for the next game, at home to Peterborough, in the League Cup, Ward replaced Maybank after 68 minutes and a 1-0 win allowed Brighton to progress to the quarter-finals for the first time. Reward for the victory was an away game at Clough and Taylor's League Champions, Nottingham Forest — the first opportunity that either would have to face the club that they had each managed.

Ward returned to the reserves and was not included in the next first team game, which was a victory over Wrexham. Restored to the bench for the next three games, he made late appearances in defeats at Sunderland and Notts County but was not used: the Seagulls beat Millwall 3-0.

On the first weekend of December, Ward was recalled to the starting eleven for the first time in seven games and Mullery praised his attitude over the past couple of months. Orient's visit to the Goldstone resulted in a 2-0 victory for the Seagulls but Mullery was far from happy with his team's performance.

◇ ◇ ◇

On the afternoon of Wednesday, 13th December, three chartered trains left Brighton station, heading for Nottingham: the Seagulls would take on the champions of England. Unfortunately for supporters in two of the trains, a broken-down train in North London put an end to their journey in Kettering rather than in Nottingham.

While the waylaid supporters did not miss another giant killing performance from the Albion, the 3-1 defeat was not without glimpses of hope for the
Seagulls and did end in victory for one Albion player. Ward recalls:

> *Going up to play Forest in the League Cup was great. They had won the
> league and were also the holders of the cup, so we knew that they were the
> best team that most of us had ever played against.*

> *I had only just got back into the team and I hadn't scored for a long time, so
> I was really keen to do well. They scored first but we were playing well and,
> just before half-time, Viv Anderson fouled me in the box. The ref wouldn't
> give a penalty. I went mad — it was such a clear foul! — and the ref ended
> up having to book me to shut me up.*

> *After half-time I equalised with a shot right into the corner past Peter Shil-
> ton — fantastic. We ran out of steam a bit after that and they ended up get-
> ting two more goals.*

> *I remember walking off at the end of the game and Shilton said to me, 'Did
> you mean that?' - meaning did I intentionally try to put my goal right in
> the corner. I said 'Yeah, of course I did!'*

> *The fans gave us a great reception after the game and when we got into the
> dressing room, we really felt like we wanted to play more games at grounds
> like this and against the best players in the country.*

> *Cloughie came into the changing room after the game and said something
> like, 'It was a waste of time for you lot to come up here.' This was typical of
> him, really: he was never one for keeping his comments to himself.*

> *Teddy was funny though; he was scared of Larry Lloyd, who had been
> marking him. Larry was massive, probably the biggest player in the league,
> and Teddy didn't fancy getting kicked about all game. At half-time he com-
> plained to Yax [Mike Yaxley, the club physiotherapist] about having a bad
> back and, in the second half, Mullery brought him off.*

> *After the game, we all went to a nightclub and Teddy, who had obviously
> made a miraculous recovery, won the competition for being the best dancer
> on the dance floor! He won an album along with some girl that he had
> pulled!*

The defeat proved to be a turning point for the Seagulls and eight wins
from the next twelve games saw them rise from seventh place to top of the
table. Unfortunately for Ward, an injury to the ligaments in his ankle cut short
his return to the team after just one more game.

◇   ◇   ◇

Galvanised by the brave display at Forest, Brighton re-commenced League Two action by welcoming Luton Town to the Goldstone Ground. Missing Maybank, who had managed to shut his arm in a door when entertaining his young cousins, Mullery recalled Gerry Ryan to the side. A 3-1 win didn't produce a goal for Ward, although his performance did earn him the Man of the Match award.

Ward injured his ankle in training as the team prepared for three games in eight days over the Christmas holiday. In his absence, the partnership of Maybank and Poskett excelled, starting with a Poskett hat-trick in a 3-0 win at Charlton.

Cardiff City visited the Goldstone on Boxing Day but left with little Christmas cheer following a 5-1 drubbing. Mullery called the performance "near perfection" and, this time, the hat-trick hero was Maybank.

Four days later, Poskett scored again as Albion defeated Newcastle 2-0 in the final fixture of 1978. Included in the Newcastle lineup was Peter Withe who had fallen out with Brian Clough at Forest after demanding a new contract. Immediately sold to Newcastle for £250,000, Withe's departure provided an opportunity for Garry Birtles to break into the Forest team. Birtles, who would eventually be part of the three-way transfer that enabled Ward to join Forest, took his chance - scoring 26 goals by the end of the season.

The four successive victories at the end of 1978 put Brighton in third place in the table, with Stoke and Palace still sitting in the top two places... one point ahead of the Seagulls.

◇　◇　◇

On New Year's Eve, the players and their partners gathered at Ward's house for a party to welcome 1979. Ward takes up the story:

> I'd invited everyone 'round but we knew that we had to travel down to Bristol the next day to play against Bristol Rovers so we weren't going to go too mad. Mullery would have gone crazy if we'd turned up for the game with hangovers.
>
> After a while, it started snowing and Gerry Ryan suggested that we should keep the party going because the game would definitely be called off the next day. We weren't so sure, but Gerry was adamant and we didn't take too much persuading...
>
> By the time midnight arrived we were all very, very drunk. Then someone looked out the window and it had stopped snowing! We panicked and Gerry got plenty of abuse, but there wasn't a great deal that we could do.

Luckily, the next morning, we got a call from the club to say that the game had been postponed, so we could stay at home and nurse our sore heads!

◇ ◇ ◇

The postponement of the Bristol Rovers game was followed a few days later by a similar outcome for the FA Cup third round clash with First Division Wolves. Taking place a week later than originally planned, Albion's cup involvement did not stretch beyond a single game: their top division guests won 3-2. Ward was still not being considered for the first team and the icy weather did little to help. A run of reserve team fixtures were cancelled due to frozen pitches; this restricted Ward's opportunities to display his sharpness.

The only league game that took place in January ended in a 1-1 draw at home to second-placed Stoke City. Poskett got Brighton's goal and substitute Ward, back after five weeks, replaced Peter Sayer with 30 minutes of the game remaining.

Following the game, Ward expressed his disappointment at not being involved in recent games and the press anticipated a showdown between player and manager. Ward commented that, as the team hadn't played well against Stoke, Mullery had no justification for delaying his return to the starting eleven.

Mullery did not agree, stating, "I don't drop players: they drop themselves." He picked an unchanged team for the next game, two weeks later, against Leicester City. Despite the fact that parts of the pitch were frozen, the referee decided that the game should go ahead. Conditions made it difficult for either team to keep possession. Ward joined the game after 67 minutes, replacing Ryan; with two minutes remaining, he smashed the ball into the net to make the score 3-1 to Brighton. The result gave Albion some payback for the hammering that they had suffered at Leicester earlier in the season. Ward's goal was his first since the cup defeat at Forest in December and his first in the league since Preston were beaten 5-1 at the Goldstone, some four months earlier.

The result lifted Albion to the top of the table, a position that they would occupy for ten of the remaining thirteen weeks of the season.

◇ ◇ ◇

The day after the Leicester victory, the players were in good spirits as they arrived at Gatwick Airport ready to take advantage of a short-trip to Jersey. This was Alan Mullery's idea of a way to relax his team in anticipation of the final three months of the season.

To the players' delight, Mullery decided that there was no need to accompany the players himself and, instead, left his assistant Ken Craggs in charge.

The manager's parting shot was "enjoy yourselves," and the players made the most of the opportunity, as Ward recounts:

> The first problem was that the flight from Gatwick was delayed so we spent two or three hours sitting in the bar at the airport before we could board the plane. By the time we did get to Jersey we were hammered and although the club had told us that we had to buy the drinks ourselves, I don't remember buying any…

> When we got to the hotel, Graham Moseley had said that he wasn't going to drink anything because he didn't want to get into trouble, but he ended up getting more drunk than anyone. We were putting salt, pepper and cigarette ash in his glass and he was still drinking it. Eventually, he went into the hotel foyer and threw up all over the place. We were sitting in one of the bars and Moseley and Teddy Maybank started to have a play-fight. They ended up on the floor, with Mose on top of Teddy, and he pulled his arm back as if he was going to throw a pretend punch and put his fist straight through a glass door that was just behind him. There was blood everywhere!

> We decided that it was a good time to all go to our rooms, but after a little while we heard that Ken Craggs was trying to get everyone together and that he was going nuts. All of a sudden Graham Moseley walked in and his arm was all bandaged up. The hotel manager arrived and he was really angry too, complaining that someone had been sick all over the floor in the reception area.

> He wasn't the luckiest chap on the world, Mose, and because of his injury he lost his place to Eric Steele and didn't play again for the rest of the season.

> For the next two or three days, we all took it easy. The club had arranged these brand-new Minis for us to drive around the island and we absolutely wrecked them — it was like something out of the Italian Job.

> When we got back to Gatwick, Mullery was waiting for us at the airport and went absolutely ballistic. Poor Craggs took the worst of it, although I may have said something because I wasn't even sub for the next game.

◇ ◇ ◇

While the Albion's players were making the most of their few days of freedom in the Channel Islands, Brian Clough's Nottingham Forest were making transfer history by signing Trevor Francis from Birmingham City for a British Record £1,150,000. The amount that Forest paid for 24-year-old Francis was more than double the previous highest fee between British clubs. In typical Clough style, Francis' first game for his new club was as a member of the Forest third team, alongside a mixture of peripheral reserve team players and members of the youth team.

◇ ◇ ◇

Despite his goal in the Leicester game, Ward didn't even make the bench for the next fixture at Preston. Mullery decided that the frozen Deepdale pitch would not suit Ward and, instead, named Paul Clark as sub. A 1-0 defeat dropped the Albion to second and probably confirmed Mullery's belief that the trip to Jersey would be the last of its kind.

On 17th February, rivals Crystal Palace, positioned immediately below the Seagulls in the league table, visited a still-icy Goldstone. Ward replaced Clark on the sub's bench and was called into action after 62 minutes, replacing Poskett. His introduction could not help to break the deadlock and the game finished nil-nil. A point for each team lifted them both above Stoke, whose game was a victim of the weather.

Ward was at last recalled to the starting lineup for the short trip to Fulham. Replacing Poskett, he partnered Maybank and made his first start in over two months. The forwards both had excellent games, although Albion's winner came from substitute Paul Clark midway through the second half.

Ward kept his place for a close 2-1 win over Burnley and then played a leading role as Brighton overcame a waterlogged pitch to win 3-1 at Oldham. The weather played a big part in Ward's goal: an Oldham back-pass got stuck in the mud and Ward raced in to nip the ball past the stranded goalkeeper, earning Brighton a 1-0 lead.

The visit to East London to take on West Ham resulted in a more exciting game than the 0-0 score suggests. In front of a capacity 35,000 crowd, Brighton matched their hosts, although they required three excellent saves from Eric Steele to ensure that a run of only one league defeat in three and a half months was maintained.

A 2-0 win over Sheffield United was marred by a sending-off for Maybank but the result kept the Albion at the top of the table with just ten games remaining.

Maybank's automatic one match ban and ongoing disciplinary problems led Mullery to look to strengthen his forward line. 34-year-old, former England international Martin Chivers signed for £15,000 from Norwich City and watched Ward score twice as Albion won 2-1 at Bristol Rovers. Ward's first goal was his tenth of the season and his second-half winner came within a minute of Rovers' equaliser. Victory gave Albion a three-point cushion over their promotion rivals, although both Stoke and Palace had played fewer games.

Consecutive goalless draws at Cambridge and at home to Notts County saw Albion's lead cut to two points. Yet again, Ward was the fall guy as Mullery looked to reignite the promotion challenge. The Brighton manager dropped him in favour of Poskett for the trip to Orient. In front of ITV's Big Match cameras Ward, spent the entire game wrapped in a long padded coat and crammed into the tiny dug-out with Ken Craggs and cigar-smoking Mullery. A thrilling 3-3 draw provided a great spectacle for the armchair viewers and kept Albion at the top of the table.

Ward was left out of the squad for the 2-0 victory over Charlton on Good Friday but returned, along with Maybank, for the trip to Cardiff on the following day. He scored the first goal of the game, but this proved to be the lone high point of the contest for Brighton as three goals from Cardiff sentenced the Seagulls to defeat — their first in a dozen games.

Bristol Rovers' visit to Hove on Easter Monday got off to a great start for the Albion. Ward was fouled within the first minute and Horton's penalty sent the home side on their way to a comfortable 3-0 win. Unfortunately, the victory was tainted by an injury to Mark Lawrenson: a broken arm meant the end of his season.

◇ ◇ ◇

Going into the final three games of the season, Albion were still top: they stood two points ahead of Stoke and Crystal Palace and, more importantly, three points above Sunderland, who sat just outside the promotion places.

The penultimate away game of the campaign resulted in a precious point from a 1-1 draw with Luton Town. Teddy Maybank's late equaliser kept Albion in the promotion places, although they dropped to second, and the three other teams battling for promotion (Crystal Palace, Stoke and Sunderland) all had games in hand on the Seagulls.

Midweek victories for Stoke and Sunderland (who had not lost a league game since mid-December) meant that as Albion took to the Goldstone pitch for the final home game of the season, against already relegated Blackburn Rovers, they were now in third place in the table.

As Peter O'Sullivan was serving a one-game disciplinary ban, Mullery recalled Poskett and played all three of his main strikers. Man of the Match Ward and Peter Sayer combined to set up Maybank for the opening goal of the game after 18 minutes and Andy Rollings doubled the lead with half an hour of the match remaining. A late goal from Blackburn gave the Seagulls fans a nervous final few minutes but Albion maintained their composure to secure victory. Celebrations at the final whistle were further boosted as news filtered through that Sunderland had been beaten at home by Cardiff and that Stoke had only drawn.

The combination of results left Albion back at the top of the table and, unlike the previous season, in control of their own destiny — victory at Newcastle the following Saturday would guarantee promotion to the First Division.

◇ ◇ ◇

While the majority of the population was focused on the General Election which resulted in Margaret Thatcher becoming the UK's first female Prime Minister, Sussex was gripped by promotion fever. As Albion fans were busily planning their trip to Tyneside, Alan Mullery took the team north:

> I decided that it would be a good idea to take the lads up to the north-east early in the week so that they could relax and get away from the excitement of the fans in Sussex. We travelled up on the Wednesday and stayed in a hotel in Washington.

> That evening, we went to watch Newcastle play Bristol Rovers: Newcastle absolutely hammered them. I thought that this was good because the players knew that Newcastle would be a tough test for them, even though a lot of people were saying that Newcastle would let us win so that Sunderland wouldn't go up.

> Sunderland let us use their training ground and the next day we did some light training. The lads then went and played golf.

> By the time the game came 'round, the players were relaxed and focused on what needed to be done. I felt that they were fully prepared.

Ward agrees that the extra two or three days away from home put the players in an ideal state of mind.

> It was a great week. We stayed in a nice hotel and played golf at a really good course at Gosforth Park. I was useless and could hardly hit the ball, so I'm not sure why I even went, but it was good fun. We had a few drinks as well and everyone was really relaxed.

> We went and watched Newcastle play and it snowed! This was in May — I couldn't believe it, it was freezing! Newcastle won easily and they looked good but we knew that there was no way that we weren't going to win that game. Nobody wanted to go through the disappointment that we had experienced the previous year.

Brighton captain Brian Horton views the preparation as a masterstroke on Mullery's behalf:

> The lead up to the Newcastle game was fantastic management. It was the biggest game in the history of the club and the days before totally relaxed the players — we couldn't have been better prepared.

88

◇ ◇ ◇

For many Brighton fans, Saturday, 5th May, 1979 was the most exciting day in the history of the club: the pinnacle of success during the 'golden years'. An estimated 10,000 Seagulls supporters made the 700-mile round trip to see the game, and the majority of them massed at the Leazes End of Newcastle's famous St James' Park ground.

Albion, in their all-yellow away kit, started the game by kicking toward their own fans, and it took just twelve minutes for Brian Horton to score the opening goal. It's a memory that he still cherishes:

> We were desperate to make a good start and we'd forced a few early corners. Gary Williams took one from the left-hand side and I connected with a great header from near the penalty spot. The goalie had no chance. I still have a photograph of that goal, hanging in pride of place in my study.

After 25 minutes, Albion scored again. This time it was Ward who sent the Brighton fans into raptures:

> Nobby had scored early on and we were playing well. I picked the ball up about 40 yards out and tried to flick it to Peter Sayer, but it came back to me off one of their players. I took on two defenders and hit the ball with my left foot from about 25 yards out. I didn't catch it very well but the keeper made a real mess of it and it bobbled under him and rolled into the net.

> I couldn't believe it and put both my arms in the air and looked to the sky — it was pure relief. Teddy came over and lifted me up and that picture was in a lot of the papers the day after. What a moment!

> We scored again just before half-time and that was it: game over. Gerry [Ryan] scored after a great move and we were all thrilled as we went in for half-time.

> When we sat down at the break, we expected Mullery to be really pleased but he went absolutely nuts! It was as if we were losing rather than winning three-nil. Nobby had to remind him that we were winning and he did calm down eventually. I guess he was feeling the pressure a bit.

> It was a really strange day because when we kicked off it was sunny but by half-time it was pouring down, and then in the second half it started to snow!

Confirming Mullery's belief that Newcastle would come back at Brighton in the second half, the home team did score one goal with ten minutes left. Albion, however, were not to be denied. The final whistle was greeted with roars from the Brighton fans and a fair amount of cheering from the Newcastle supporters, who were appreciative that Brighton's success meant that their rivals, Sunderland, may well have (and did) missed out on promotion.

Ward recalls the post-match celebrations and the journey home with a big smile:

> *Mullery came running onto the pitch and we all celebrated in front of the Brighton fans — it was incredible.*
>
> *The train journey back was quite something. It was a great big train and it was full, but we had our own section, although we didn't stay in there for too long.*
>
> *Everyone was over the moon: we had won promotion, there were loads of bottles of champagne, and there were women everywhere. It was an orgy!*
>
> *It was unbelievable, it was brilliant — one big party. Some of the players would nip away somewhere with one of the girls for a little while — it was crazy.*
>
> *And then, when we got back, there were thousands of fans at Brighton station; this was at two in the morning!*
>
> *I think that we went straight to Sergeant Yorke's Casino, which was right by the station.*
>
> *That was a great ride back, unbelievable, brilliant. We didn't want it to end — superb.*

Albion full-back Gary Williams has equally positive memories of the train journey:

> *We went through every carriage, sang with everybody, danced with everybody. If we could have got on top of the train, we would have done. It was unbelievable — what a day!*

The journey that Alan Mullery refers to as the "champagne express" is one of Albion fan David Dresch's fondest memories from over forty years of supporting the Seagulls:

> *When we came out of the ground after the game the police had all disappeared because we'd been celebrating in the ground for so long. We tucked our scarves into our pockets and started to walk to the station. I was with a couple of friends and we had to walk past this pub that was full of Geordies. All of a sudden this great big Newcastle fan with a pint in both hands stepped into my path and said, 'Brighton?'*
>
> *I didn't fancy my chances of getting away with a Geordie accent and thought to myself that if I was about to get beaten to a pulp, at least I had seen Brighton get promoted. So I said 'yes' and he replied 'Well, get these down you, man, and well done for keeping Sunderland down'. He handed*

*me the drinks and gave me a pat on the back. You wouldn't believe how re-
lieved I was!*

*It was quite a surreal journey. I was one of the club stewards on the train
and as we were pulling into York there was an announcement that all of
the stewards had to go to the buffet compartment. We didn't know if there
had been some trouble or something like that, but when we got there we
saw that the players had left a big case of champagne for all the stewards
— which was great.*

*We had a wonderful time. Chris Cattlin and Gary Williams came into our
compartment and Gary was so drunk that he just collapsed in a corner.
Chris said that he couldn't be bothered to take him back so he was left in the
corner for an hour or so. I remember Chris saying to me 'Enjoy this, make
the most of it and remember it, because you'll never win promotion to the
First Division for the first time again.'*

*Alan Mullery got off the train at Croydon, as he always did, and got a fan-
tastic reception as he walked down the platform alongside the train. It was
an amazing day.*

The following day, more than 100,000 fans lined the streets to see the Albion
players tour the town in an open-top bus. The team and management were pa-
raded in front of 25,000 jubilant supporters inside the Goldstone Ground and
then attended a civic reception at Hove Town Hall.

Albion's promotion had been achieved with a final tally of 56 points, the
same as the previous season, in which they had missed out by such a narrow
margin. Ward's total of 13 goals in league and cup made him the clubs' leading scorer for the third successive season. Brian Horton was the leading league
scorer with 11 goals, which was one more than Ward, Maybank and Poskett,
who each finished with 10. Mullery's quandary over which two players made
up his best forward combination had caused Ward to miss more games than
either of his counterparts and his total of 27 league appearances was 10 less
than in the previous campaign.

◇ ◇ ◇

*On reflection, that season was personally the least productive that I had at
Brighton; yet, in terms of what the team achieved, it was the most memorable.*

*I missed a number of games and that was frustrating at times because I
always believed that if I played, I would score. I was young and I wanted to
play, and I wanted to be involved with England again. That was never going to happen if I was sitting on the subs bench or playing for the reserves.*

I didn't really fall out with Mullery or anyone else but if we hadn't gone up I don't know if I would have still been at Brighton the following season. However, as everyone knows, we did get promoted and the prospect of playing in the First Division was incredibly exciting. As things turned out, I only missed one league game the following season; staying was definitely the right decision.

I couldn't wait for the fixtures to come out: Highbury, Anfield and, of course, Old Trafford. Incredible!

CHAPTER 8

Top Flight Survival and a full England Cap

*It was only five years after I'd left Burton Albion, so
to go from non-league to winning a cap in that
amount of time was quite special.*

– Peter Ward

A week after the jubilation at Newcastle, the Albion players, their wives and the club officials headed to America for a three week trip. Touted by Albion Chairman Mike Bamber as the trip of a lifetime, the excursion left the players and the Albion manager with mixed memories.

Gary Williams remembers that the trip consisted of a series of conflicts between the players and the management:

> There was some kind of deal between the club and Bob Bell, who owned the San Diego Sockers. They took us and the wives and girlfriends over for 2 or 3 weeks and the club told us it would be the holiday of a lifetime and that we'd be treated like kings.
>
> However, when we got there, we found out that the club had arranged 6 or 7 games for us in 18 days. They wanted us to train all the time and we were saying 'Hang on a minute. We've just got promotion to the Premiership and been playing hard for nine months: this is supposed to be a holiday.'
>
> We were hardly seeing anything of the girls and so we had a team meeting one evening. It was like a mutiny. We all got together and went to see Mullery; we said that we weren't going to train all the time and leave the wives and girlfriends to amuse themselves for days on end. The club cancelled three of the games, so it wasn't too bad in the end.
>
> The singer, Leo Sayer, came to one of the matches and came to see us after the game and invited the team out for a drink — he was a massive star at the time. The club wanted us to leave the party after twenty minutes but most of us stayed for a few hours, which didn't go down too well.

Alan Mullery views the trip as the start of the end of his relationship with Mike Bamber:

I had a feeling that the chairman wanted everything his way and there were a few petty things which spoiled it. There was too much drinking on the trip because the players were still celebrating, but we also had games to play. It was a difficult balance and, to be honest, I was glad when it was over.

The tour was Peter Ward's first visit to the USA and, despite the unrest between the players and the management, he remembers it as a fascinating experience:

We were tired after the season, but we were still excited about going to the States. We had to do a lot of travelling around and we played San Diego, Portland and California Surf.

We went to Portland first and then we stayed in the Hotel Circle in San Diego for two weeks. Whilst we were staying in San Diego, I remember that we managed to really upset the waitresses in the hotel. We didn't know what the problem was but we found out that they were going crazy because no one was leaving them any tips. It wasn't because we were tight, we just didn't know in those days that it was the normal thing to do.

Overall, though, we had a good trip. We went to Vegas but had to drive from San Diego to Vegas in a bus. It was about seven hours through a desert. Halfway through the journey we stopped at a place called Barstow where there's a burger bar and a motel but nothing else. I remember, we'd been sun bathing and a couple of the women were really badly sun burnt — typical English.

We got on this bus which was air conditioned and it was absolutely freezing. There were only a few blankets and people were so cold — we'd never been on a bus with air conditioning before, it was unbelievably cold.

Chris Cattlin's wife, Maureen, got sick because she was so sun burnt. That coach journey was one of the worst parts of the trip. When we got to Vegas, though, it was great; we were there for four days. We saw Shirley MacLaine in a one woman show; she was fantastic.

We used to wind Teddy Maybank up by saying that he was Mullery's baby. We were in the bus going to one match on the trip, and Teddy Maybank needed to go to the toilet and not just to have a pee... Mullery loved Teddy and got the coach driver to find somewhere quiet to stop. We pulled up by the side of a field and Teddy got out but didn't have anything to wipe himself with, so Mullery took his handkerchief out of his pocket and gave it to Teddy to wipe his arse with. I'm pretty sure Teddy didn't give it back to him!

It was during the trip that Mullery said that I'd never play for the team again. My wife at the time, Sue, was pregnant so she had to go back to England early — leaving me in San Diego. It was our wedding anniversary on

31st May and she had to go home a couple of days before that. On our anniversary we were all invited to a party at the house of Bob Bell, was who was organising the trip.

Within a couple of hours I was paralytic — I was being sick on the lawn and everything. Chris Cattlin and his wife made me sleep in their bed because they were scared that I would be sick in my sleep and choke myself.

We were playing two nights later and I still hadn't recovered. I started the game but Mullery took me off — I was still drunk. I was terrible and he went crazy at me.

To make things worse, Mullery ended up getting sent off in that game because he ran onto the pitch to have a go at the referee after Peter Sayer had been stamped on by Juli Veee (who was a big star for the Sockers).

Mullery and I fell out after San Diego and I asked for a transfer when we got back.

Whilst her husband was suffering from the after-effects of far too much alcohol and feeling the wrath of his manager, Sue Ward experienced a sobering return flight to the UK:

We were staying in a hotel in San Diego and there were lots of air crew staying at the same place. We spent quite a lot of time in the bar and a number of the players had been talking to the American Airlines stewardesses. I had to go home before Pete because I was pregnant and the doctor at home had advised me that I shouldn't stay away for too long. The day before I was due to fly home there was a plane crash at Chicago Airport and nearly 300 people died, including some of the stewardesses who had been sitting in the San Diego bar with us.

Mark Lawrenson was also flying back early with me because his arm was broken and he had to go and have some more work done on it. It was awful on the flight back — very sombre.

When the team arrived back a couple of weeks later it was the last day that the particular type of planes were used because of the crash, so it was a relief for everyone to get back safely.

◇ ◇ ◇

On 30th May, while the Albion were enjoying American hospitality, Clough and Taylor added the European Cup to their roll of honour. A goal from the million pound man, Trevor Francis, was enough to give Forest a 1-0 win over Malmo of Sweden in the Olympic Stadium, Munich.

◇ ◇ ◇

On his return to England, Ward was greeted by fresh rumours concerning his future. Malcolm Allison, Manchester City's flamboyant, fedora-topped manager, had been given a £1,000,000 transfer budget and offered Brighton half of it for Ward. Later in the season, Allison told The Sun that Brighton had verbally accepted the initial offer but had increased the asking price to £700,000 on their return from the States.

Allison envisioned Ward as the ideal strike partner for Michael Robinson, whom City had just signed from Preston. City paid a staggering £750,000 for twenty-year-old Robinson, who didn't have any top division experience and who had played fewer than fifty games for Preston in the Second Division.

By paying such a high price for Robinson, City had set the transfer market spiralling. The Brighton board may have felt that if an inexperienced youngster such as Robinson was worth three-quarters of a million pounds, Ward, with 72 goals in a little over three seasons, was worth significantly more than the initial £500,000 fee that Allison said had been agreed.

Within a season, Robinson's Manchester City career was deemed a failure and, ironically, Allison's ideal partnership came together at Brighton when Mullery signed Robinson for the Seagulls.

Although he failed to capture Ward, the City manager's high spending continued and, a month into the season, he paid a British record £1.44 million for Wolves' Steve Daley. If Robinson's purchase was seen as a failed gamble, Daley's City career was a disaster. Failing to justify a price tag that far exceeded his own valuation of his worth and struggling to perform consistently for City, Daley lasted less than two years in Manchester. He was sold to the Seattle Sounders of the North American Soccer League for just £300,000, where he would eventually be joined by Peter Ward.

As Brighton's renewed valuation cooled City's interest in Ward, the next enquiry came from further afield. German Bundesliga club Werder Bremen were reported to be keen on making a double swoop by signing on Manchester City and England defender Dave Watson and Ward. Werder, nicknamed The Millionaires following a series of costly, high-profile transfers, had watched their league rivals SV Hamburg prosper, following the signing of Kevin Keegan. Werder, therefore, turned to England for their next targets. Watson agreed to sign, although he returned to England after just six months, but Ward did not get the opportunity to discuss the move with any Bremen representatives:

> I had heard that Bremen offered £350,000 for me but Mullery wanted a lot more. Keegan had been doing really well over there and it was his agent who was involved in trying to get me to Bremen. The money that they were paying at the time was great, much better than I was getting at Brighton, and I would have gone if I'd been offered the chance.

Peter David Ward - aged about
6 months.

Cavendish Close Junior School
1964-65. Peter is front row,
second from the left. Andy
Rowland is front row, second
from the right.

Dream Debut at Hereford - Ward celebrating the first goal of his professional career with Steve Piper.

At home with Great Dane, Sumi, in 1976.

Peter Ward, Alan Mullery and Brian Horton at training.

Celebrating a goal against Preston in February 1977.

Catch me if you can... captivating the East Terrace against Mansfield in March 1977.
Goal number 31 of the season, scored against Portsmouth in April 1977.

6th September 1977, England Under-21 debut, England 6 - 0 Norway.

Picture: The Evening Argus

Next stop Brighton... Peter with Mark Lawrenson and Gary Williams.

Theatre of Dreams. Centre stage at Old Trafford, watched by United's Martin Buchan and Gordon McQueen.

Peter Taylor and Brian Clough welcome their new signing.
Forest photo call and picking oranges in Valencia.

© Ken Smales

Falling foul of the referee in the World Club Championship in Tokyo, February 1981

Below: At Seattle, watched by Carlos Alberto.

Right top: With Mark Peterson and Pelé at the 1982 NASL Awards ceremony

Right bottom: Parading the 1982 NASL MVP awards.

Picture: Joanie Komura

The uncertainty about Ward's future was a worry to Albion fans and Sue Ward found herself questioned about any possible moves in the most unexpected situations:

I was pregnant and one day I went to have a check-up with our Doctor; he asked me if I was going to have the baby in England or Germany! Pete and I did discuss the possibility of a move and, even though we would have had the language barrier, it would have been quite an adventure.

The news that many Albion fans had been dreading broke in the last week of July as the Evening Argus reported that Ward had been put on the transfer list:

After the USA trip, I came home and there were lots of rumours about different clubs wanting to sign me. Teams were suddenly spending lots of money, more than ever before, and I thought that it might be the right time to leave. I had a meeting with Mullery and told him that I wanted to go on the transfer list. He was fine, he knew that it might be in the best interest of the club to cash in on me whilst the market was booming.

Mullery was empathetic to Ward's situation and knew that money generated by the player's transfer could help develop the Seagull's squad:

Peter came to me and said that he wanted to move. We weren't under any financial pressure to sell him but in the back of my mind I did wonder how he would get on in the First Division. His size and pace had been a huge asset in the Third Division and less so in the Second, but in the First Division the defenders had a lot more guile and it would be more difficult for him.

We certainly would not have let Peter go unless we had a replacement for him. As a manager, I always looked to replace players with better players, which, with Peter, would have been difficult.

What Peter did say was that if he ever had the opportunity to go to Derby or Nottingham so that he was nearer home that he would want to go. I told him that I understood and that I would let him know if either of those teams made an enquiry about him.

◇　◇　◇

With their newly acquired First Division status, the Albion embarked on a pre-season programme that was somewhat more glamorous than trips to Brentford and Torquay, the norm in the preceding seasons. During the first week of August, Albion participated in the fourth annual Tennant Caledonian Cup at Glasgow Rangers' Ibrox Park stadium. Ward's goal gave Brighton a 1-1 draw with Scottish Premier League side Kilmarnock in the first semi-final,

97

although the Scottish team progressed to the final with a 6-5 penalty shootout victory.

Kilmarnock's spot-kick expertise led them to win the tournament following a 2-2 draw with Rangers in the final; Albion beat West Ham 3-1 in the third and fourth play-off. Transfer-listed Ward was relegated to the substitute's bench for the West Ham game and replaced Teddy Maybank for the final 30 minutes of the match.

On the day of the West Ham game, *The Sunday People* reported that Arsenal, Albion's opponents in the first league game of the season, were watching Ward with an interest in signing him as a replacement for Malcolm MacDonald. 'Supermac' had suffered a career-ending knee injury and *The People* suggested that, by the time the season started, Ward would be lining up for Arsenal rather than for Brighton.

The pre-season programme continued with a ten-day trip to Holland. The first game saw Albion lose 2-0 to what Mullery labelled a "world class" East Germany national side. The Germans, who were reigning Olympic champions, were fiercely competitive and Ward's patience eventually ran out after consistently receiving rough treatment from opposing defenders:

> *I had been getting kicked about all over the pitch by this great big German goon. Just after half-time I had the ball and I goaded him, did a Georgie Best saying, 'come on then,' and knocked it past him. He took me out neck-high and I lost it. I pushed him and then kicked him in the nuts. The referee sent me off straight away.*

> *After the tournament there was a big banquet and all the teams were there. Mullery told me that I should apologise to the guy that I'd kicked, but I said 'no chance.' That was the only time that I was ever sent off, playing for Brighton.*

The tour continued with a 3-2 defeat against Sparta Rotterdam and ended with Ward's sixth minute goal, giving the Seagulls a 1-0 victory over Den Haag.

Albion returned to England with just one week to go before the opening First Division fixture against FA Cup holders Arsenal at the Goldstone Ground.

◇　◇　◇

The day before Arsenal's visit, Ward came off the transfer list, much to the relief of Brighton fans and players alike:

Mullery had told me that he didn't feel that he could pick me if I wasn't committed to the club, which was fair enough although I was still training hard and wouldn't have let anyone down.

We had reached stalemate, I suppose, but then Mike Bamber came to see me and he persuaded me to come off the list and sign an improved contract.

There were reports that I had signed a ten-year contract but I hadn't. We changed a couple of things on my contract but it wasn't extended.

It was a big relief: I really didn't want to miss the Arsenal game, having been such a big part of our efforts to get to the First Division. I went home happy that my immediate future was settled and looking forward to a good night's sleep in preparation for the big match the following day. It didn't quite work out like that, though.

Peter's second daughter, Rebekah, was born at 6.45 a.m. on the morning of the Arsenal game. Sue Ward takes up the story:

At 1:30 in the morning, I told Pete I needed to go to the hospital. He must have been quite focused on the game because he took me to the hospital and then went home again!

The nurse had told him that they would call about 30 minutes before the baby was going to be born so that he could drive back in. But when they did call, it only took 15 minutes for me to give birth so he arrived just after Rebekah was delivered.

Chris Cattlin's wife came and sat with me. Rebekah was born at a quarter to seven in the morning. I thought we were going to call her Sarah so I told the reporter that this was going to be her name, but Pete changed his mind and told BBC radio that she was going to be called Rebekah. I heard on the radio what he had said and I was thinking 'What? Her name's not Rebekah' but it was too late.

He wanted her middle name to be Arsenal! I said he had to be kidding.

After the match, Pete came to visit us and brought Rachael with him. He'd got her dressed and managed to put her dress on inside out — it was quite funny!

◇　◇　◇

The Seagulls' First Division debut proved to be a stark reality check, ending in a 4-0 defeat to Arsenal. Despite the score, however, Ward remembers feeling encouraged by the performance:

We started off really well and I had a couple of early chances. After 30 minutes or so we were thinking 'we could be ok here' but, all of a sudden, Arsenal had three chances and scored each one.

We were 3-0 down at half-time and Mullery threw in the towel. He told us that we would never get it back against Arsenal and although it was strange hearing him say this with half the game to go, he was right.

Away defeats at Aston Villa and Manchester City left Albion without a point from the first three games. Teddy Maybank scored Albion's first-ever Division One goal in the 2-1 defeat at Villa and scored again in the 3-2 loss at Maine Road. Ward scored his first top-flight goal against City when he hit a shot past Joe Corrigan in the final few minutes.

It was nice to get my first goal but disappointing that we didn't get something from the game as we had played well.

I remember the night before the game: all the team had gone to the cinema to watch the first Alien film. There was a really scary bit and one of the players screamed like a woman at the top of his voice because he was so scared. It was either Gary Williams or Mick Kerslake who did the screaming — it was really funny.

Ward got his second goal of the season in a two-nil League Cup win against Cambridge United at the Goldstone. The Seagulls went into their second home league game against Bolton Wanderers confident that they could achieve their first-ever Division One victory.

Fittingly, Ward put the Albion in front after twelve minutes with Brighton's first home top flight goal. Paul Clark scored the second before half-time and Brian Horton completed a 3-0 victory in the second half.

Ward failed to impress the watching England manager, Ron Greenwood, in a goalless draw with Southampton and, after an impressive 2-2 draw at West Bromwich, Brighton went on a barren run of nine games without a win.

The poor form saw the Seagulls drop to the bottom of the table and, by 10th November, they had amassed just seven points from fourteen games. Ward failed to score during this period but was still savouring the new challenges of Division One:

We were having a really hard time and sometimes looked out of our depth. We played at Manchester United and there were over 50,000 there — even though we lost, it was still a fantastic day. We got hammered twice at Arsenal and then lost 4-1 at home to Liverpool.

Teddy was really struggling and he fell out with Mullery in a big way. Eric Steele also fell out with Mullery and left. Malcolm Poskett wasn't getting much of a look-in either, so it seemed like Mullery wanted to make some changes.

We played Norwich at home and lost 4-2 after being 2-1 up. Andy Rollings got sent off for whacking Justin Fashanu and I think Andy only played one more game for us after that. So things were really changing, but Mullery had no choice really as we were struggling.

Despite Ward's goal drought, further reports that a move was likely for the striker started to appear. Mullery denied that he had contacted Luton about a player plus cash deal but confirmed that he had approached Derby about another swap deal. Mullery was keen for Republic of Ireland international Gerry Daley to come to Brighton, and for Ward to move to Derby. Daley rejected the move, saying that he didn't want to join the team at the bottom of the table, although, five months later, Derby were relegated, having finished places below the Seagulls.

On 4th November, 1979, a day after a 3-0 defeat at Arsenal, the Sunday Express reported that Spurs and Luton were both interested in signing Ward but were unlikely to pay the £600,000 fee that Brighton were supposedly demanding. According to the Express, Nottingham Forest were prepared to meet Brighton's price and were keen to sign Ward as a replacement for Tony Woodcock, who was on the verge of a £650,000 move to FC Köln in Germany.

A week later, Albion suffered an embarrassing 4-1 defeat at home to champions Liverpool. Brighton's lone goalscorer was new signing Ray Clarke. Clarke had spent the early part of his career with Spurs, Swindon and Mansfield but had made his name by scoring 38 goals for Dutch giants Ajax during the 1978-79 season. Clarke's arrival signalled the end of Maybank's Brighton career and he was sold back to Fulham (who ended the season being relegated to Division Three) for £150,000.

Clarke was regarded by many as the ideal partner for Ward and Mullery hoped that signing the tall target man would help Albion to overcome what he regarded as their biggest problem — not converting chances to goals. Clarke's arrival at the Goldstone Ground owed much to a shared connection with Mullery:

I'd been playing abroad but was looking to come back to England because my wife wasn't very well. I nearly signed for West Ham but then I heard that Brighton were interested too. I had been at Tottenham when I was younger and Alan Mullery was the captain then, so when we met it didn't take long to tie up the deal. When I joined, the team had played 14 games but had only seven points and were bottom of the table.

Wardy and I got on really well — we just hit it off. We complemented each other: he was sharp and quick, and I could get him the ball. He was a good finisher and a great lad — if I think of him now it just makes me laugh — he was great fun.

We had a decent side and it was a very friendly club. All the lads were great — from day one you felt like you'd been there for years. The supporters were fantastic and I really enjoyed myself.

When we were near the bottom of the table, we would stand in the tunnel waiting to come onto the pitch and someone would start to sing 'Always Look on the Bright Side of Life' and then we'd all be singing that as we came out. The team spirit was fantastic.

With Maybank gone, Poskett out of favour and Martin Chivers making little impact during his only three appearances of the season, Ward and Clarke were the only two strikers being considered for the first team. Injuries permitting, this created for the pair the unusual situation of knowing that, unless any new signings were made, they were pretty much guaranteed a place in the starting eleven. Ward enjoyed lining up alongside Clarke:

Ray was a good player — not at all flash, just a sound, straightforward target man. I liked playing with him and after he joined and Teddy left, we played every game together. I hadn't had a regular partner since Ian Mellor in the Third Division and it helped to have some consistency. When I played alongside Ray I probably played the best football of my Brighton career — it was a shame that he left so soon.

Ray was a nice lad although he never went anywhere without his wife — she was his biggest fan! It made it a little bit difficult sometimes: when we went out with just the lads, he wouldn't always be invited because his wife would normally turn up too — which was a bit awkward.

It was fair to say that some of the boys enjoyed the freedom of being away from their wives and girlfriends, although I'm not naming any names! When I first got into the team I couldn't believe what would go on at away games — it seemed like everyone was making the most of a few days on the road.

At one time, one of the players came home from a trip abroad with the sort of disease that you really don't want and gave it to his wife. I'm not sure how he explained that one.

When I came back to the club on loan, one of the team was actually keeping a hooker in a flat in Hove. He invited some of the lads round and asked if we wanted to, how shall I say, take advantage of this girl's hospitality, but I politely refused.

We were all very well known around town and girls would just throw themselves at us. We would get all sorts of offers and it was hard to resist: we were young lads and I suppose that we enjoyed the limelight. We wouldn't have to queue to get in at any of the clubs and we were treated like celebrities, which I suppose we were in those days.

We had a girl who used to babysit for us; she was the daughter of a friend, and about 15 years old. One night I was driving her home after she had been looking after our little ones and she just flung herself on me — I couldn't believe it. I had to push her off and tell her that I wasn't interested. I guess that would have been quite a good story to tell her friends at school the next day!

Another time, our neighbours told me that the girl they lived next door to had bet them £100 that she would sleep with me within a month. £100 was a lot in those days — if she'd told me, I could have split it with her! Only joking; she ended up losing the bet.

I would get quite a lot of fan mail from women and Lawro [Mark Lawrenson] used to get lots of letters from gay men. I'm not sure what his girlfriend thought about that, but it was quite amusing for everyone else.

The club was really keen for players to settle down and get married; lots of the players married when they were too young and ended up getting divorced. Looking back on it, I suppose that I was one of those who got married too early but we have three beautiful daughters and I wouldn't change that for anything.

◇　◇　◇

Two days after the defeat to Liverpool, Alan Mullery announced that Brighton had accepted a bid from Forest for Ward. The fee was believed to be around £500,000 and Mullery told the press that the decision was now Ward's to make:

I went into training and Mullery told me that they had accepted Forest's offer and that I could join them if I wanted to. I thought that was it and I was on my way. We were bottom of the table and it looked like we were going to go down; Forest were near the top and were European champions. It wasn't a hard decision in many ways, but we really loved it in Sussex.

I went home and waited for Forest to call me but I didn't hear anything. A couple of the national papers reported that I had been up to Nottingham but I hadn't. Nobody from Forest or Brighton contacted me and I didn't know what was going on.

While his Brighton colleagues travelled to Highbury to face Arsenal in the League Cup, Ward stayed in Sussex anticipating that the next stage of his career was about to begin. Ken Gutteridge, who had been instrumental in bringing Ward to Brighton, told the Daily Express that a move to Forest was just what the striker needed. When Forest announced that they had agreed Woodcock's transfer to Germany, the scene looked set for the deal to be rubber stamped:

The lads went up to Arsenal on the Tuesday night and got hammered 4-0, so that wasn't the worst game to miss. The next day I read in the papers that Brighton had even lined up a replacement, so I just sat at home waiting for someone to let me know what was happening, but the call never came.

Ward's potential replacement was named in the Daily Mirror as being Morton striker Andy Ritchie. Ritchie had been top scorer in the Scottish Premier League for three consecutive seasons and had been described by football journalist Chick Young as "the epitome of the Scottish footballer - a fat, lazy bastard, but with great ball skill." In fact, the player Mullery wanted to replace Ward was another Andy Ritchie, Manchester United's nineteen year-old striker, who had made his First Division debut two years earlier.

On Thursday, 14th November, two days after Forest's bid had been accepted, their Chairman, Stuart Dryden, announced that the deal was off. Neither club offered explanation for the u-turn but Mike Bamber insinuated that Brian Clough was behind Forest's change of heart, saying that Clough was "a difficult man to deal with."

Clough's assistant, Peter Taylor, later admitted that he had been the driving force behind the deal and that he saw Ward as the perfect player to slot into Woodcock's position, with Trevor Francis playing just behind the strikers. In his book With Clough, Taylor wrote that he had agreed to a £300,000 deal with Mike Bamber for Ward but found it difficult to make contact with the Brighton chairman or Mullery to complete the deal. During this delay, Clough questioned Taylor's judgment ("for the first time in our partnership") with regards to Ward, which led Taylor to storm out of the City Ground, feeling "insulted."

Mullery contacted Ipswich manager Bobby Robson to sound out the idea of a swap involving Ward and Ipswich's Eric Gates but Robson rejected the idea. With the Forest deal officially dead in the water and no other confirmed interest, Ward met with Mullery and Bamber to discuss his future:

We had a long, honest meeting and worked out how we were going to move forward. Mullery wasn't convinced that I was trying as hard as I could and he was very frank. He knew that we were in trouble: we had only won two out of fourteen games and we needed to make some changes. I was very disappointed that the Forest move was off but I understood that I just had to get on with my football and do all that I could to help Brighton get off the bottom of the table.

Strangely enough, the next game was away at Forest and I had been expecting that to be my debut for them!

Mullery felt that the confusion was down to one man:

Cloughie let Peter down. We had agreed that Peter could go and all Clough needed to do was send someone down to pick him up. I think Peter was very disappointed but, rather than let it have a negative effect on him, he used it as motivation and, for the rest of the season, played —probably— the best football of his life.

◇ ◇ ◇

With Ward's immediate future no longer in question, Mullery looked to make other changes to his team. He signed Peter Suddaby from Blackpool, who came straight into the team for the visit to Forest. Lawrenson was moved into midfield and Ward was recalled. Forest, the reigning European champions and League Cup holders, had not lost at home for a staggering 51 games and Brighton were still searching for their first Division One away victory.

In a game dominated by the home side, Gerry Ryan skidded through the mud and hit a low shot through Viv Anderson's legs and wide of Peter Shilton to put Brighton in front after twelve minutes. Just before half-time, Brighton keeper Graham Moseley saved a John Robertson penalty and the Seagulls hung on to achieve an incredible victory. The game did not prove to be a fitting Forest finale for Woodcock who, kept quiet by Suddaby and Steve Foster, was substituted at half-time.

Ward had what Mullery described as "his best game for a year" and the manager admitted that the striker was looking to prove a point to both Forest and to Mullery himself for having doubted Ward's commitment. Mullery told the assembled journalists that he thought "Brian Clough would like to buy [Ward] now — but he can't."

Manchester City manager Malcolm Allison would have read Mike Bamber's post-match comments with a sense of irony, as the Brighton chairman told the Daily Mirror that Clough had verbally agreed to sign Ward but had pulled out, and that "it certainly isn't the way we do business at Brighton."

The victory over Forest proved to be the turning point that the Seagulls had so desperately needed. Full-back Gary Williams remembers Mullery's after-match team-talk, which gave the players renewed belief:

We had all found it hard in the first year. We were playing big teams and virtually all of our players had come up from the Third Division.

The defining moment was the win at Nottingham Forest. We were all doubting ourselves and losing confidence; we were losing all the time and we weren't really competing.

Beating the European champions turned it all around. After the game, Mullery drilled it into us that we'd just beaten the best team in Europe: that made us all stand a little bit taller.

We played like champions for the rest of the season and went into games not expecting to get beaten. We were winning at home and drawing away and ended up finishing well away from the relegation zone.

◇   ◇   ◇

The victory over Forest lifted Brighton off the bottom of the table for the first time in a month and was followed by an encouraging one-all draw at seventh-placed Middlesbrough. On 1st December, Ward finally broke his three month goal-less spell with a goal in a 2-0 victory over Derby at the Goldstone.

A trip to an icy Molineux to take on Wolves four days before Christmas gave the Seagulls an early Christmas present. Ward played one of his most memorable games:

It was a Friday night and it was absolutely freezing. The pitch was rock hard and I had a really good chance early on. I was right in front of the noisy Wolves fans and the ball came to me inside the six yards box. Some-how I managed to put it over the bar, and it was probably the worst miss of my career. The Wolves fans thought it was hilarious and started to sing 'He shot, he missed, he must be f****** pissed. Peter Ward, Peter Ward.'

They probably thought that they were hilarious, but they weren't singing for long…

Emlyn Hughes was marking me. He was still in the England team but I ran rings around him that night and ended up with a hat-trick.

The next day, one of the papers carried the headline "Peter Pans the Wolves" and when my youngest, Louisa, was looking through some old scrap books she thought that was hilarious: she still calls me Peter Pan!

Ward's first Division One hat-trick, and his first away from the Goldstone, gave Albion an unexpected but very welcome 3-1 victory. His first goal came after 36 minutes and he got another just before half-time. Ward completed his hat-trick with twenty minutes remaining before Wolves got a late consolation goal.

◇   ◇   ◇

The Boxing Day visit of Crystal Palace gave the Seagulls an opportunity to secure their first victory over their rivals since Mullery had taken charge. England manager Ron Greenwood was once again in the crowd and witnessed a fine performance from the re-invigorated Ward.

After just five minutes, Ward was fouled in the penalty area and Brian Horton scored the spot-kick. Thirty minutes later, Ward scored Albion's second, his fifth goal in five games. Ward set up Albion's third, scored by Ryan, after an hour and a three-nil victory took Brighton out of the relegation zone for the first time since early October.

Terry Venables, experiencing defeat to Brighton for the first time in three and a half years, picked out Ward as being the difference between the two sides. Man of the Match Ward remembers Venables as a long-time admirer of his talents:

> *Venables tried to sign me a couple of times, once when I went to Forest and again when I was in the States. He liked me even when he was at Palace. When we beat them on Boxing Day, I was having a really good game and just after half-time Kenny Sansom had to go off because he was injured. Terry Fenwick, the Palace sub, came on and tried to mark me man for man. I gave him a really hard time and about 5 minutes after he came on I went past him and set up a goal for Gerry [Ryan].*

> *A little while later we had a throw in by the dugouts and I pointed to Fenwick and shouted to Venables 'Why have you got him marking me? He's crap!'*

> *Venables and Mullery didn't really get on, so it was great to beat them at last.*

Greenwood was impressed with Ward's display and told The Argus that "there was no reason why Ward should not be knocking on the international door."

Brighton welcomed Manchester City to the Goldstone for the final game of 1979. With only 34 seconds gone Ray Clarke put Albion in front and further goals from Ward and Clarke put them 3-0 up after just thirty-five minutes. City pulled one back before half-time but Ryan secured Albion's biggest win of the season with a fourth goal after 75 minutes. City's lineup included three of Ward's future Seattle teammates: Joe Corrigan, Steve Daley and Nicky Reid.

◇ ◇ ◇

With four and a half seasons of league football under his belt, Ward had scored 82 first team goals. The football magazine Match Weekly ran a story in its first issue of 1980, titled "Most Wanted," which detailed the Football League's top 100 most consistent strikers. Ranked at joint second in the list with a goal every 1.94 games, Ward was the only current Division One striker in the top 5. Coincidentally, Ward shared the second spot with Fred Binney, the player whom he had replaced at Brighton. Recently-retired Malcolm MacDonald topped the list with a goal every 1.93 games.

A visit to bottom of the table Bolton Wanderers, in front of the Match of the Day cameras, gave Ward further opportunity to show that he was well and truly back to his goalscoring best. He didn't fail to deliver and a goal in each half from the striker gave Albion a vital 2-0 win and their first double of the season. Ward had now scored eight goals in the last eight league games.

Ward's brace against Bolton caught the eye of Manchester United striker Jimmy Greenhoff, who told the Daily Express that he thought Ward was 'sheer class' and that Brian Clough must be regretting his decision to call off Ward's transfer.

Further good news for Ward came when he was named the Daily Mirror's Footballer of the Month for December — an award he dedicated to his teammates with special mention for Mark Lawrenson and strike partner Ray Clarke.

A home defeat to Tottenham and an FA Cup exit at Arsenal gave the Seagulls a disappointing end to January; February saw Albion fail to win. However, three draws from four games kept them just above the relegation places.

At Ipswich, Ward turned in another Man of the Match performance but Albion needed a last-minute equaliser from former Ipswich trainee Gary Stevens to secure a one-all draw. This was followed by Albion's heaviest defeat for six seasons, 5-1 at third-placed Southampton, where Ward's goal, his thirteenth of the season, was the only bright spot in a dismal afternoon for the Seagulls.

Two days after seeing their team hammer Brighton, Southampton fans were further excited by the news that Lawrie McMenemy had secured the signing of England captain Kevin Keegan. Keegan had also been a target for Brighton but the club could not meet his wage demands.

A trip to Yorkshire to face Leeds came after a goalless draw with West Brom. Ward's equaliser, with only three minutes remaining, gave Albion another vital point. Leeds captain and England defender Trevor Cherry was impressed with Ward and said the he looked "sharp and back to his best and should be back in the England squad soon."

The Leeds game had special significance for Ward:

> My Grandad, on my mum's side, lived in Harrogate and only ever saw me play twice. Once was in the Third Division when I scored the winner at York, and the other time was when I got the equaliser at Leeds. It was nice scoring and knowing that he was watching. Sadly, he died not too long after that game at Leeds.

After the Leeds game, Albion headed to Israel for a short break and a game against the Israeli national team. Despite the Jersey debacle of the previous season, Mullery decided to stay in the UK: Ken Craggs and George Aitken took joint charge of the team.

◇ ◇ ◇

Ward's memories of the trip focus more on the off-field antics than the game against the Israelis:

The trip was quite eye-opening because we were just a bunch of lads and didn't know much about the situation in the Middle East.

On the flight over, John Gregory had an argument with two Orthodox Jews who were in the seats in front of us. We were playing cards and one of them turned around and asked John to go and get a drink for him! John thought he was joking, but he wasn't and they ended up having a real shout at each other.

*The day after the game, we were due to go on a bus tour around Jerusalem. We were in the hotel bar waiting for the bus and it took ages to arrive, and by the time it did we had all had a few drinks. The tour guide was trying to point out all these places of historical significance and Gerry Ryan shouted 'For f**** sake, cut the crap and just get us to f****** Jerusalem!' I'm not sure we did too much for international relations on that journey.*

We eventually got to Jerusalem and were in a big building, which I think was the Israeli Parliament building. There were four of us in a lift and Gary Williams wasn't too keen on being in confined spaces, so the other three of us started to muck about. We were jumping around just to annoy him. All of a sudden, the lift stopped between floors. Our messing around had broken it! It was quite funny at first but we ended up being stuck in it for 3 or 4 hours. It was awful; really hot, and all we could hear were these Israeli security guards shouting things at us and trying to wedge the doors open with their guns.

When we got out all hell broke loose. The security guards wanted to arrest us but we weren't in the mood for co-operating because we'd had a few drinks and just wanted to get back to the hotel.

BBC Radio ran a story about the players all going on a drunken rampage in a sacred Israeli building — it was really blown out of proportion and the club banned them from the Goldstone for a while.

Overall it was a great trip — the sort of place I would never have gone to otherwise and a good break from February in England!

For the record, the game against the Israeli national team finished in a 2-1 win for Brighton. Ward scored a fantastic solo goal for the Seagulls.

◇ ◇ ◇

Albion welcomed second-placed Manchester United to the Goldstone on 15th March with a seven point cushion between themselves and Bristol City, who occupied the final relegation spot. Just short of 30,000 fans witnessed Albion earn another point in a nil-nil draw. The Seagulls had now lost just one of their last nine home league games following the thrashing at the hands of Liverpool in November.

Following the United game, Albion's next two fixtures pitted them against the two teams who, between them and by the end of the season, would have won the European Cup for four consecutive years. The trip to Anfield to face Liverpool, who had been champions of Europe in 1976-77 and 19'77-78, preceded the visit to Hove by reigning European Cup holders, Nottingham Forest.

◇　◇　◇

Five days before the Albion were to face Liverpool, Ward's improved form was rewarded by a return to the international scene as Ron Greenwood announced that he (Ward) was included in the England 'B' squad for the forthcoming game with Spain.

Greenwood cited that, in addition to witnessing Ward's performances himself, recommendations from other England regulars had convinced him to bring the striker back into consideration after a break of two and a half years. For Ward, the news was a welcome surprise:

I had been playing well but I wasn't necessarily expecting to get back into the England squad. We were still at the wrong end of the table and had been drawing a lot of games and I hadn't scored that many goals in the couple of months before.

As it turned out, I didn't actually get on the pitch in the game against Spain. Greenwood had picked Paul Mariner and Gary Birtles up-front but a defender, Russell Osman, ended up getting the only goal of the game. Just before he scored, I had started to warm-up because I was going to go on, but after the goal I was called back to the bench because they didn't want to put another forward on.

◇　◇　◇

The Seagulls battled hard in an unfortunate 1-0 defeat at Anfield. Mark Lawrenson had an outstanding game against the team with which he would later enjoy considerable success.

The imminent arrival of Clough's Nottingham Forest to the Goldstone was eagerly anticipated by Brighton's supporters. With the team in much-improved form and a chance to "do the double" over the European champions, the scene was set for a memorable encounter.

The unlikely hero of the day, and scorer of the game's only goal, was Albion full-back Gary Williams:

> *It was one of those days: the sun was shining, the crowd was buzzing and we were really up for it. We'd beaten them once and we knew that Clough would have made it quite clear to his players that losing to us again would be unacceptable.*
>
> *The goal itself was probably the best that I ever got, although, to be fair, I didn't get many! There were only a couple of minutes left and Wardy had the ball. He had played brilliantly and had run Larry Lloyd and Kenny Burns all over the place. For once, he knocked it back to me. I had one touch and then hit it from about 25 yards out. It flew into the top corner and Shilton couldn't get near it. Clough later said it was a 'fluke' and I suppose that it was. After it went in, the players just all piled on top of me. What a day!*
>
> *The game was on Match of the Day and I've got a DVD of the programme - the fifteen minutes of fame was quite nice. People still stop me to talk about 'the goal'!*

England manager Ron Greenwood was once again in the Goldstone crowd and witnessed Ward torment Forest defensive duo Burns and Lloyd. Burns was eventually booked after a string of scything tackles on Ward, who was also booked following his complaints to the referee about the treatment that Burns was dishing out.

Eleven days later, an identical Forest team beat Dutch champions Ajax 2-0 in the first leg of the European Cup Semi-final. Ten of the eleven Forest players who experienced defeat at the Goldstone featured in the team that eventually retained the European Cup by defeating Kevin Keegan's SV Hamburg 1-0 in Madrid on 28th May.

◇   ◇   ◇

Ward impressed again as his fourteenth goal of the season gave Albion a share of the points in a one-all draw at Crystal Palace on Easter Saturday. The point lifted the Albion to sixteenth position and meant that, unless their final six games drew a disastrous run of results, First Division status would be maintained for the following season.

A surprise 1-0 home defeat to second from bottom Bristol City left Brighton boss Alan Mullery fuming that his players had become complacent. He complained that Ward had played his "worst game of the season." The manager's harsh words were still ringing in the ears of the Albion players as they took to the Goldstone the following day to play Wolves.

In sharp contrast to the previous day's disappointment, Albion achieved their third double of the season with an emphatic 3-0 victory. Ward and Ray Clarke dazzled again, while Steve Foster and Peter Suddaby kept a tight rein on Wolves' £1.5m British record signing Andy Gray. A goal in each half for Ward took his total against Wolves to five in two games.

A 3-0 defeat at doomed Derby County sent Albion into their penultimate home league game against Middlesbrough; they were still not mathematically certain of avoiding relegation. Ray Clarke's goal (his ninth of the season and last ever for Albion) just after half-time was cancelled out by 'Boro's Micky Burns after 57 minutes. With two minutes remaining, Albion were awarded a penalty when Lawrenson was fouled and, although Ward's spot-kick was saved, he tapped in the rebound to secure a 2-1 victory. The two points gave Albion the security of knowing that they could no longer be caught by the three teams in the relegation places and that their Division One status was secure.

Ward's eighteenth goal of the season earned him his second-best season total and he received recognition of his achievements when he was named as an over-age player in the England Under-21 squad to face East Germany later that week.

That was a good trip. Steve Foster had also been picked, so that made it even more fun. It was the second leg of the Under-21 European Championship semi-finals and the Germans had won the first leg 2-1 so we had to win to stand a chance of going to the final.

We landed in West Berlin and had to go through Checkpoint Charlie to get into East Germany. We got off our nice posh bus on the West German side and into an old East German school bus — it was horrible. Cyrille Regis and Justin Fashanu decided that they would play a joke on the security guards and swapped passports before we went through the checkpoint. All of a sudden these armed police appeared from everywhere and demanded to know what was going on. Cyrille and Fash had assumed that the East Germans wouldn't be able to tell the difference between two black people. They tried to get Vince Hilaire to join in too, but he was frightened to death that they would get caught — which proved to be quite sensible!

As we drove through East Germany, we were going past rows and rows of houses where the windows were broken or boarded up — it was very strange.

In the hotel, the water was brown. I walked into Fashanu's room and he was in the bath with the door open. The bath water was all dark and murky and I said 'Holy crap, you're melting!' Luckily, he found it quite amusing!

We lost the game 1-0. We'd played ok. Terry Venables was the manager: he played me up front with big Cyrille; Gary Owen and Vince Hilaire were on the wings. Fozzie [Steve Foster] came on late in the game in place of Terry Butcher but it was pretty much over by then.

After the game we went back to West Berlin and stayed in a nice hotel. We were playing cards and I was winning, killing everybody and making quite a lot of money. Butcher and Russell Osman from Ipswich were playing and Glen Hoddle was playing too — he was alright back then. I was knackered and decided to go to bed; quit whilst ahead, for once.

At around three in the morning, somebody, I think it was Vince Hilaire, was roaming around the corridors shouting 'I want my money back, let's play again'. He was making a real racket, although he was one of Venable's stars at Palace so he probably didn't get into any trouble. I just kept my head down and my door locked and waited for him to go away.

◇ ◇ ◇

The final two games of the season saw Albion lose 1-0 at Stoke and draw nil-nil with Everton. A total of 37 points was enough for the Seagulls to finish in sixteenth place - an excellent achievement, considering their poor start to the season.

Before the Albion players jetted off for the traditional end-of-season holiday in Majorca, Ward discovered that he had been included in Ron Greenwood's preliminary forty-player squad for the European Championships, which were to be held in Italy the following month:

I didn't really expect to be included in the final party to go to Italy, as there were ten or so forwards in the first squad he announced. But 'you never say never,' and if there had been a couple of injuries, who knows what might have happened?

I was invited to go up to London to be measured for my England blazer but I couldn't make it as I was in Majorca with the lads.

We'd had a good season, considering the start, and we just went to let our hair down. The directors and managers went too but we would do our thing and they would do theirs — we'd avoid each other. We just had a great time; it was a fantastic way to end the season.

On return to the UK, Ward received further good news: he was named in the full England squad to travel to Australia, to take part in an international match marking a centenary of football in Australia:

The squad had to meet at the Post House Hotel at Heathrow, or London Airport as it was called then, on the Monday evening for dinner. On the Tuesday morning we did a couple of hours of training and then we had lunch; after that, we could do whatever we wanted for a few hours. We flew out on Tuesday evening and arrived in Sydney on Thursday morning.

The rock group, Queen, were on the same plane as us. I'm really into my music, so to share a flight with them was very exciting. I got their autographs on a Qantas menu and I kept that for years — although I think that it was a victim of my divorce!

We stayed in a hotel just outside Sydney. The day before the game, we had a short training session and then we went to a press reception at the Hilton.

The game took place on Saturday the 31st; we found out who was playing, that morning. There were sixteen of us in the squad and there were four forwards, so I wasn't that surprised to be named as a sub.

The game was England's last before the European Championship Finals in Italy and Ron Greenwood used it as a final opportunity to cast an eye over a number of fringe players who were still under consideration for the final squad.

The match was held at Sydney Cricket Ground and 45,000 fans packed in to watch England take on the Australian underdogs. Greenwood took a back seat during the game and let Bobby Robson take charge of the team. Ward has fond memories of Robson, who died in July 2009:

Sir Bobby was a really nice man and a pleasure to be around. It was very sad when he died, and I felt privileged to have played under him.

At the time, the Ipswich players were quite funny and they used to call him 'Mogadon' after the sleeping tablets. They would say that he would call a meeting to tell them that he was calling a meeting! Both Terry Butcher and Russell Osman made their debuts in that game and they were both Robson's players at Ipswich.

There were some good players in the team — Hoddle, Bryan Robson, Paul Mariner, Trevor Cherry, Big Joe [Corrigan] in goal.

The game actually took place on my wedding anniversary. The previous year, I had been in America and now I was in Australia, whilst my wife was at home.

When you are sub, the game goes really slowly. We were two-nil up at half-time, Hoddle and Mariner had scored, and with about twenty minutes left I got the nod to get ready to go on. It seemed to take forever for play to stop but eventually I came on for Alan Sunderland. England's number 16, Peter Ward — fantastic!

Just after I came on, Australia scored a penalty but we ended up winning 2-1.

Somebody put a video of the game on YouTube recently: it was the first time that I'd seen it. I played bloody well! I was quite surprised — but I was never picked again!

Ward's fleeting appearance made him only the second Albion player in history to win an England cap whilst being with the club. Official records set his appearance at between 7 and 8 minutes, so, for a number of years, Ward was the answer to a popular pub quiz question: which player had the shortest-ever England career? Not that this has ever bothered him:

Lots of very good players never get to play for England. It was an honour and one of my proudest moments. It was only five years after I'd left Burton Albion, so to go from non-league to winning a cap in that amount of time was quite special.

For the record, Blackburn Rovers full-back Stephen Warnock is the current holder of the shortest England career, having amassed just 6 minutes of international action when come on as a sub for England against Trinidad and Tobago in 2008.

◇ ◇ ◇

Before departing for Australia, Ward had signed a new contract with Brighton. The eight-year deal increased his weekly wage to £620 and included the promise of a testimonial after ten years of service. The contract also committed the club to paying the mortgage on Ward's new house in Woodland Drive, Hove and followed a similar ten-year deal signed by Mark Lawrenson.

Despite the long-term agreement, Ward's Brighton career would come to an end within five months.

CHAPTER 9

JOINING THE DOUBLE EUROPEAN CHAMPIONS... AT LAST

I said 'I want a £50,000 signing-on fee'. Clough looked at me
and said 'Son, if you were Peter Shilton, you wouldn't get that.'

– Peter Ward

Before the Seagulls started their second Division One campaign, Steve Foster, who had impressed during the first season, joined Lawrenson and Ward in signing a long-term contract. Alan Mullery correctly predicted at the time that Foster would be part of Ron Greenwood's England squad for the 1982 World Cup Finals in Spain.

As the players gathered for the pre-season team photograph session, there were two obvious changes from the previous season. The blue and white stripes were replaced with an all-blue kit complete with sponsors British Caledonian emblazoned across the shirts; and Peter Ward was now sporting an impressive moustache. Whilst the new kit lasted for three seasons, Ward's moustache has proved to be rather more enduring and remains to this day.

◇   ◇   ◇

Ward lined up alongside new signing Michael Robinson for the opening league game of the season at home to Wolves. When signing for the Seagulls, Robinson remarked that he was looking forward to teaming up with Ward, having seen his new teammate score twice against Manchester City during Albion's 4-1 win a few months earlier.

Although Ward could not add to the five goals that he had scored against Wolves during the previous season, a comfortable 2-0 win for the Seagulls was an encouraging start.

Ward's first goal of the season came after four games as he scored Brighton's third in a 3-1 win over Tranmere Rovers in the League Cup.

By the end of September, only one further league victory had been achieved, against Norwich, and the Seagulls sat at 16th place in the table after eight games. Although Mullery kept a fairly consistent team, neither Ward nor Robinson were hitting the net. Robinson's goal in the win against Norwich was the only goal that either striker had managed in the league.

Despite the lack of goals, on 4th October, Ward was named in the England B squad to face the USA later that month. On the same day, Gordon Smith's late hat-trick gave the Albion an excellent point in a 3-3 draw at Coventry and put the team in good spirit for the midweek visit of third-placed Everton.

After a goalless first-half, Everton dominated the game and were leading 3-0 by the time Ward pulled one back for the Seagulls with seven minutes left. Unfortunately, his first league goal of the season was the lone bright spot in a 3-1 defeat.

Albion's next game was against Clough and Taylor's Forest, who had successfully retained the European Cup by beating SV Hamburg a few months earlier. In the days preceding Forest's visit, the newspapers were once again reporting that Ward was a possible target for the European Champions. Rather than a straight transfer, this time Ward was being touted as one part of a three-way transfer; Forest's Garry Birtles would go to Manchester United and United's young striker Andy Ritchie would replace Ward at Brighton.

Clough was keen to sell Birtles, having fallen out with the striker during the summer, after Birtles' request for time off to move house was denied. Although Birtles had scored nine goals in the opening months of the season, Forest were willing to cash in as United was offering a reported £1,200,000.

Initially, Mullery told the press that he was keen on signing Ritchie to add competition for his forwards rather than as a replacement for Ward. It soon became clear that unless Brighton could generate money by selling Ward, they could not afford to pay United's asking price of £500,000.

Mullery viewed Ritchie as an ideal replacement for Ward:

> *Andy Ritchie was only 19 or 20 at the time and he was already established in the First Division. I knew his manager, Dave Sexton, very well because he had lived in Brighton too.*

> *You always have to be on the lookout for players who you think will be better. You can be loyal to players but you always have to be looking to improve. We did have a lot of stability at the club during my five years there and Peter Ward was the first of the stars to leave.*

> *There was never any financial pressure to sell Peter. I wasn't going to let him go until we had a replacement, but after Clough and Taylor —well, mainly Taylor, actually— had decided that they wanted Peter, I spoke to Dave Sexton and he was willing to sell Ritchie for the same amount. We were getting a 19-year-old to play in our first team who had played at a very high level since he was 17 — that was the difference between Ritchie and Peter, really.*

When I signed Michael Robinson it was because I thought that Ward was struggling in the First Division and that Robinson could help take the pressure off him. Robinson was big, strong and powerful, and he ended up scoring 22 goals in his first season with us.

We were always looking to make the squad stronger with people like Gordon Smith and Neil McNab but my assessment of Ward after that first season in the First Division was that it would be difficult for him to be consistent at the higher level. I suppose that his time at Nottingham Forest justified that view.

With United, Brighton and Forest all seemingly keen on completing the deal, Ward took his place in the Brighton team to face Forest anticipating that it would be his final game for the Seagulls:

Even though I had been through the on-off transfer saga with Forest the previous year, I did think that this time it would all go through. Mullery had said on TV that he was confident that Ritchie would join Brighton, and Peter Taylor had said that Forest were waiting on Ritchie's decision before they would make any moves. In the tunnel before the game, though, John Robertson asked me if I was going to be joining Forest and I told him that I had no idea!

Forest won the match 1-0 thanks to a goal from Scottish striker Ian Wallace. Wallace had become the fourth million pound player, following Trevor Francis, Steve Daley and Andy Gray, when Forest paid Coventry £1,250,000 for him during the close season.

As the teams left the field, and to the surprise of Argus reporter John Vinicombe, there was no 'special ovation tinged with pardonable nostalgia' for Ward. Albion fan David Dresch remembers the lack of acknowledgement for Ward as a disappointing end to the striker's Albion career:

I was sorry to see him go because I felt that we hadn't seen the best of him. After the last home game, there weren't any chants about keeping Ward; the talk was of Andy Ritchie, who was young and exciting. I suppose we weren't even really sure that the transfer would take place because it hadn't been confirmed and Forest had mucked us around before.

Peter definitely deserved a better send-off. I remember John Vinicombe telling me that he was hoping that someone would stand up in the crowd and say 'Thank you very much Peter, well done' but everyone just melted away.

Although the deal looked likely to happen there were two potential sticking points: the first was that Andy Ritchie was not keen on moving away from his Manchester home and had already rejected a move to Chelsea because he did not want to live in London; the second was a certain Mr. Clough, who was still not convinced that Taylor's positive appraisal of Ward justified the price that Brighton were demanding.

◇　◇　◇

The day following the Forest match, Ward travelled to Manchester to meet up with the England B squad. As he trained with the England players at Manchester University's athletic ground, negotiations between Mullery and Clough started to falter:

> It was extremely difficult to deal with Clough and Taylor, to say the least. That week was an absolute nightmare with discussions between me and [Brighton director] Harry Bloom and those two. Mike Bamber was away on business in America at the time so it was left to us to try to make the deal happen.
>
> There were promises made and then they would phone up and say the deal was off; then it would be back on again. Luckily, we protected Peter from this, although I had told him that Forest wanted to buy him because I'd promised him that we'd let him go back to that area if he had the chance.
>
> Peter was in Manchester with the England B team and Clough and Taylor said they would go over to see him but they didn't.
>
> Whilst this was going on, I was negotiating over Ritchie with Manchester United and had convinced him to sign. On the Monday following, I got a call from Clough saying that we were asking for too much money for Ward so the deal was off. I went mad and told the papers that as long as I was manager of Brighton, we would never do a deal with Nottingham Forest.
>
> The next day Peter Taylor phoned me and told me that the deal was back on and that I should tell the papers that Ward was going to Forest.
>
> Andy had agreed to come to Brighton and had trained with us and had his medical. We were keen to get him signed because other teams were interested in him too.

With the deal still hanging in the balance, Ward took his place on the England bench at Old Trafford:

> It was a strange night. Old Trafford was a fantastic place to play but there were fewer than ten thousand fans there so it felt really empty. We won 1-0; I went on as sub for Alan Sunderland with about twenty five minutes to go and played quite well.
>
> The FA never gave me a cap for that game and when I enquired about it they said that I hadn't played! I've got an old newspaper report from The Times that mentions me playing, so maybe I'll send them that and get my cap after all.
>
> The next morning, the papers said that the deal for me to go to Forest was back on but by the time I'd returned to Brighton, it was off again!

119

With Clough and Taylor seemingly unable to agree on Ward's value, Mullery's patience was running thin. He was relieved when Mike Bamber returned from his business trip:

Mike came back on the Wednesday and by that time Clough had phoned again to say that the deal was off and that it was up to him and not Taylor. Mike spoke to Forest and finally decided on a fee with them.

Dealing with Cloughie and Taylor was an absolute nightmare from start to finish.

Still in limbo, Ward trained as usual with Brighton on Thursday morning and found out that the deal had finally been completed, from a television report that evening:

I was at a friend's house and we were watching the news and it said the transfer has gone through between Brighton and Forest for Peter Ward. So I thought, 'oh right' — it was a strange feeling. On one hand, I loved being at Brighton and on the other hand, I was signing for the European Champions.

I went into the office at the Goldstone the next day to check that everything was ok and then Sue and I drove up to Derby to meet Clough and Taylor to do the deal.

Sue's clearest memory of the meeting is the Forest manager's opening question:

Forest put us up in a hotel in Derby and Sheena Easton, who was a big star, was staying in there at the same time so I was quite impressed. They treated us very well.

The first question Brian Clough asked was directed to me. He said 'Do you like [Peter's] moustache?' I told him that I did and Clough said 'OK, he can keep it then!'

In a way it was nice to go back to the Midlands but I much preferred Brighton.

Before travelling to Derby, Peter had sought advice about the financial demands that he should make of his new employers:

I spoke to an agent. I was earning about £600 a week at Brighton, and he said that I should ask Forest for £750 a week. So I sat down with Clough and Taylor and said 'I want £750 a week' and expected them to come back with a lower figure to negotiate. Straight away, though, they both said 'OK'. I thought, 'oh f****** hell' and wished that I'd asked for lots more!

So then I said 'I want a £50,000 signing-on fee'. Clough looked at me and said 'Son, if you were Peter Shilton, you wouldn't get that.'

120

I got £20,000 or so and put that straight in a pension. I still get a good return from that.

With a four-year contract signed, Ward, Clough and Taylor posed for pictures with an unusual prop —a vacuum cleaner. The Wards stayed in Derby overnight and then returned to Sussex to say their goodbyes and to organise the move north.

In a little under five years since breaking into the first team, Ward had scored 92 goals for Brighton in exactly 200 games, and had been the biggest star during the club's most successful period.

Summing up Ward's time at Brighton, Alan Mullery says:

In the time that I had him he was, for me, Roy of the Rovers. He was as good as anybody at scoring goals — he was absolutely brilliant. It was a joy to be with him and a joy to work with him.

◇ ◇ ◇

The Brighton team travelled to Stoke on the Friday night without Ward. The journey had a sad ending: Albion director, Harry Bloom, suffered a fatal heart attack on the team coach. Alan Mullery had regarded Bloom as the perfect buffer between himself and Chairman Mike Bamber, and partly attributes Bloom's death to the anxiety caused by the Ward transfer negotiations:

I'm sure that the business of trying to deal with those two men [Clough and Taylor] and the amount of stress that it caused killed Harry. I was sitting next to him on the coach and he'd won some money playing cards and then, all of a sudden, he slumped forward and that was it. Our medical staff did what they could but they couldn't save him. Harry was a great character and a good friend.

CHAPTER 10

IN AND OUT AT FOREST

*Cloughie told Larry Lloyd to stand by the door and make sure
that nobody was coming and then he emptied the boxes
onto the table. They were full of video recorders and money.*

– Peter Ward

Peter Ward's transfer to Nottingham Forest was met with delight by his father. Colin Ward hoped that his son's move back to the East Midlands would provide an ideal platform for Peter to further his career:

> *I was really thrilled that Peter was coming to Forest. They had just won the European Cup for the second time and he would be closer to home.*
>
> *Cloughie used to go to the same hairdresser as I. One night, I was about the last customer and my hairdresser said that I should hang on because Clough was coming in and he would usually bring a bottle of champagne with him.*
>
> *So after I'd had my hair cut I waited and, sure enough, Clough did arrive. He said to me 'When's your Peter coming to play for us then?' I said 'I don't know, you'd better ask him.'*
>
> *I told Clough how I'd been drenched watching Forest play Man United a couple of weeks earlier and he said 'Leave it to me, I'll make up for it and send you a couple of tickets.' So he took a note of my address and a few days later two season tickets courtesy of the generous Brian Clough arrived in the post.*
>
> *I assumed that Peter would get on with Clough, but evidently it didn't turn out that way.*

Two weeks before Ward had finally become a Nottingham Forest player, they had been knocked out of the European Cup in the first round by unfancied CSKA Sofia. The defeat ended Forest's two-year reign in Europe and was an early indication that the club's gloriously successful run was drawing to a close.

Since Peter Taylor left Brighton to team up with Brian Clough in 1976, Forest's achievements had been spectacular; promotion to the First Division in 1976-77 had been followed by the Division One Championship and victory in the League Cup Final in 1977-78. During the next season, Forest won the Charity Shield, retained the League Cup, won the European Cup and finished second in Division One. In 1979-80, Forest reached the final of the League Cup for the third successive season: they lost to Wolves in the Final, but won the UEFA Super Cup and became the second British club to retain the European Cup.

Seven trophies in four years was both a phenomenal achievement for a club that had won only one in the previous eighty years and a testament to the impact that Clough and Taylor had at Forest.

Nottingham-born Viv Anderson, MBE, was an integral part of the team between 1976 and 1984 and made over 300 appearances for Forest. The right-back puts Forest's success down to a combination of a great group of players and a unique management team:

> *To turn a provincial club like Forest into League Champions and then European Champions —twice— was incredible. It was quite a story.*

> *We had a lot of excellent players and a fairly consistent side. We would only ever see Clough and Taylor on a Saturday, but during that time they could motivate us enough that we could, and did, beat anyone.*

Gary Mills, another player who came through the ranks at Forest (making his debut at just 16 years of age), had become the youngest player to appear in a European Cup Final when drafted as replacement for the injured Trevor Francis for the 1979-80 final against Hamburg. Mills' view of Forest's success is similar to Anderson's:

> *The approach was simple, really - we were taught how to win and how to play as a team. There weren't any complicated tactics or secrets. It was all down to Clough and Taylor's management.*

> *Of course, we also had quality players and an excellent spirit, which was a great combination.*

Clough and Taylor tried to maintain the success by spending considerable amounts of money on transfer fees but the slow dissolution of the 'Forest Giants' resulted in a more fragmented squad: the social togetherness of the previous years was lost.

Club record signing Ian Wallace joined Forest from Coventry for £1.25m before the start of the 1980-81 season and found the contrast between his new and old club quite noticeable:

> *I had been at Coventry for four years and was more ambitious than the club. I wanted to move to a bigger and better club and Forest came in for me. They were European champions so it was an easy move.*

> *Socially, it wasn't such a close knit group at Forest as it had been at Coventry and people tended to stick to their own small group. It could be a lonely club at times and the players tended to live in quite a spread out area. At Coventry we would often go out golfing and virtually all of the team would go - it wasn't like that at Forest.*

Viv Anderson puts the change in atmosphere off the pitch down to the declining fortunes on it:

> *During the successful years we would hang out a lot together, going for lunch or a drink. It was a family-orientated club but a lot of the great players had started to leave. It was a difficult time for me and for the club. We'd had four or five fantastic years and a lot of new players were coming in who hadn't shared the same successes. Of course we'd try to make new players welcome and we still had plenty of laughs but it was a lot easier to enjoy ourselves when we were getting good results every week.*

Peter Ward's early impressions mirrored those of Wallace:

> *At Brighton, we'd been very close knit and there hadn't been any cliques. At Forest, it was different: there seemed to be little groups who would hang out together but we wouldn't do much as a team.*

> *The players made me feel very welcome and generally they were better players than there had been at Brighton. All the players were very good; they were a better team [than Brighton]. There were some really strong personalities in the dressing room: Kenny Burns was a leader, Larry Lloyd was a leader, Dave Needham, when he played, was a leader.*

> *John Robertson set an example by the way he played — he was fantastic, probably the best I ever played with. He couldn't run, he wasn't very fast, but he used to go around people as though they weren't there.*

> *John McGovern was underrated too. Even though he was captain, I don't think many people rated him. He was a good player, a very good player. Trevor Francis was injured when I joined but he was excellent too.*

> *We had a lot of Scottish internationals — Frank Gray, Robbo (John Robertson), Ian Wallace, Kenny Burns —John McGovern was a Scot too — and there was quite a lot of England-Scotland rivalry. The Scottish team were much better in those days than they are now and the Home Internationals were still taking place, so England and Scotland would play each other every year.*

> *In training we would play the 'Blocks' against everyone else. The 'Blocks' were the blacks and the jocks, so it would be all the Scottish lads plus Viv and Justin Fashanu after he'd joined. These games would tend to be on a Friday afternoon and they could get really competitive.*

> *Kenny Burns and Peter Shilton really didn't like each other and Kenny would always give Shilton a hard time, so even when we went away Shilton wouldn't come over to sit at the same table as us if we were drinking with Kenny and Robbo. He would choose to sit in a corner on his own drinking his half-pints. Mind you, he was still playing for England when he was forty so he looked after himself pretty well!*

124

Shilton got caught by the police with his pants down, sitting in his car with a girl called Tina. Every morning, Kenny would shout to him 'Have you still got that Cor-tina?'

And then, when they were at Leicester together, Frank Worthington had supposedly had a fling with Shilton's wife and the fans used to shout 'Worthy's shagged your missus, Worthy's shagged your missus'. Burnsy would come in and say 'Have you been out with Worthington recently?' It was horrible, but Shilton wouldn't have a go at him because Burnsy was a very tough man and would have killed him.

The rivalry wasn't confined to the changing rooms and the training pitch, and I remember one league match: we were defending and the ball came over. Shilton was shouting 'Away! Away!' but instead of clearing it, Kenny controlled the ball on his chest and volleyed it straight to him, with power, right at his chest. I thought that was brilliant. You could see the glaring looks they were giving each other.

Apart from the players, there wasn't that much difference between Brighton and Forest. The facilities were a little better at Forest — the ground was bigger, the dressing room was a little bigger and there was generally more space but it wasn't that different.

The training facilities were no better, though. We'd get changed at the ground and then jog down the side of the Trent to the training ground.

In my first training session I chipped Peter Shilton and scored. He screamed 'Damn it, Peter!' I thought 'shit, what have I done,' but one of the other players told me that he was shouting at himself for letting a goal in.

Clough didn't get involved in training. Occasionally, he would turn up with a big stick, thinking he was Robin Hood, but Ronnie Fenton used to take all the training sessions.

◇　◇　◇

The summer signing of Wallace and Ward's arrival, coupled with departure of Birtles two months into the season, left Forest with the smallest strike force in the division. Gary Mills did not see the lack of a traditional big target man as an issue:

It didn't really hit me. Gary Birtles had done unbelievably well and was a great player and it was difficult to replace him. I don't think the big man/little man issue really made much difference. We played the ball on the ground mainly anyway — so as long as you could play you were ok.

Viv Anderson remembers that change in personnel had a more significant impact on the team:

> We had to change the way that we were playing because we had always played with a big centre forward — first, we had Peter Withe and then we had Garry Birtles. It was a completely different way of playing with two smaller players. To be honest, we found it hard to adjust to playing without a target man.

> Birtles, in my view, was pound for pound one of the best centre forwards I played with. He was good in the air, could hold the ball up and score goals. He also worked very hard for the team so when Peter Ward came in to replace him they were big shoes to fill.

> I knew Peter because we had been in a few England squads together. He was really skilful and had a low centre of gravity. He was very slight but manipulated the ball well and could go past people with ease. He had an eye for a goal and had done really well at Brighton.

> We knew that Peter Taylor had seen a lot of him and Forest paid what was a lot of money at the time to sign him.

The newspaper headline writers had a field day, coming up with a variety of names for the pairing, such as the "Tiny Terrors" and "Wee Ward and Wallace." The two strikers joined up for the first time in Ward's debut on 22nd October, 1980, five days after he had signed:

> I made my debut on the Wednesday night. We played Leeds and I played up front with Ian Wallace — we won 2-1. Wallace was even smaller than me, about 5'7", so we must have been the smallest pair of forwards in the league by a long way!

> Clough was really pleased that we had beaten Leeds and, although I didn't score, he actually said that it was one of the best debuts he'd ever seen.

Ward had played with a variety of strike partners during his time at Brighton and Sammy Morgan, Teddy Maybank, Ray Clarke and Michael Robinson had all provided physical stature to complement Ward's turn of pace and quick feet. Similarly, new partner Wallace had also been used to playing alongside a ball-winning target man:

> I had always played with a big man: Mick Ferguson at Coventry and then, for a short while, Birtles at Forest. I was more physical than Peter but he was probably sharper than me. We were both penalty area players but neither of us were target men in the traditional sense. However, Forest had good players on the wing, who could get the ball in the box.

> Peter and I gave the defenders a hard time even though we were two little guys. I think we did as well as we could in that system.

126

◇ ◇ ◇

The following Wednesday, Forest travelled to Norwich and earned a point in a one-all draw. A satisfactory result left Ward reasonably pleased with his first two appearances for his new club and looking forward to a quick trip back to Sussex to tie up a few loose ends:

> After the second game, away at Norwich, I was planning to head back down to Brighton rather than go on the team bus because I still had quite a lot of organising to do. After the game, Clough said to the team 'Do you think he deserves to go back down to Brighton for the weekend after that performance?' Luckily, the boys said yes!

Fortunately, Ward was cup-tied for the midweek trip to Watford in the League Cup. Graham Taylor's Second Division side made light work of Forest with a 4-1 victory, thereby ending Forest's attempt to reach the final for the fourth consecutive season.

Recalled for the league visit of Southampton, Ward scored his first Forest goal:

> We won 2-1 and I got the first goal after just seven minutes. It was a massive relief to get a goal, especially at the City Ground. George Courtney, who was one of the top referees, was in charge of the game. There were seven bookings and a Southampton's Malcolm Waldron got sent off for fouling me twice in about five minutes.

A goalless draw at Anfield against league champions Liverpool was a creditable result and Ward's performance drew a special mention from Clough, who professed to being "very pleased with Ward's all-'round game."

As Ward was earning praise from his manager, his old team-mates at Brighton were suffering the 1-0 defeat at home to Middlesbrough that sent the Seagulls to the bottom of the table. The defeat, their fourth on the run since Ward had left, was played out in front of just 12,000 spectators — the lowest First Division gate the club had experienced at that point.

Three days later, Forest lost 2-0 at Birmingham City; this was Ward's first experience of defeat as a Forest player. His memories of Clough's reaction to the result demonstrate how quickly a player could go from hero to villain in the manager's opinion:

> Frank Worthington scored both goals for Birmingham and Clough used to hate Worthington. Frank was a real showman — birds and booze — he thought he was Elvis Presley! Clough couldn't stand all that.

> On the coach on the way home I wanted to be dropped off at a service station near Derby where I had parked my car. I went down to ask the coach

driver to stop for me but Clough told him to carry on driving, go past my
stop and drop me off a mile or so up the road.

I'll never forget what Clough said: 'with a bit of luck, the little c**t might
get run over.' I couldn't believe it! It was dark and pouring down too; I had
to walk a mile back down the side of the motorway to get my car.

◇ ◇ ◇

Sandwiched between home defeats against Tottenham and Ipswich, Ward made another appearance for the England B team in what proved to be his final international call-up:

We played Australia at St. Andrews in Birmingham. It was virtually the
same Australian team that I had played against for the full England side in
the summer. This time, we won 1-0 and I played up front again with Cyrille
Regis.

Ward's first taste of European club football came with Spanish side Valencia's visit to the City Ground for the first leg of the European Super Cup. The two-legged final pitted the European Cup Winners against the UEFA Cup Winners.

A physical game ended in a 2-1 victory for Forest. Two second-half goals from Ian Bowyer, the first set-up by Ward, gave Forest a slight advantage going into the second leg four weeks later. Ward's performance returned him to his manager's good books ("He told me that I was man of the match"). It also drew praise from a number of football writers, who commented on the courage shown by both Ward and Wallace when suffering some harsh tackling from the Spaniards.

In the next game, Wallace scored against his old team; Forest maintained their 8th position in the league with a one-all draw at Coventry. A week later, Crystal Palace visited the City Ground. Much had changed for the South London club since they had been infamously christened the "Team of the Eighties," following a modest run of success under Terry Venables. Venables had left for Queens Park Rangers and Palace has slumped to the bottom of the table. In what proved to be a failed attempt to save the club from relegation, Palace appointed Malcolm Allison, recently sacked by Manchester City, for his second stint as manager. Allison lasted just two months in the hot-seat and neither he nor his successor, Dario Gradi, could lift Palace off the foot of the table during the last six months of the season.

A goalless first half led to a half-time rocket for his players from Clough, and the manager's words resulted in an improved performance from his team. Goals from Frank Gray, debutant Colin Walsh and Ward secured a comfortable 3-0 win for the home side.

My second goal was against Palace — I got a few extra boos from the Palace fans although they were really struggling, so there weren't that many of them at the game.

I remember my goal: Jim Cannon or one of the defenders tried to clear it and I sort of blocked it and it flew over the goalkeeper's head into the net — it wasn't a classic, put it that way.

Following a 1-0 defeat at Leeds, Ward lost his place in the side to fit-again Trevor Francis. The million pound man returned to the team for the Super Cup second leg in Valencia and Ward was relegated to the substitutes' bench.

Another rugged encounter resulted in a 1-0 defeat for Forest and an aggregate loss on away goals. Despite the result and having lost his place in the team, it was still a memorable trip for Ward:

On the flight to Valencia, we were playing cards at the back of the plane and one of the stewardesses came over and said 'He says you need to get him a drink'.

We said 'What?' and the stewardess pointed at Cloughie and said that he says you need to get him a drink. I told her to tell him that he could get his own drink and we carried on playing.

A little while later she came back past us and said the same thing to Gary Mills. He ended up getting Cloughie's drink for him, taking it to him and then pouring it for him. Typical Cloughie…

I remember, in the tunnel before the game, walking side by side with Mario Kempes, who had been the star and leading scorer when Argentina had won the World Cup a couple of years earlier. He had his socks sort of pulled half up like in the World Cup — I thought wow, this is great! It was experiences like that which made the move to Forest the right thing for me to do.

We deserved to win the game but lost 1-0: we just couldn't score.

◇   ◇   ◇

For the final three league games of 1980, Clough picked his two million-pound strikers — Francis and Wallace — and Ward was banished to the reserve team. Two wins and a draw lifted Forest to fifth in the table but Ward returned to the first team for an FA Cup replay at Bolton on 6th January. When Ward replaced Wallace, Peter Taylor's preferred combination of Ward and Francis could finally play together.

The pair eventually combined for the game's only goal, when Ward's header sent Francis through on goal with just seven minutes remaining of extra time.

Ward retained his place for the visit to second-placed Ipswich Town but both he and Francis were subdued by Town's defensive pairing of Terry Butcher and Russell Osman. Ipswich won comfortably, 2-0, and the defeat all but ended Forest's tenuous chance of recapturing the Division One title.

Following the game, the Forest team travelled down to London in preparation for a flight to Paris the next morning. The game against Paris St.-Germain was, in Ward's opinion, an unnecessary distraction and did little to improve Clough's attitude toward him:

> It was crazy — in the middle of the league season and the day after a game against one of the best clubs in the country, Forest scheduled a friendly in France!

> We would play a lot of friendlies, which I didn't mind because I just wanted to play football, but we didn't have big squads like now. The games were organised to raise money for the club, or for the managers anyway.

> The trip to Paris was a disaster for me. I played in the first half but had a nightmare. At half-time, Clough came up to me and said 'What was that? Pathetic! Get off!' and he took me off. We lost two-nil and I stayed out of his way on the way back.

◇ ◇ ◇

Ward was banished to the reserve team for the next two months and his sole first team appearance during this period came 6,000 miles from Nottingham, in Tokyo, Japan.

The World Club Championship (WCC) was contested between the reigning champions of Europe, Forest, and their South American counterparts, Nacional Montevideo from Uruguay. The competition was the forerunner of the FIFA Club World Cup: the winners had the distinction of being able to call themselves the World Champions.

Mindful of an FA Cup fifth round tie in Nottingham just three days after the Tokyo match, Brian Clough decided to leave Bryn Gunn, Gary Mills and Colin Walsh at home along with injured skipper John McGovern. This opened a place for Ward in the squad and an epic journey started with a coach trip from Nottingham to Heathrow:

> Pete Taylor had taken some medical advice about how we could avoid jet-lag and decided that the best way would be if we stayed on British time. We left Nottingham early on Sunday morning and took a nine-hour flight from Heathrow to Alaska. We spent an hour or so there and then took another flight which lasted for eight hours to Japan. The club gave us all sleeping tablets and by the time we got to the hotel in Tokyo we were all wide awake.

130

It was strange because we stayed up all night and then slept during the day. The second night that we were there, most of the players were in a bar having a few drinks. We were talking to some Japanese girls and Kenny Burns decided that it would be funny to take his teeth out and give the girls a big gummy grin: it frightened the life out of them and we all found it very amusing.

I was sub for the game and it was the first time that I'd been involved with the first team for a while, so it was good to be back. The National Stadium was fantastic and there were 62,000 people there — the biggest crowd that I had ever played in front of.

The game was actually a bit of a disappointment. We played well and I came on in the second half but we couldn't score and ended up losing 1-0.

When we got back to Nottingham we were told to meet in the old board room and Clough and Taylor came in with these two great big boxes. Cloughie told Larry Lloyd to stand by the door and make sure that nobody was coming and then he emptied the boxes onto the table. They were full of video recorders and money. Cloughie told us to help ourselves; there was a video recorder for everyone and a bunch of money too — it was great!

The only other time that I had been given money under the table, so to speak, was at Brighton, from a boot rep. He would come in and put cash inside your boots if you were wearing the right brand.

When I came to Forest, I had a contract with Gola. They paid me about three or four grand a year to wear their boots - which I thought was great. When I went to the States and we got to the Soccer Bowl Final, Adidas paid me five grand to wear a pair of their boots for just one game!

Taylor's plan to minimise the impact of jet lag paid off and after a twenty-five hour trip home Forest came from behind to defeat Bristol City 2-1 in the FA Cup and progress to the quarter-finals.

Peter Ward did not feature in the squad for the Bristol City match and returned to the reserve team. By the end of February, and with Forest's good form moving them up to fifth in Division One, Ward's future at the club was reported to be on the verge of being over after just five months. The News of the World printed an article suggesting that Ward was likely to be part of a deal that would see Norwich City striker Justin Fashanu join Forest and Ward and Martin O'Neill head in the opposite direction. While Fashanu and Ward stayed put, O'Neill signed for the Canaries and he was soon followed out of the City Ground by defensive stalwart Larry Lloyd, who joined Fourth Division Wigan Athletic as player-manager.

◇ ◇ ◇

After being knocked out of the FA Cup at Ipswich Town, Forest looked likely to end the season without winning a single competition for the first time in five seasons.

Ward was once again thrown a first team lifeline when he was named as substitute for Brighton's visit to the City Ground — Ward's first chance to play against his old teammates. With an unsettled Trevor Francis falling out of favour with his manager, Clough decided against giving Ward a starting place and opted to replace Francis with Gary Mills.

An early goal from Giles Stille gave Brighton a surprise lead and the possibility that Forest would succumb to the Seagulls for the third consecutive game grew. A John Robertson penalty and Ian Wallace's first goal in a month gave Forest a 2-1 half-time lead and further goals in the second half from Mills and Kenny Burns gave Forest a resounding 4-1 victory. Ward replaced left-back Frankie Gray for the final eight minutes of the game but had little chance to show his old club any of the skills from which they had grown so accustomed to profiting:

> Before the game, Mark Lawrenson had said to me, 'come back, Whizz — all is forgotten.' They really seemed to be struggling. It was a shame that I didn't get to play more of the game against them but that is how it was at the time.
>
> I was playing well for the reserves and scoring lots of goals but that didn't seem to make any difference. Cloughie had even talked about playing Kenny Burns up front again rather than picking me.

In a candid interview with the Evening Argus, Peter Taylor explained that he still expected that Ward would become a hit at Forest, despite the fact that the other coaches at the club were not confident that he was up to the expected standards.

Ward made another substitute appearance in the following game and Forest gained a point in a one-all draw at Manchester United. United had not won a game since January and former Forest striker Garry Birtles had struggled to make an impact. He had yet to score a league goal in the five months since his move to Old Trafford.

◇ ◇ ◇

A recall for Francis put an end to Ward's hopes of a return to the starting lineup, despite Peter Taylor telling the national papers that Ward's form in the reserves was making it nearly impossible to keep him out of the team. Ward did not even make the bench for the visit to West Brom as a 2-1 defeat put a dent in Forest's hopes of finishing in a UEFA Cup qualifying place.

A hat-trick for the reserves in a 3-0 victory over Sheffield United and another goal in a 2-0 win over Preston supported Ward's quest to regain a first team place; he was finally rewarded with his first start for ten weeks as Forest faced fifth-placed Liverpool on 11th April. A crowd of 27,363, Forest's biggest home gate since December, watched the two teams largely cancel each other out in a nil-nil draw. Despite the scoreline, Ward played well and delivered a confident and lively performance.

Ward retained his place for the trip to leaders Aston Villa on Good Friday but a good performance from Forest produced little reward: Villa won 2-0. Easter Monday's visit of Wolverhampton again saw Ward paired with Trevor Francis, and Francis' sixth league goal of the campaign gave Forest a 1-0 win.

The game against Wolves was Ward's final appearance of the season as Forest completed their schedule with a win over relegated Crystal Palace and a one-all draw with Coventry.

Forest finished the season in seventh place with fifty points, ten fewer than champions Aston Villa. Kevin Keegan's Southampton also finished with fifty points but the Saints qualified for the final UEFA Cup spot, two points ahead of Forest.

Ward's season had been inconsistent at best. In 16 league and cup games for Forest, he had scored two goals to add to the two that he had scored for Brighton at the start of the season. Ward's replacement at Brighton, Andy Ritchie, had fared slightly better and had scored five league goals. The most important of Ritchie's goals came in the final game of the season as a 2-0 victory over Leeds gave Albion their fourth consecutive victory and secured an unlikely escape from relegation.

Replacing a player as popular as Ward had been a big challenge for Ritchie, but Mark Lawrenson remembers the young Mancunian as a successful addition to the Brighton team:

> *Andy Ritchie was a different sort of player — he wasn't a player who would drop his shoulder, beat three people and curl it into the bottom corner like Wardy. He was more clinical — he had a great first touch and was a good finisher but he didn't have Wardy's flair.*
>
> *Andy Ritchie was a thinking man's player and he was very good but completely different than Peter.*

Incredibly, the other player involved in the three-way transfer, Garry Birtles, ended the season still searching for his first league goal for Manchester United.

CHAPTER 11

FASHANU ARRIVES AS FOREST UNRAVEL

When Peter [Ward] and I played together, we would look for
the same kind of ball but wouldn't get in each other's way,
whereas Justin was used to playing on his own and didn't look
to play as part of a partnership — he just did his own thing.

— Ian Wallace, Nottingham Forest

Ward's first pre-season as a Nottingham Forest player got off to a fly-ing start with a hat-trick in a 5-1 victory over Linfield in Belfast. Returning from Ireland, Forest prepared for a trip to Spain, to participate in the four-team Zaragoza tournament, by signing Norwich City's 20-year-old striker Justin Fashanu. Fashanu became Forest's third million-pound striker in a deal that Brian Clough later referred to as 'dropping a mighty clanger'.

Peter Taylor hailed the arrival of Fashanu as the start of Forest's plan to build a new, young side, and stated that one of the other three strikers at the club — Ward, Wallace or Francis — would be moving on. In contrast, Clough insisted that all four strikers would be staying with the club and that there was no need to raise money to finance Fashanu's signing by selling any of the other players.

Ward continued his good form with Forest's first goal in a 2-1 win over Spanish side Osasuna and the victory put Forest into the tournament final where they faced the hosts, Real Zaragoza. A brilliant goal from new signing Mark Proctor gave Forest a 1-0 lead but Fashanu marked his first start for the club with a red card in the 78th minute. The Spaniards equalised with four minutes left and the game was decided on penalties, with the home team se-curing a 4-2 victory.

Fashanu's red card was an unhappy start to what proved to be a disastrous eighteen-month spell at the City Ground. Viv Anderson remembers the new signing's first trip with Forest as a strange few days:

*We roomed together on the trip and, as well as getting sent off, Fash gave
me one of the frights of my life. It was the middle of the night and I was fast
asleep. Suddenly, I was woken up by a massive banging noise. I looked at
the door and it looked like someone had broken it down with an axe. Fash*

had been having a nightmare and smashed the door down in his sleep with
his bare hands - he was an incredibly strong lad.

The Forest squad flew back to the UK for a couple of days before setting off
for Italy to take on Napoli in their final warm-up game. Napoli had finished
third in Serie A the previous season and included Ruud Krol, the Dutch captain, in their lineup.

A fine performance from Forest failed to produce a goal, although Ward
was disallowed what would have been a game-winning effort:

I remember that game: I scored a great left foot volley but the linesman put
his flag up. I was onside but Fashanu was offside right over on the other
side of the pitch. It wouldn't have been disallowed today.

To Ward's surprise, the Italian supporters gave Brian Clough a torrid time
throughout the match and, as the players attempted to get to the team coach
after the game, the situation threatened to get out of hand:

We came out of the stadium after the game and we had to have a police
guard so that we could get through the crowd to the coach.

The Italians weren't giving us (the players), any grief but they hated
Cloughie. They were booing him and throwing all sorts of things at him.
At the time I didn't realise what all the fuss was about but I later found out
that when Clough had been at Derby he had called the Italians 'dirty cheat-
ing bastards' in a press conference after Derby had been beaten by Juventus.

◇　◇　◇

With a successful pre-season under his belt, Ward had justifiably earned his
place in the starting eleven for the first league game of the season. With Ward
partnering Fashanu and Trevor Francis also in the team, it was Ian Wallace
who found himself left out of the side. A brace from Francis secured a 2-1 victory over the visitors, Southampton, but the reports after the game focused on
rumours surrounding Francis's future at the club rather than his match winning performance.

An unchanged Forest side visited Old Trafford and gained a point in a goalless draw in front of 51,000 spectators. Fashanu acquitted himself well against
United's giant defender, Gordon McQueen, and Ward and Francis were both
denied by fine saves from United keeper, Gary Bailey. United striker, Garry
Birtles, had yet to score a league goal for his new club: he eventually took just
shy of eleven months to hit the back of the net.

The United game was Francis's last for Forest and, despite Clough's earlier
assurances that the club did not need to sell any of their star players, a fee of

£1.2m moved the 27-year-old to Manchester City in a deal that Clough admitted Forest made to 'balance the books'.

Despite playing a significant role in Forest's unbeaten start to the season, Ward was dropped for the trip to Birmingham City in favour of Ian Wallace.

Wallace marked his first start of the campaign with a hat-trick but still ended up on the losing side as Birmingham ran out 4-3 winners. Wallace and Fashanu kept their places in the side for the next two months and Ward, once again, found himself playing reserve team football.

Clough dropped Wallace after he had been sent off for fighting against Birmingham in the League Cup in late October and recalled Ward to the first team squad for the visit of Leeds United. A familiar face in the Leeds team was Kenny Burns, who had been signed from Forest for £400,000 a month earlier.

Playing against Burns, who had a well-deserved reputation as a no-nonsense defender, didn't give Ward any undue worries:

> It was a little strange playing against Burnsy but I'd played against him when I was at Brighton and always done well.

> He was a big loss to Forest because he was a very imposing player. He was a hard man, though, and on a couple of occasions he went a bit too far.

> He hit me once: I was on his team during training and went past a couple of players and had only the goalie to beat. The keeper came out and I dummied to pass to Burnsy and went round the goalie instead, but then I hit the post. Burnsy wasn't impressed and shouted, 'Gimme the ball!'

> I said, 'Shut up, you ugly so and so' which, looking back, was a bit of a mistake. He came after me and threw a punch; I saw it coming, though, and it just caught me but I still went down because I didn't want him to punch me again.

> So the coach, Ronnie Fenton, says 'Both of you, go!' and pointed to the club building. By the time we had got to the office we were having a laugh about it but we still both got fined £25.

> Fenton asked me, 'Why didn't you stand up to him?' I said, 'You f*****g stand up to him: do you think I'm crazy?!'

> On another occasion, we were training with the apprentices, which we hardly ever did. We were playing a little match and one of the kids caught Burns in the face with an elbow by mistake. Within ten minutes Burnsy had got his own back and the kid was on his way to hospital. 'That'll teach him,' he said, and it probably did.

In his first start for two months Ward soon made his mark. His header after twenty-two minutes gave Forest the lead and was his first goal of the season. Leeds equalised just before half-time, but a John Robertson penalty midway through the second half was enough to secure two points for Forest and lift them to fifth place in the table.

Clough's post-match address to his team left Ward feeling somewhat bemused:

> We'd beaten Leeds — which should have made him happy — and I'd scored a goal, so I thought I might get a 'Well done, Peter' or 'Good game, lad' but, instead, he decided to have a go at me for celebrating my goal too much. I'd run to the Trent End when I scored and he thought I'd made a meal of it.

> By this time I knew that whatever I did, even if I scored a hat-trick every game, he wouldn't be happy with me. But what could I do apart from just get on with it?

Despite performing well in a Forest victory, Ward lost his place to Wallace for the next game. A goalless draw with West Ham saw neither Wallace nor Fashanu looking likely to score and *The Times* rather damningly described Fashanu's ball control as "unspeakably poor for someone so costly."

Wallace's suspension for the fight at Birmingham came into force for the next game and Ward replaced him for the League Cup third round game at Blackburn Rovers. Fashanu's header from Ward's cross, his second goal of the season, gave Forest a 1-0 victory and a place in the last sixteen.

Ward kept his place for the trip to Arsenal but, although Fashanu scored again, Forest could not prevent their hosts from gaining a sixth consecutive victory with a 2-1 win.

A long midweek trip to Sunderland saw Ward and Fashanu link up for the third consecutive game. Fashanu's third goal in as many games gave Forest a two-nil lead just after half-time. Bottom-of-the-table Sunderland battled back with two goals but David Needham scored the winning goal for Forest with no more than five minutes remaining.

Fashanu's goal at Sunderland, his third league goal of the season, proved to be the last that he would score during his uneasy stay with Forest. Ward's memories of Fashanu, who committed suicide in 1998, are of a young man who struggled with the expectations of a big-money transfer and who found it difficult to integrate with his team-mates:

> It must have been very hard for Fashanu: he had signed for a lot of money and he really struggled to score goals. In a way, it was similar to my situation, but he had the added complication of his social life and constant rumours about his sexuality.

> I remember one day in the changing room, it was either Kenny Burns or John Robertson said to Fash, 'There's a rumour going 'round that you're gay.' Then it went around the room, lots of the lads saying 'I've heard it too.' Fashanu said something like 'Well, what do you think?' but nobody

was brave enough to say 'Yeah, I think you're gay' because he was huge and a very strong lad.

In one game against Man City, we had a corner and I was on the near post and Fashanu was behind me. Robbo was taking the corner and just before the ball came over I heard a 'crack' and looked 'round: Tommy Caton [Man City defender] was lying on the floor with a broken nose and there was blood pouring everywhere. Fashanu had just elbowed him.

When I had been at Brighton, Fashanu had done something similar to Andy Rollings. He had been a good amateur boxer and I remember that, after we played at Villa, Ron Saunders, who was the Villa manager, said that Fashanu should decide whether he wanted to be a boxer or a footballer because he was too aggressive on the pitch.

Fashanu had a sponsored car at Forest and there was space along the side so that they could add a little ball sticker every time he scored a goal. It stayed on three balls for ages and he used to get slaughtered by the boys for that.

Cloughie would give him a really hard time sometimes too. After Fashanu hadn't scored for a while, Cloughie came into the changing room before training and he had a photograph in his hand. It was an old black and white picture of Cloughie scoring a goal, a diving header, and he went over to Fashanu put it in front of his face and said, 'Son, this is what you have to do to score a goal.'

Cloughie found it hard to deal with Fashanu's lifestyle and he later admitted that he wished that he had treated him differently. A week or so after he had brought in the photo of him scoring the goal, I think Cloughie's patience finally ran out. We were all in the changing room getting ready for training and Fashanu's training kit wasn't there. Ronnie Fenton was taking training, as he usually did, and Fashanu said to him, 'Where's my stuff?'

Fenton told him 'You're suspended with pay. You can't play and you can't train — Cloughie said.' Fashanu replied, 'But I want to train.'

Fenton said, 'No, you can't' and Fashanu responded, 'Are you going to stop me?'

There was nothing that Fenton could do; he certainly wasn't going to physically stop Fashanu from going to the training pitch, and he went to get Fashanu's kit. So Fashanu went out training and all of a sudden two police cars pull up by the training pitch. Two of the smallest policeman you'll ever see got out and came over to Fashanu and marched him off the field. Cloughie suspended him for two weeks - it was ridiculous.

A 3-1 defeat at defending league champions Aston Villa dropped Forest to seventh in the table and brought Ward's short run in the side to an end. Villa's third goal was scored by ex-Forest striker Peter Withe, who would go on to finish the season by scoring the winning goal in Villa's European Cup Final victory over Bayern Munich.

◇ ◇ ◇

Forest made four changes for the League Cup tie with Tranmere Rovers, including the debut of new signing Jurgen Roeber. Midfielder Roeber, a West German B international, would later fall victim to a Peter Taylor one-liner that still brings a smile to Ward's face:

> Taylor could be very funny and was brilliant company at times. Jurgen had come over from Germany and was struggling to find any sort of form. We were sitting in the changing room after one game and Peter went over to him and said, 'I know what's the matter with you... You've been watching too many war films and you never win!' I'm not sure that Jurgen saw the funny side of it, but it helped lighten the mood.

The icy British weather put paid to a number of fixtures during December but the month did not pass without incident for Ward:

> My sponsored car was a white Mazda with a big red tree, the Forest emblem, on the bonnet. The car had 'Peter Ward drives a Mazda' down the side.

> At Christmas time, I was driving home to Derby —I lived in the countryside— and I hit some black ice and skidded off the road and hit a tree. I wasn't hurt but the car had a big dent in the front.

> I had to get a taxi to training and when I later went to the garage to see how the car repair was going it was still all muddy and one of the mechanics had written 'did' with their finger between 'Ward' and 'drives'.

> Because I was living in Derby and Forest were their big rivals I would get all sorts of abuse when I was driving around the town. People would spit on the car, stick their fingers up at me and shout abuse — I couldn't believe it.

◇ ◇ ◇

Two days after Christmas, Brian Clough was taken to hospital complaining of pains in his chest. Whilst Clough, who was 46 at the time, suggested that the pains were brought on by "too many brandies over Christmas or too many bad signings over recent months" the medical staff at the Derbyshire Royal Infirmary took a somewhat more serious view and ordered the Forest manager to take the next month off work. With typical mischief, Clough issued a statement saying that he was feeling absolutely fine and that he had gone into hospital for a check-up because he was thinking about making a playing comeback in an attempt to improve Forest's goalscoring record.

With Clough sidelined, Peter Taylor took over full responsibility for managing the team and for Ward this proved to be a new opportunity to be part of the starting eleven:

> *When Cloughie had his murmur, Pete selected the side and he would pick me and drop John McGovern, who was the club captain. Then Cloughie would come back and I would be out and McGovern would be playing. It was quite frustrating, because it didn't seem to matter whether I played well or not: it was just down to who was picking the team.*

The first game during Clough's absence would have done little to help his recuperation. An embarrassing 3-1 FA Cup defeat at Second Division Wrexham was a woeful result for a team who, less than eleven months earlier, had been 90 minutes away from being crowned the best club team in the World.

With Fashanu's disciplinary record leading to a three-match ban, the Wrexham game was the first time in the season that Ward and Ian Wallace started a game together. Wallace welcomed the opportunity to partner Ward rather than Fashanu:

> *I found it hard to play with Fashanu. Both Peter and I had been in and out of the team and had been used as partners for Justin, but I found it difficult to get a partnership going with him. I found it easier with Peter and thought that we got on as well as two small guys could.*

> *When Peter and I played together, we would look for the same kind of ball but wouldn't get in each other's way, whereas Justin was used to playing on his own and didn't look to play as part of a partnership — he just did his own thing.*

Ward agrees:

> *I preferred to play with Wallace because he was a much better player than Fashanu. Fashanu was big but he wasn't anywhere near as good as Wallace. It didn't make much of a difference that we were both small: if you're playing with good players, it doesn't matter how big they are.*

A week later, Forest faced Birmingham for the fourth time in the season and there was a welcome return to scoring for both Ward and Wallace:

> *We played Birmingham and won 2-0. Wallace and I both scored and it was the first league goal that he had got for about three months.*

> *Afterwards, on the TV, Gary Newbon, who was the presenter on Midlands football, was interviewing Jimmy Greaves about goal droughts and he was asked Jimmy if he'd ever gone through a bad spell without scoring. Greavsie*

said 'Yeah, I had a few.' Newbon asked him 'How long did they last?' to which Jimmy replied 'About 20 minutes!'

I still use that joke now when I talk to some of the kids that I coach.

The victory was Forest's first home league success since Ward's goal had helped them beat Leeds back in October.

◇　◇　◇

Clough's first game back in charge was the League Cup Fifth Round clash with Tottenham. Fashanu was still banned, so Ward and Wallace kept their places but, with midfielders Mills and Roeber primarily used to shadow Spurs' Glen Hoddle and Ossie Ardiles, chances for the Forest strikers were few and far between. Peter Shilton did his best to keep Forest level but was finally beaten when Ardiles scored the only goal of the game midway through the second half.

Fashanu returned at Ward's expense for the local derby with Notts County but was subjected to constant jeering from the Forest supporters as County outplayed their neighbours in a two-nil victory.

A goalless home draw with Stoke and a defeat at West Brom dropped Forest to eleventh position in the league. Substitute Ward scored Forest's goal in the 2-1 loss at The Hawthorns and was recalled to the starting lineup for the next seven games.

Brian Clough was spending more and more time away from the club and communication between the manager and his assistant, Taylor, at times appeared to be non-existent. On 5th February, Clough told reporters that although Justin Fashanu had been having a hard time, Clough would get him scoring again. Within a week, Taylor had put Fashanu, Ian Wallace and club captain John McGovern on the transfer list.

Defeats at table-topping Southampton and Wolves were followed by a trip to Brighton — Ward's first chance to play in front of the Albion fans since his transfer sixteen months earlier:

It was strange, coming back, and I got a big ovation at the start.

I scored a header and we (Forest) won 1-0. I hardly ever scored headers either — I think it actually came off my shoulder.

When I scored I went to the West Stand, as I used to do when I had scored for Brighton, and some of the fans were booing. I thought, 'Oh that's nice,' but I guess I had just scored against them so it was understandable.

A lot of changes had taken place at Brighton; Mullery was gone, Nobby Horton had gone to Luton, Mark Lawrenson had gone to Liverpool. That

*was the heart of the promotion team, so it was strange. They were doing
well though — the new manager, Mike Bailey, had a system and they had
been getting good results.*

*That was the only time that I played against Brighton at the Goldstone, so I
suppose it had to happen that I would score the winner.*

A draw at Middlesbrough followed, then a narrow home victory over Coventry. Ward scored Forest's goal from the penalty spot in a one-all draw with Manchester City to bring his season tally to five. The goal was the last that Ward ever scored for Forest.

Ward's last Forest appearance of the season came on March 17th with Ipswich Town's visit to the City Ground. Ward had a penalty saved after half an hour and, despite an Ipswich player being sent off in the first half, could only manage a 1-1 draw.

Fashanu's return to the team at Ward's expense did not seem particularly significant to him at the time:

*I had been in and out all season so I didn't think at the time that I wouldn't
be playing for Forest again that season. In fact, I never started another game
for them.*

*I went back to playing for the reserves and just tried to play as well as I
could.*

◇　◇　◇

Ward's doggedness paid off after a particularly impressive performance against Man City's reserves. He scored five goals in a thumping victory for Forest and among the spectators was ex-Forest, Derby and England winger, Alan Hinton. Hinton had relocated to the US in 1977, having helped County to two League titles under Clough and Taylor, and had played a season for both Dallas Tornado and Vancouver Whitecaps in the North American Soccer League (NASL). After a season as coach of the Tulsa Roughnecks, Hinton's next move was to become coach of the Seattle Sounders in 1980. His trip to England was aimed at finding new players to add to his Sounders squad for the upcoming 1982 NASL season. Peter remembers:

*We played Man City and I scored five. I had watched Alan Hinton when
I was younger —when he had played at Derby— and after the game he
asked me if I'd like to go to America. I thought 'Yeah, why not?' It was good
money for three or four months and it was a chance to play.*

*I didn't know much at all about the NASL, to be honest. A lot of stars had
gone over there toward the end of their careers —people like George Best,*

Pele, Beckenbauer — and we had played some of the US teams when we toured with Brighton, but apart from that I was in the dark, really.

Hinton said, 'we'll give you so much — an apartment, car, flights and a signing-on fee - tax free, and then you get paid on top of that.' I went home and spoke to Sue and she agreed that it sounded like an exciting way to spend the summer, so I agreed to go.

They wanted to sign me permanently but before I left, Cloughie's agent called me and said 'You've got to ask for £5,000 more.' I asked him why and he said 'For Cloughie, else he won't let you go.'

So I called Alan and said I needed another £5,000 more but he said that Seattle couldn't afford it. So instead of a transfer I went on loan.

When I got back after the first season, Clough called me into his office and told me he would sue me for slander if I told anyone about his agent's demand. I said, 'What are you talking about - you asked for it!'

Clough and Taylor were both good opportunists. They rarely missed a chance to make a few extra pounds for themselves.

Hinton had ticked off one of his main pre-season objectives by signing Ward:

I was looking for a striker and at the time it seemed to me that big target men were going out of fashion. Peter was small and quick and I thought that his style would really work for us. The English game wasn't in a good financial state and clubs were keen to loan players out, so it wasn't hard to convince Forest to let us have Peter. I liked him a lot — he was bubbly, liked a challenge and he was a Derby boy too!

In addition to securing Ward's services, Hinton signed his teammate Gary Mills, who was also experiencing a frustrating season at Forest:

I had had a great time at Forest when I was 16 to 19 years old, with the European Cup and the success of the team, but then I wasn't in the team consistently and I was offered the chance to go to Seattle.

I'm not sure if I would have gone if Pete hadn't been going too. I was only 20 at the time and it was a little bit daunting, really.

When we arrived it was easy to settle down because most of the team were English. Pete and I had an apartment together for a while until Pete's family came over.

It suited Pete and he loved the lifestyle but I was still a little unsure and wanted to be playing the highest level of football in England. After I settled in, though, I thoroughly enjoyed it.

It wasn't until we went to Seattle that we got to know each other and we got on really well. My relationship with Pete was fantastic and at times he was like a father-figure to me, which I really appreciated.

As Ward and Mills headed to the Pacific Northwest, Forest stuttered to a twelfth-place finish in Division One, only winning three of their final eleven games. Remarkably, Ward's five goals made him Forest's second leading league scorer behind Ian Wallace, who had scored nine.

CHAPTER 12

Pelé, Beckenbauer, Cruyff... Ward

*Pete grabbed the opportunity in America superbly and did
really well. He was made for America. The lifestyle suited him,
he liked the way that Americans do things and his laid-back
approach was completely suited to the way of life.*

– Gary Mills, Seattle Sounders 1982

The Seattle Sounders joined the NASL in 1974 and, although they had experienced limited success, were one of the league's best-supported teams. Prior to Alan Hinton's appointment as Head Coach in 1980, the pinnacle of their achievements was a trip to the Soccer Bowl in 1977, where they were defeated 2-1 by the New York Cosmos team that included Pele and two World Cup winning captains, West Germany's Franz Beckenbauer and Carlos Alberto of Brazil.

In Hinton's first year at Seattle, he guided the team to first place in the Western Conference (the first time that the Sounders had won their conference) and the highest number of wins in NASL history (25), but a play-off defeat to Los Angeles closed the season in disappointment. Hinton's policy of building a squad that focused on experienced British players who were supplemented by young Americans reflected that of the majority of teams in the league.

For his first year achievements, Hinton was crowned NASL Coach of the Year (1980) and his ex-Derby teammate and Seattle's top scorer Roger Davies was voted league MVP, having scored 25 goals in just 29 games.

1981 proved to be less successful for the Sounders despite the addition of experienced First Division players Steve "Six Million Dollar Man" Daley and Kevin Bond. The team slipped to fourth in their division and suffered a first round play-off defeat to Chicago Sting, who eventually defeated defending champions New York Cosmos in Soccer Bowl '81.

The arrival of Ward, Mills and Nicky Reid from Man City were the major additions to Seattle's roster for the 1982 season and helped offset the loss of former Scotland captain Bruce Rioch, as well as Kevin Bond and Tommy Hutchinson. Ward was pleasantly surprised by the quality of his teammates and soon settled into life in Seattle:

145

When I arrived, [Seattle] had some great players. We had Steve Daley, Big Roger Davies, Ray Evans (who had played at Spurs with Alan Mullery) and Alan Hudson; he was still amazing and only 30 when I joined— one of the best players that I've ever played with. He was like a right leg to me: every time he had the ball I got it. I made a run and it was there.

We used to call Alan and Ray Evans 'Team Hollywood' because they would always be driving around like film stars in convertible cars with their sunglasses on.

We had a very good team with players who had been successful First Division players and some who had been internationals. You only had to have four North Americans in those days and we had a goalie, Paul Hammond, who had played for Crystal Palace, then married an American and had become a US citizen. Most of the time, we only had to have two or three American players on the pitch.

We played on astroturf, which took some getting used to. The ball bounced more than on grass but if you had basic control and could play the game you were ok.

It was pretty easy settling in. Gary (Mills) was just a young lad and I had to look after him a little bit, but we shared an apartment and had a great time. The Seattle climate is very similar to England and as there were so many British players, it felt like a home from home. Seattle was a wonderful place to live and it started my love for living in the US.

Hammond, who at Tampa Bay had been part of the NASL's very first championship side, remembers Ward's arrival:

I knew Peter because I had played against him a few times in the mid-70s when I was at Crystal Palace and he was at Brighton. Whenever I see him I remind him that he never scored against me for Brighton. There weren't many Third Division goalies in the 1970s who could say that!

Peter came from Derby, Gary Mills is from Northampton and I'm from Nottingham, so we were three Midlands lads and had a good connection. The camaraderie amongst the players was fantastic.

Peter was a great lad — he sometimes got carried away and thought he was Gerd Müller or Franz Beckenbauer, but that doesn't matter — he was a fantastic person and is still a great friend.

◇　◇　◇

The NASL was still home to many quality, mainly non-American, players but it was in what proved to be terminal decline and, between the end of the

1981 season and the start of the next, seven teams folded. This left the league with just fourteen active franchises. National TV network ABC cancelled its contract for the 1982 season. Even though the league was losing its appeal to the national media, fan interest remained stable: the average league match attendance held firm at around 14,000.

The New York Cosmos were Seattle's biggest rivals nationally, with the Vancouver Whitecaps and the Portland Timbers providing local rivalries that guaranteed the largest crowds at Seattle's Kingdome stadium. The Kingdome was a huge covered arena and was opened in April 1976: 58,000 fans watched the Sounders take on the Cosmos in the first game.

Seattle-based journalist David Falk started following the Sounders when they were accepted into the NASL in 1974 and remembers that the signing of Ward at the start of the 1982 season was greeted with hope rather than expectation by Seattle's supporters:

> *Peter was fairly well known amongst the Seattle fans for his previous seasons in England. However, we'd had a pretty big set of stars such as Bobby Moore, Geoff Hurst, Mike England, Alan Hudson, Roy Greaves, Bruce Rioch, Roger Davies and Steve Daley who came over with more buzz.*
>
> *Since the Sounders played on 'Astroturf,' most Sounders fans took a wait-and-see attitude about foreign attackers rather than expecting them to replicate the same form that they had with their previous clubs.*
>
> *Peter would have big shoes follow in, as Davies had led the NASL in goals in 1980.*

◇ ◇ ◇

Seattle opened the season with a visit by local rivals, Portland. In front of a crowd of 14,000, Ward had 3 chances to open the score in the first quarter of an hour. His first shot was saved and the next two went, narrowly, over the bar. Early chances wasted, the Sounders were eventually beaten by a single goal.

Missed chances and narrow defeats were the story of Sounders' first four games, although the poor start was not a surprise to Falk (who now runs the Sounders Museum website, www.GOALSeattle.com):

> *The Sounders of those years almost always got off to slow starts. The previous season had been a wash, so a slow start was not a surprise.*
>
> *Peter showed signs of progress right from the start but he and Mark Peterson had yet to become a team. We didn't win a match until our fifth try, but Peter did score one of the goals in the 4-3 win over the Tulsa Roughnecks that saw Steve Daley notch the winner.*

147

The disappointing start had resulted in a drop-off in interest from the Sounders fan base, and the win over Tulsa and Ward's first goal were witnessed by fewer than 6,000 fans at a near-deserted Kingdome. The second victory of the season came two nights later with a 2-1 win over San Diego.

A road trip to Florida resulted in two further narrow defeats at Tampa Bay and Fort Lauderdale. Following the defeat to Tampa, coach Hinton called a team meeting:

> We had a horrendous start to the season and, against Tampa, Peter had missed some really good chances when he was clean through the middle with only the goalie to beat. After the game, we had a team meeting because I wanted to try to find out what was going wrong. It had gone on for half an hour when Peter got up and said 'Coach, let me ask you a question. Would we be having this team meeting right now if I was scoring all the chances that I was missing?'

> I said, 'No, we wouldn't' and Peter replied, 'Well it's down to me then, and I take responsibility for the bad start we have had. If I had been scoring we wouldn't be in this position.'

> I said, 'Peter, I admire you for taking the responsibility - meeting over.'

> Not long after that, we turned the season around and Peter couldn't stop scoring.

A Seattle newspaper had also picked up on the striker's poor start and, after an overtime defeat at Montreal, printed an article about Ward's failures in front of goal and christened the striker "The undisputed king of the near-miss". The report detailed how Ward had taken 42 shots in the first nine games of the season but managed just two goals.

> It was a frustrating time. I was getting lots of chances but they just wouldn't go in. I was hitting the bar or a post or the goalie was saving it with his legs. There's nothing that you can do apart from keep playing and waiting for the next chance.

> Roger (Davies) hadn't scored at all and we had lost seven of the first nine games, so it was looking like it was going to be a hard season.

> Alan Hinton offered me plenty of encouragement and told the papers that he knew it wouldn't be long until I started to score regularly.

The Sounders coach did not have to wait long for his prediction come true. As Ward and his young American strike partner, Mark Peterson, started to forge an understanding, the goals finally started to flow.

A first road victory of the season at Jacksonville was followed by a three-nil victory over reigning champions Chicago and a goal each for Peterson and Ward. Including the Chicago game, Ward and Peterson went on to score thirty goals between them in the remaining twenty-two games of the regular season — there were only three games in the run where neither striker scored.

Somewhat taller than Ward but similar in style, Peterson proved to be a worthy strike consort. With Peterson just 22 years old and Ward rediscovering his confidence, the Sounders strikers proved to be a tough assignment for many of the league's defenders:

> Mark did well: he was a good player. I think that if there wasn't the rule about having to include American players then Roger Davies would have been first choice, but Mark took his chance very well. Mark adapted quickly to playing with me and the other English players.

It wasn't only NASL defenders who found the pair hard to contain. In May, the Sounders took part in a four-team tournament known as the Europac Cup. Seattle hosted the event which also included Vancouver, Yugoslavian side Hajduk Split and Ron Atkinson's Manchester United.

At the pre-tournament dinner, Alan Hinton bet the United manager that Seattle would finish higher in the tournament than the English First Division side. The reward for winning the wager was to pocket the other team's prize money. Hinton's logic was simple but his team were still surprised by the manager's confidence. Ward remembers the players' reaction:

> Alan came in and told us that he had bet the prize money with Big Ron. We asked him if he was crazy because United had a very good team and had finished fifth in the First Division a few weeks earlier. Alan told us that we needed to remember that United were on holiday, whereas we had just started our season and were in a competitive state of mind.

Seattle opened the tournament with a 3-1 victory over Split, with Ward scoring once; Vancouver scored an equally impressive 3-1 win over United. The second round of games saw Vancouver and Split draw two-each and Seattle achieve a memorable three-nil victory over the holidaymakers from northeast England. With United beating Split and Seattle and Vancouver drawing one-each in the final round of games, the Sounders were crowned tournament winners and pocketed their prize money as well as that of United.

After the final game, the teams enjoyed a post-tournament reception and Ron Atkinson reminded Ward of a previous encounter:

> We were in the lounge upstairs in the stadium and I was talking to Ron. He said, 'You never did anything against me.'
>
> I said, 'When did I ever play against you?' and he replied, 'Cambridge United Reserves. I had you in my pocket all afternoon!'
>
> Then he pointed to big Gordon McQueen, whom I had punished on the astroturf, and said, 'See him over there? He wants to come over here to play. Did you see him today? He can't even walk on the astroturf, let alone play!'

◇ ◇ ◇

Home defeats to Montreal and Vancouver at the start of June left the Sounders with just four wins from the first thirteen games as they prepared for a tough four game excursion to the East Coast.

Ward enjoyed the road trips, although the scheduling of away games often meant that the players would be away from their families for over a week:

Sue and the girls came over to Seattle after I had been there for a month or so and we got an apartment in the Bellevue area, which was really nice. Originally, we had wanted to live on Vashon Island but because the only way from the island to the main part of the city was via ferry, and sometimes the bad weather would keep the ferry from running, the club told us that we couldn't live there.

As I was only on loan, we kept our house in Derby and we had to leave our Great Dane dog, Sumi, in England.

Not long after Sue came to Seattle, I had to go over to the East Coast to play Chicago, New York, Tulsa and Toronto - so I was away for about fourteen days.

That was exceptional because, normally, if you were going to the East Coast you'd play just two or three games and be away for a week or so.

The travelling was fine: we would fly everywhere, so it wasn't like we were sitting in a coach for hours on end. I used to enjoy the road trips, they were good fun. We used to say that going on the road was brilliant but the games f*** it up!

Sounders' first game of the trip was at 1981 Soccer Bowl champions, Chicago Sting. On the same day, England started their España 1982 World Cup fixtures with a 3-1 victory over France. England's goals were scored by Bryan Robson (2) and Paul Mariner: both players had played alongside Ward when he won his full cap against Australia some two years earlier. An unused substitute for England was Ward's ex-Brighton teammate, Steve Foster.

A 4-2 victory over the Sting put Seattle in a positive state of mind ahead of the first clash of the season with the Cosmos. Despite goals from Peterson and defender Jeff Stock, 27,000 New Yorkers went home happy as the Cosmos secured a 3-2 victory.

The Sounders bounced back as a Ward goal helped them to defeat Toronto 2-0. Three days later, Ward scored again as Seattle hammered Tulsa 4-1 for their second consecutive road victory.

Three wins from four games was an encouraging outcome from the journey east. Seattle returned to the Kingdome with a 2-1 victory over Toronto and achieved their fourth win on the spin with a 5-4 success against struggling San Jose. Ward scored the first goal of the game against San Jose and, midway through the second half, the Sounders were seemingly cruising to victory with a 4-0 lead. However, a bizarre 25-yard own-goal from Gary Mills breathed new life into the Earthquakes. Sounders eventually prevailed, despite two late goals from the visitors.

The San Jose game marked the first start for Sounders new signing, mid-fielder Kenny Hibbitt. Hibbitt joined on loan from Wolverhampton Wanderers, where he had played over 400 games and scored more than one hundred goals. Ward remembers Hibbitt's arrival as a timely boost for the Sounders:

> *Kenny came in with a dozen or so games to go and he was terrific. He just loved to play and he was full of energy. The crowd loved him and he played a really big part in the success that we had in the second half of the season.*

Ward's four goals and five assists saw him named the NASL's Player of the Month for June, and it was no coincidence that his upturn in form had helped the Sounders move from the bottom of the division to third place.

The good run ended with defeat at Western Division leaders San Diego, although the Sounders soon got back to their winning ways with a single-goal victory over last-placed Edmonton.

The visit of the struggling Jacksonville Tea Men gave the Sounders a further opportunity to move up the table: they took full advantage, with a 6-0 victory. The Tea Men, who included former Scotland captain Archie Gemmill and Norwich striker Keith Bertschin, were outplayed from start to finish; both Ward and Peterson scored twice.

Tampa Bay visited the Kingdome on 17th July and completed a double over the Sounders with a 4-3 victory. Despite the two successes over Seattle, the Rowdies would finish the season outside the play-off places for the first time in their history.

Once again, the Sounders bounced back from a defeat with two victories. A 4-2 win over Edmonton included Ward's 10th goal of the season and Peterson's 12th.

A short trip to local adversaries, Portland Timbers, proved to be an excellent night for Seattle. Coming back from an early goal down with a Kenny Hibbitt equaliser, the Sounders dominated the rest of the game and Ward's first NASL hat-trick lifted the team to the top of the Western Division:

> *I had a great game against Portland. They didn't like us much and we were all fired up before the game. They scored early on with a goal that should have been disallowed because the linesman had his flag up, but Kenny equalised. I had three chances and scored three goals — two of them were headers.*

> *Steve Daley had a great game too; he set up three of the goals.*

After that, we went to the top of the table, which was amazing because a few weeks earlier we had been rock bottom.

The day after Ward's twenty-seventh birthday, Seattle suffered a shoot-out defeat to Edmonton in front of less than 3,000 spectators. A second victory over Portland in a week kept Seattle on course for the Western Division crown, as two second-half goals from Ward and another from Peterson gave the Sounders a three-nil win. Ward's goals moved him into second place in the NASL scoring table (which combined goals with assists) behind Giorgio Chinaglia of New York.

July had been an excellent month for the Sounders and Ward, with eight goals and five assists, was named the NASL Player of the Month for the second consecutive month.

◇ ◇ ◇

Going into the final month of the regular season, the Sounders were in an excellent position to capture the Western Division title for the second time in their history.

August started with a visit from the toughest opponent of all, the New York Cosmos. 24,000 fans made their way to the Kingdome to see the league's top 2 scoring players go head-to-head. Avenging the narrow loss in New York two months earlier, Seattle defeated their rivals 3-2. Ward, Daley and Ray Evans scored the Sounders' goals as the Western Division leaders put one over their Eastern Division counterparts.

Three nights later, Seattle's third consecutive victory came at San Jose, with Ward scoring again in a 2-1 victory.

The next visitors to the Kingdome were the Southern Division leaders, Fort Lauderdale Strikers. Fort Lauderdale were another side with a heavy British influence and included Brian Kidd, Ray Hudson and Keith Weller in their line-up. The Strikers looked likely to be Seattle's biggest obstacle in the approaching play-offs but another impressive Sounders display saw them triumph four goals to none.

Seattle's biggest crowd of the season, 29,488, hoped to see the home side clinch the Divisional title and, in the process, defeat Vancouver for the first time that season. However, a 2-1 defeat left the supporters temporarily frustrated and aware that San Diego could still beat the Sounders to the Divisional title if Seattle failed to beat Portland in the final game of the season.

Mark Peterson's seventeenth goal of the season was enough to beat the Timbers and to ensure that Seattle finished at the head of the Western Division. Seattle had actually won fewer games (18) than second-placed San Diego (19) and third-placed Vancouver (20), but the unusual point system adopted

152

by the league — which awarded teams for high scoring and winning without the need for over-time or shoot-outs — meant that Seattle's 166 points was 4 more than San Diego achieved and 6 more than Vancouver.

◇　◇　◇

Sounders' reward for winning the Division was a first round play-off match-up with Toronto Blizzard, who had finished behind New York and Montreal in the Eastern Division. The Blizzard had won 17 games during the regular season —their best ever total— and had an experienced roster. The play-off format for the first round and semi-finals was the best of three games: the first team to secure two victories would progress irrespective of aggregate score or away goals.

The play-offs were a new experience for Ward but he relished the challenge:

> The first game was just two days after the final regular season game but, luckily, we were at home, so we didn't have to travel to Canada straight away. The return leg in Toronto took place just two nights after the first game and then, if needed, we would play the deciding game at the King-dome.

> Toronto had some familiar faces, including 'Super-Sub' David Fairclough, who had won the European Cup with Liverpool; Jimmy Nicholl, who had just played in the World Cup for Northern Ireland; and David Needham, who was at Forest with me.

> We had played them twice that season and won both games, so we were fairly confident that we could get through to the next round.

The Sounders eased to a comfortable 4-2 victory in the first game with Ward scoring twice. The away tie was less straightforward and Toronto forced a deciding game with a 2-1 overtime victory. Ward and his teammates were, maybe, too complacent and were rocked by the result:

> Losing at Toronto was a shock and meant that if we lost the deciding game that our season was over. The Toronto fans must have expected us to win because only five thousand turned up for the second game. That was one of their smallest crowds of the season.

Over seventeen thousand Seattle fans attended the third and deciding game of the series and witnessed their side progress to the semi-finals with another 4-2 victory.

Seattle's opponents in the next round were the Fort Lauderdale Strikers, who had won the Southern Division with an identical win/loss record to the Sounders. The teams were well matched and had beaten each other once during the regular season. While Ward and Peterson were the obvious threats to the Strikers' goal, Fort Lauderdale had their own goalscoring danger man in Brian Kidd, who had scored fifteen times during the season.

Fort Lauderdale drew first blood by winning the opening game 2-0 at the Kingdome. For the first time since the first week of the season, the Sounders failed to score at home; the defeat left them with no option but to win in Florida to force a third and decisive game.

If ever there was a time for the Sounders experienced stars to perform this was it. Ward and his teammates were well aware of their precarious position:

> We had to win — plain and simple. Roger Davies was back from injury and made a big difference for us, scoring two goals. We were losing 3-2, I'd scored and Roger had scored, and it had been a really exciting game with both teams going at each other. It looked like our season was over and with less than a minute to go they had the ball down near one of our corner flags. Instead of holding the ball and letting time run out, this guy crossed the ball and it went straight to our goalie, Paul Hammond. Paul launched the ball down the pitch, Ian Bridge headed it on to me, and I ran at the guy who was man-marking me. I went past him on the outside and crossed from the left. Roger ran to the near post and scored with a great header to send the game into overtime.

> Four minutes into overtime, I had the ball on the edge of the area again and took on the right back and chipped a little cross over to Big Roger at the back post. This time, he nodded it back across the goal and Kenny Hibbitt scored the game-winner with a diving header. That was it, game over and we went crazy. I ran over to Alan Hinton and gave him a massive hug and Big Roger came over and hugged us both. It was an incredible relief and must have destroyed the Fort Lauderdale boys, who had been thirty seconds away from the Soccer Bowl.

> After the game, we all got in the coach and Alan Hinton said 'Straight to the bar.' So we went and celebrated before flying back to Seattle the following morning.

Hinton remembers well Hibbitt's goal and the ensuing celebrations:

> I always used to nag Peter about his crossing and kept telling him that he wasn't a very good crosser of the ball. The cross for Kenny's goal in the semi-final was beautiful. When we were celebrating I grabbed him and said, 'I always told you that you could cross a great ball!'

Incredibly, Hibbitt's overtime heroics were not finished, as Sounders fan David Falk fondly recalls:

The Fort Lauderdale series was the swan-song highlight of the NASL years for Seattle. Even though the club returned in 1983 before folding, the real magic came in the play-off drama against the Strikers.

The 4-3 overtime win at Fort Lauderdale to stay alive was televised back to Seattle and created a buzz that led to 28,000 fans returning to see the club play the last leg. Crowds had dwindled to around 12,000 in 1982, so to get that many back in the stadium was exciting.

Then, Kenny Hibbitt sent everyone into ecstasy with his unlikely long-range shot in overtime. The old love for the Sounders was back, and there were echoes of 1977 when Seattle had edged George Best and Los Angeles Aztecs 1-0 before 56,000 fans to make Soccer Bowl 1977.

Before Hibbitt's goal sparked the celebrations, the Seattle fans had sat through a nail-biting encounter in which neither team could make the break-through. Hibbitt's late strike was a worthy way to win any game, let alone the deciding match in a semi-final series: collecting a headed clearance on the edge of the penalty box, he dummied to shoot with his right foot, let the ball bounce once and then hit a curling left-foot volley into the bottom corner of the net — cue pandemonium on and off the pitch.

For Ward, it was a memorable moment and the high point of his first year in the NASL:

It was an incredible goal and a wonderful way to win a semi-final. We all piled on top of Kenny as soon as he had scored and then we did a lap of honour. It was one of those moments where you didn't really want to leave the pitch - in many ways similar to winning promotion for Brighton at Newcastle.

◇ ◇ ◇

On the day that Kenny Hibbitt's first overtime goal won Game Two of the semi-final series for the Sounders, Peter Ward's former and current English teams played each other in the First Division at Forest's City Ground. A crowd of less than 14,000 saw Brian Clough's team beat the Seagulls 4-0.

Much had changed at Forest since Ward had headed to Seattle. Two weeks before the end of the 1981-82 season, Peter Taylor resigned, bringing the most successful managerial double act to what proved to be a permanent end. Taylor told Clough that he had run out of energy and wanted a complete break from football. Sensing that there was little chance that he could change his assistant's mind, Clough negotiated a big money pay-off for him.

Peter Shilton, another established face, left to sign for Southampton for £325,000 after returning from World Cup duty with England.

The turnaround of playing staff at Forest had been so marked that on the opening day of the 1982-83 season, only two players, Viv Anderson and John Robertson, remained of the team that had defeated Hamburg in the European Cup Final just two years earlier.

One familiar face making a return to the City Ground was striker Garry Birtles, the player that Ward had replaced at Forest. The two years that Birtles had spent at Manchester United had been a phenomenal disappointment: he had produced just 12 goals in 64 games. Securing Birtles' return cost Forest just £250,000 — a staggering million pounds less than United had paid to sign him.

◇ ◇ ◇

Seattle's opponents in Soccer Bowl '82 were to be the New York Cosmos, who had defeated Tulsa and San Diego in the play-offs to reach their fifth Soccer Bowl in six years. Cosmos were led by the 1981 NASL MVP and top scorer in the league, Giorgio Chinaglia — one of the league's most high-profile and successful players.

Chinaglia's path to becoming one of the NASL's biggest names started in the unlikely surroundings of Swansea City in the English Third Division. Released on a free transfer by the Welsh club, Chinaglia returned to Italy to rebuild his career. Playing for Lazio, he became the top scorer in the Italian Serie A and helped the Rome-based team to win its first-ever championship in 1974. Chinaglia was rewarded with 14 Italian caps and appeared in the 1974 World Cup Finals in West Germany. Two years later, he joined Pele at the New York Cosmos and went on to score an incredible 193 goals in 213 games over eight seasons.

Despite being joint top scorer in the NASL in 1982, the fifth time in seven seasons that he led the league, Chinaglia lost his Most Valuable Player crown to none other than Peter Ward:

> *I found out in the week before the Soccer Bowl that I'd won the Player of the Year Award or MVP, as they call it. There were two awards, one voted for by the media and the other by the players, and I won both, which was fantastic and a real surprise.*

> *Previous winners of the award included Pele, Franz Beckenbauer and Johan Cruyff, so I was in pretty good company.*

In the week preceding the Final, Seattle coach Alan Hinton received a phone call from Brian Clough:

> *Cloughie was quite happy to do me a favour and let Wardy come to us on loan but when we reached the Final he phoned me up and said 'Where's my player?'*

Peter's loan had run out because it only lasted until the end of the regular season. Cloughie was being mischievous and threatened to have Peter sent back to England before the Soccer Bowl.

San Diego's Jack Murphy Stadium had been picked to host Soccer Bowl '82 and the Sounders' success in reaching the Final caused a flurry of activity back in England, as Sue Ward recalls:

I had taken the girls back to school in England by the time that the play-offs had started. Pete called me to tell me that Seattle had won the semi-final and would be playing in the Soccer Bowl. The club wanted me, and the other wives of the English players, to come back over to watch the game.

I said that I was only going to come if I could bring the kids too, and the club agreed to fly us all back.

We were in San Diego for a few days and the award ceremony was held at Sea World. It was hosted by Bob Barker from The Price is Right, who is a legend in America. Pele was the guest of honour and presented Pete with his MVP award — wow!

I got Pele to sign my invitation envelope. Pete told me that Pele had shaken his hand and wished him good luck before the game.

◇ ◇ ◇

The game itself proved to be a disappointment for the Sounders players and their supporters, despite the fact that the team got off to a good start. With Steve Daley and Kenny Hibbitt both going close within the first thirty minutes, it looked like Seattle might avenge their 1977 Soccer Bowl defeat to the Cosmos.

After 31 minutes, the only goal of the game was, unsurprisingly, scored by 35-year-old Chinaglia. The goal, which came against the run of play, changed the flow of the game and Seattle struggled to build any momentum against the more experienced Cosmos team.

Seattle keeper Paul Hammond regrets that he didn't do more to prevent the goal:

It was disappointing — we had a great team and we thought we had a chance. I didn't have a particularly great game — I should have got the cross that led to their goal but I made a schoolboy error. Chinaglia scored and that was it.

Ward and Mark Peterson were kept quiet by New York defenders Jeff Durgan and former Brazilian captain Carlos Alberto. Peterson was substituted after 67 minutes and Ward had one chance in the first half, but could not replicate his late season form:

> It was a great occasion but a disappointing game. Cosmos were good but they were no better than us — it was just one of those days. Carlos Alberto marked me and he had a great game. As we were leaving the pitch I asked him if I could have his shirt and he said 'Only if I can have yours.' I thought he was joking but he came into our changing room and we swapped shirts.
>
> It wasn't the perfect way to end the season, but I'd had a great time during the year and just enjoyed playing regularly.

Ward's Forest teammate, Gary Mills, had also enjoyed his first taste of the NASL:

> The format of the league took a while to get used to, with the conferences and play-offs. We were literally two minutes from being knocked out in Fort Lauderdale but managed to score in the last minute of the semi-finals; we got through and went all the way to the Final.
>
> Soccer Bowl was superb, even though we lost. Overall, it was a fantastic experience and I've never regretted going to Seattle.
>
> Pete was immense in that first season and won Player of the Year — he was happy and you could really see that in his game.
>
> Pete grabbed the opportunity in America superbly and did really well. He was made for America. The lifestyle suited him, he liked the way that Americans do things and his laid-back approach was completely suited to the way of life; you could see it from day one.

Once again, Ward demonstrated that, given the opportunity, his durability was a big asset: and he played in every single game for the Sounders. His total of 21 goals was the best on the squad and two more than Mark Peterson, who set a record for the highest number of goals scored by an American player - Peterson was rewarded with the North American Player of the Year Award.

In addition to the 18 goals that Ward scored during the regular season, he also contributed 13 assists, which put him third in the leading scorer table behind Chinaglia and Chicago's Karl-Heinz Granitza. Ward was named in the NASL All-Star First Team along with Chinaglia and, surprisingly, was the only British player in the team.

CHAPTER 13

RETURN TO BRIGHTON, FINISHED AT FOREST

Son, I've never been to a Cup Final and neither will you.
– Brian Clough, March 1983

Seven days after crossing swords with a Brazilian World Cup winning captain in North America's showpiece football final, Peter Ward took his place on the away team bench as Nottingham Forest took on Tottenham Hotspur at White Hart Lane:

> *I arrived back in England on the Thursday and went into training at Forest the day after. Clough came up to me and said 'You're going to Spurs tomorrow.'*

> *I thought 'Jesus.', I was so tired. I was sub and came on after about 20 minutes because Stuart Gray got hurt. We lost 4-1 but I played well.*

> *I remember Spurs keeper Ray Clemence chasing me across the penalty area because I went for a ball and got him right in his chest with my studs — I saw it on TV and it looked quite funny, he was really angry.*

> *Ian Wallace was back in the team and Garry Birtles was back at the club, so they were the first choice strikers. Fashanu was still at Forest but had been loaned out to Southampton. He had been sent off in pre-season for the second year in a row, which didn't help his cause much.*

> *It was odd going back because there were lots of new faces and plenty of players had left. The new keeper, Hans Van Breukelen, thought that I was an American and John Robertson eventually told him, 'He's not a f****** American!'*

The defeat left Forest with four losses from their first seven games and in thirteenth place in the league. Ward kept his place on the bench for the next game, Stoke's visit to the City Ground, and came on for Ian Wallace. Garry Birtles had rediscovered his goalscoring touch and his third goal in consecutive games gave Forest a much-needed 1-0. Ward's brief appearance alongside the player he had been signed to replace, was his final contribution as a member of Forest's first team and he returned to the familiar role of reserve team player.

159

Newspaper reports the following week indicated that Forest were on the verge of selling Ward to Seattle in a permanent transfer valued at around £200,000. Keen to recapture his star performer, Alan Hinton travelled to England and tentatively agreed a deal with Clough. The deal was not finalised because there were still six months until the start of the new NASL season and if Ward signed a contract with the Sounders it would have made any temporary move to another English club difficult:

> It was clear that I still wasn't going to get a decent chance from Clough. Pete Taylor had left while I was in Seattle and that made it even more difficult for me because, without him fighting in my corner, Clough could do what he wanted.

> Pete called me after I got back. He told me that he was going to be the new Derby manager and said that I should go there on loan. He knew that Brighton were keen on taking me back and said that Derby would pay me more money.

> It was a tough decision — Derby were in the Second Division and were near the bottom but Pete was joining and it meant that we wouldn't have to move again, whereas it was hard to resist Brighton because I had loved my time there.

> They say you should never go back but I decided to go to Brighton. In some ways, it is one of the few regrets that I have. Maybe if I had gone to Derby, I could have built my career in England again but there you go — it was one of those things.

◇ ◇ ◇

Ward's return to Brighton on a five month loan deal was confirmed days before Brighton welcomed second-placed West Ham to the Goldstone Ground. Ward took the return to Sussex in his stride:

> Going back to Brighton was not that strange: it had changed, there were lots of different players, but it still felt very familiar. The club put me up in a hotel on the seafront and they would fly me down a couple of days before a game so I could train and then I would fly back to Derby after the match.

> I suppose the biggest change was that Mullery had gone and Mike Bailey was the manager. They were completely different and Bailey liked to play much more defensively.

Brighton had enjoyed a reasonable start to their fourth Division One campaign and, with thirteen points from the first ten games, were positioned mid-table. However, Bailey's tactics, construed by some as negative, were undoubtedly a major contributing factor to the stark drop in attendances at the

160

Goldstone. Despite home results being good, with 3 wins and 2 draws from five games, support had dwindled: crowds hovered around the 10,000 mark. Financially, the small crowds were of huge concern to the Seagulls and it was hoped that the arrival of Ward would rekindle interest from the locals, as well as produce results on the field. The move had an instant impact:

My first game back was against West Ham, who were flying at the time. I replaced Andy Ritchie in the side and I got a tremendous reception from the crowd. We won 3-1 and we played really well. I put over 9,000 on the gate — which the club must have been very pleased with.

The crowd of 20,490 was Albion's largest of the season to date and double that of a league game with Birmingham a month earlier. Three days later, Albion's bank balance was further boosted by another 20,000 plus gate. Unfortunately, Albion lost 1-0 to Spurs to end their interest in the League Cup.

Albion midfielder Jimmy Case welcomed the addition of another striker and was impressed with Ward's impact:

I knew that Peter had been a prolific goal-scorer for the club before, so when he joined I knew that he would add another dimension to the team. He had been very popular at the club but he didn't come in just to get people to the games; there was more to it than that. He came in to do a job on the pitch and to earn his money. I thought he was great when he came back to the club.

The next game saw Albion travel to Anfield to take on Case's former club, Liverpool, the reigning League Champions, who included former Brighton star Mark Lawrenson in their line-up. A one-sided game ended in a predictable 3-1 victory for the home side who eventually went on to successfully defend their league title.

Ward's first goal in his second spell with the club came a week later on 6th November. A goal that Ward remembers as 'one of my favourites' came against Manchester United in front of a packed North Stand:

The ball came to me in the area; I controlled it on my chest and volleyed it past Gary Bailey into the top corner. There were only 20 minutes to go and we managed to hang on for the win. It was the first time that Brighton had ever beaten United, so it was a special goal. I found out recently that the goal was the one hundredth of my professional career in England, which is a nice coincidence.

The goal is on YouTube and Tarpon; the team that I coach for now have a link to it from their website. It is a shame that more of my goals weren't on TV because I got some really good ones, especially in the early years at Brighton.

Albion failed to build on their maiden victory over United and a run of four defeats dropped the team into relegation trouble and spelled the end of Mike Bailey's reign as manager. Chairman Mike Bamber told the press that Bailey was a "victim of the modern style of play, which was too negative for spectators."

With rumours circulating of a possible Goldstone return for Alan Mullery, Albion's chief scout, Jimmy Melia, and coach, George Aitken, took temporary charge of the team. Seemingly as keen to generate media coverage for himself as he was to consolidate Brighton's Division One status, Melia looked to bring fresh life to the Seagulls by recalling Andy Ritchie and playing with three strikers — Ritchie, Michael Robinson and Ward.

The changes had the desired effect and, in the first game after Bailey's departure, Norwich were soundly beaten 3-0 at the Goldstone. The change of management failed to spark a reaction from the Albion fans, though, and the victory was witnessed by fewer than 10,000 fans.

Replacing Bailey with Melia (who Ward describes as "a nice fella, but clueless and as soft as s***") was not perceived by the players as having made much difference, as Jimmy Case remembers:

> It wasn't a big change - there were a lot of strong characters and experienced players at the club: myself, Steve Foster, Tony Grealish, Gary Stevens, Neil McNab. It was just a question of Jim (Melia) carrying on and being a figurehead with the press.

> I wouldn't go so far as to say that the older players picked the team because there were some good young players too, but there were a number of players who, if they were fit, you knew they would play.

The on-pitch revival was short-lived and the final three games of 1982 produced a single point from a 1-1 draw at Manchester City. At the turn of the year, the Seagulls were precariously positioned just one place above the relegation zone and had won only once in the previous eight games.

◇　◇　◇

Albion's visitors on New Year's Day, 1983, were Watford, who, under the guidance of future England manager Graham Taylor, occupied second place in the table. A one-all draw was a respectable result for the Seagulls and the game marked Ward's last goal at the Goldstone Ground and his last-ever goal in English League football. Fittingly, with Ritchie dropped to the subs bench, Ward had been restored to the number 8 shirt for the Watford game; he had worn number 10 in all of the previous games of his loan spell.

The following game saw Nottingham Forest visit the Goldstone and provided an opportunity for Ward to help his current, temporary employers further damage Forest's remote chance of catching league leaders Liverpool. In a performance that reflected their superior league position, Forest dominated the game and only an inspired display from Brighton keeper, Perry Digweed, prevented Clough's side from building on a first-half lead given to them by Willie Young.

Despite Forest's continued possession in the second half, Albion snatched a draw, and an unlikely point, when Michael Robinson scored his fourth goal of the campaign after 71 minutes.

◇ ◇ ◇

On 8th January, the third round of the FA Cup saw the First Division teams enter the competition. The draw had paired Clough's Forest with a mouth-watering trip to East Midlands rivals Derby County, now under the management of Peter Taylor.

Struggling at the foot of the Second Division, County were a shadow of the team that Clough and Taylor had guided to two league championships ten years earlier. Taylor's appointment as Derby boss had irked Clough, coming so soon after Taylor had resigned from his post at Forest, citing the need for a complete break from football. In a bid to lift County from the bottom of the table, Taylor turned to two players he knew well; his first signing was Archie Gemmill, who had played for Clough and Taylor at Derby and Forest, and his second was the loan capture of Gary Mills from Forest.

Gemmill, scoring the first goal, and Mills, who marked John Robertson out of the game, played a large part in Derby's shock 2-0 victory. The result left Taylor elated and Clough, for once, speechless.

Brighton's own FA Cup campaign started with a visit from Division Two Newcastle United. Although they were sitting in a disappointing mid-table position in the league, Newcastle had an experienced and highly talented team which included Kevin Keegan, Terry McDermott, Imre Veradi and a gangly, young winger named Chris Waddle.

An evenly balanced game finished one-each with McDermott's late goal cancelling out recalled Andy Ritchie's opener. An evening replay at Newcastle's famous St. James's Park beckoned and many sports writers wrote off Albion's chances of progressing to the fourth round.

32,000 expectant Geordies headed to St. James's in anticipation of seeing their team claim the scalp of Melia's First Division side. A small group of Brighton fans made the journey on the official supporters' coach. Among them was David Dresch, who remembers the evening well:

I was one of two stewards on the coach and there were only nineteen people booked for the trip. We were getting ready to set off from the bus station when someone from the bus company came on board and asked if there was a steward on the coach. I was sitting near the front so I asked him how I could help.

He told me that there was a phone call from the club, so I went to the office to take the call. Albion's promotions manager, Tony Millard, was on the other end of the line and he asked me if there was any room on the coach. I told him that there was and he asked me if we could bring somebody back from the game. This wasn't particularly unusual because we often bought supporters back on the coach who had travelled up to the game on the train.

Anyway, Tony said to me that the person we were bringing back only had to go as far as Derby — which was a little strange. I asked him who it was and he said it was Peter Ward. So, jokingly, I said that we would take him on the coach as long as he scored the winning goal!

The chance of any Brighton player scoring, let alone notching the winning goal, looked somewhat unlikely as Newcastle dominated the game. When a rare Brighton attack led to the game's only goal after 62 minutes, it was Ward who stunned the home fans with a clinical finish:

They completely hammered us and we'd hardly had a kick before I scored. Neil Smillie crossed the ball from the right wing and one of their centre backs cleared it straight to me. I took one touch and placed it in the bottom left hand corner with my left foot.

I watched a tape of the game recently when my dad came over and the commentator only mentioned my name twice — once when I scored and again at the end when I cleared the ball out of our area!

After the goal they came at us even more — they hit the bar twice and then had two goals disallowed in the final few minutes. I don't know how we managed to hang on but somehow we did.

Following the game, the Newcastle supporters vented their frustration with the result by showering Albion's loyal band of followers with a variety of missiles. David Dresch was relieved to eventually get back on to the supporters coach:

The Geordies were throwing all sorts of things at us after the game. We were kept in the ground for thirty minutes and when we got back on the coach Peter Ward was sitting there in his big coat. He smiled at me and said 'So it's alright for me to travel back with you then?' Tony Millard must have told him what I'd said about scoring the winning goal.

On the way back, we stopped at a motorway service station to get some food and to watch the game on Midweek Sport Special. It was quite funny because all of these truckers were sitting in the restaurant and one of them noticed Peter and told him that he looked just like the bloke who plays for Brighton. Wardy found that very amusing!

It was a great journey; Peter was very friendly and talked to everyone on the coach. It really made the night special.

◇   ◇   ◇

Two further league defeats, at Ipswich and at home to Luton, dropped the club into the relegation places where, with only three league victories achieved during the next four months, the Seagulls remained for the rest of the season.

An injury kept Ward out of the team for the next three games. Initially, his teammates seemed to be coping admirably without him, as they defeated Manchester City 4-0 in the fourth round of the FA Cup to set up a fifth round tie at Liverpool.

An almost inevitable league defeat at Arsenal and a point at home to West Brom was not enough to prevent Brighton from slipping to the bottom of the table and they travelled to Anfield knowing that Liverpool had not lost at home in any cup competition since 1974 — a run of 63 cup ties.

Ward, fit once more, was recalled to the starting line-up at the expense of Ritchie, who had been the subject of a failed transfer bid by Coventry City during the preceding week. Brighton took a shock lead after half an hour when Michael Robinson out-paced the Liverpool defence and crossed for Gerry Ryan to side-foot the ball into the net from eight yards out. Heroic defending from Steve Foster and Gary Stevens, and an inspired performance from Albion keeper Digweed, kept Liverpool at bay until twenty minutes remained, when Craig Johnston's spectacular volley levelled the scores.

No sooner had the home fans stopped celebrating than Jimmy Case's deflected shot flew past Bruce Grobbelaar to restore Albion's lead. With Phil Neal missing a dubious penalty with 15 minutes to go, Albion kept hold of their lead and progressed to the quarter-finals for the first time in their history.

For goalscoring hero Case, the win was especially poignant:

Steve Foster recently gave me a DVD of the cup games and it certainly brought back the memories. We were underdogs at Newcastle and massive underdogs at Liverpool but sometimes you just had to have a good go at it.

We seemed to have a dream ticket for the FA Cup Final.

The Liverpool game was very special — to score the winner in a 2-1 victory at a place like that, where I used to maraud... you don't really realise what you have done until afterwards. That was a really big win for us.

165

The win was the final highlight of Peter Ward's Brighton career and, with his loan period over, he returned to Forest a week later. He played one last game for the Seagulls:

> *The game at Liverpool was incredible. Nobody gave us a hope in hell but we just outworked them and took our chances. For the first goal I was screaming at Michael Robinson to pass me the ball but luckily he passed to Gerry who scored!*
>
> *After they had equalised you got that feeling that worse was to come but Jimmy hit a great shot and we were back in front. Liverpool then got a typical 'Liverpool penalty' — in front of the Kop, no real foul — but they put it wide and that was that.*
>
> *I played one more game; we lost at home to Stoke, and that was it. I went back up to Forest hoping that I would soon be on my way back to Brighton but it wasn't to be.*

Ward's departure was soon followed by that of Andy Ritchie, who joined Leeds United in a swap deal for Terry Connor. The loss of two of the club's three top strikers plus the distraction of the cup run proved to be two critical factors in Albion's failed fight against relegation. Jimmy Case recalls the difficulty in focusing on league survival during the cup run:

> *When there is an FA Cup game coming up, you can sense the excitement around the town and the league would take a little bit of a back seat. We just wanted to win games — nobody goes out and thinks that they won't have a go at this game because there is a cup game in a couple of weeks. We were still striving to win.*
>
> *Without a shadow of a doubt, we wanted to stay up but it was like a snowball effect and the momentum of the whole town seemed to take over as we got nearer to the final.*
>
> *It was a big loss to lose Peter and then Andy Ritchie. We still had some good players —Michael Robinson was still there and Gerry Ryan and Gordon Smith could play up front— but losing forwards is especially difficult to overcome.*

◇ ◇ ◇

With his loan spell at Brighton over, Ward's future was unclear and was thrown into confusion by a change of ownership at Seattle. With his short-term preference being a move back to Brighton, Ward weighed up his options and knocked on his manager's door, hoping that an agreeable resolution could be found:

When my loan finished at Brighton there were still a few weeks to go before the NASL season started and because we'd got through to the Cup quarter-final I really wanted to go back to Brighton for the rest of the season.

Alan Hinton had got the sack at Seattle, which was unbelievable, and the new owners had been speaking to Forest to try to get the transfer fee down. In addition, when I was in Brighton, I had a call come through at the hotel from Johnny Giles who was manager at Vancouver. He told me what was going on at Seattle and asked whether I would like to go to the Whitecaps instead. He said that Vancouver had spoken to Forest and thought they could make a deal happen.

I wasn't sure what to do but thought that, if I could, I would go back to Seattle for a second year.

I went to see Cloughie and explained the situation and told him that I really wanted to go back to Brighton and then to honour the deal with Seattle. At first he said that Seattle were quibbling over money so that deal might not happen. So I told him about the cup run at Brighton and said that I would have a chance of getting to Wembley if I went back on loan for the rest of the season.

I'll never forget what he said to me:

'Son, I've never been to a Cup Final and neither will you.'

That was it. I was so pissed off. I told him that I wanted to leave and walked out of the office.

CHAPTER 14

BACK FOR SEATTLE'S FINALE

We looked over and saw Big Joe hiding behind the restaurant
door. Every time that someone came into the restaurant he
would jump out in front of them, start to scream and wave his
arms around to scare them away!

– Peter Ward

Two weeks after Clough rejected Ward's request to return to Brighton on loan, a deal between Forest and Seattle was finally agreed and Ward's two and a half years at Forest came to an end:

I loved my time at Forest: I played with great players and I wouldn't change that. Perhaps I should have stayed a little longer and put up with [Clough]; I don't know..

He always says I was one of his bad buys, but he spent a million on Fashanu and a million on Wallace and I wasn't a million, I was only £400,000 or whatever. I scored a few goals, not loads of goals, and had some good games and some bad games. The experience that I had at Forest was fantastic.

*Cloughie was a great manager: he got good players and he didn't really have to coach. He would sometimes come into the changing room before the game with his squash stuff on and his racquet, pretending he was making squash shots, and he would just say 'Hold it, play it. Hold it, play it. Hold it, play it. Hold it, f****** play it!' and that was it and we were out onto the pitch. It was different...*

If you get players who can play together, you've got a chance and that was what Taylor and Clough could do.

Cloughie used to try and scare us a little bit and Pete would try to relax everyone again and make us laugh. I wasn't scared of him; I just thought he was a little bit strange.

One time, I was talking to Viv Anderson and someone said something to me from behind me. I said 'Hold on mate,' not realising who it was and Viv game me a strange look. I turned 'round and it was Cloughie; he said to me 'Son, as long as I live, you'll never be a mate of mine.'

He could be really cruel to people but I think that was just his manner. Once, after a game, he said to Mark Proctor, 'Son, the way you are playing, you must be retarded.' A few days later, Proctor went to see him in his office. Mark was nervous and had second thoughts. He hesitated and Clough said 'What is it?'

Mark replied, 'Oh don't worry, I'll come back.' But Clough wouldn't let him go and said 'Come on, what do you want?'

'I want a transfer.'

'Done. F*** off.'

And that was it for Mark: he was sold soon after.

Clough was always trying to keep you off-guard and he would keep the team waiting for hours sometimes. On a Friday, we'd train at 10 o'clock in the morning for about half an hour and then go up to the boardroom for a team meeting.

The boardroom was a long room with a kitchen at one end, with a counter and double doors. Quite often we'd wait three, four or even five hours for Cloughie to turn up for these meetings. Sometimes he would come in after 5 or 10 minutes, say a few words and other times you would wait for ages and he'd come in and say 'the team sheet is on the board [in the changing room]' and then leave. It could be very frustrating.

One day, we were in our Friday meeting and the double doors were closed and Peter Taylor heard a noise in the kitchen. He said 'What's that? Who's there?' It was some maintenance guy fixing something in the kitchen but Taylor accused him of being a spy from Derby.

After that, every time we had a team meeting we'd always make sure the doors were just closed to annoy Taylor, who would go and open them and check the kitchen for "spies".

Taylor was great and I got on a lot better with him. They wouldn't say much before the games but I remember Pete getting confused before one game against West Ham. He was talking about the West Ham players and kept saying 'Look we've got to watch this Davenport player.' We all started laughing and he asked what everyone found so amusing. We told him that it was Devonshire who played for West Ham and that Peter Davenport played for us.

Clough's last years at Forest were overshadowed by an alcohol problem that he later admitted had, at times, "impaired his judgement." Ward is a little reluctant to discuss the subject of Clough's drinking and whether it was evident during his time at Forest:

I don't know if he was drinking when I was there, maybe he was, I wouldn't like to say.

There was one occasion when I was sub and sitting on the bench with Clough, Taylor and Ronnie Fenton, the coach. Cloughie was not in a good mood and had possibly had a drink.

Ian Wallace was sent off and Clough said something and I disagreed. Taylor immediately nudged me to keep me quiet. Clough turned to me and said 'What did you say?' So I told him and he said 'Get out!' He made me leave the dugout and go and stand in the tunnel for the rest of the game.

A bit later on, Clough sent an apprentice to go running down to me, to tell me that I had to get warmed up because he wanted me to go on.

Another time, I remember going into car park after training and one of the young players was loading a couple of boxes of booze into the back of Clough's car. I asked where it was from and he told me it was from the club lounge, but maybe Cloughie was just having a party, I don't know...

Asked whether he felt that he was given a fair crack of the whip at Forest, Ward hesitates to bemoan the stop-start nature of his time at the club and views his difficult relationship with his manager as the determining factor for his lack of opportunities:

I don't know that Clough had really wanted to sign me and I'm sure that he was the one who called off the transfer the first time around. I think that he felt that Taylor had almost forced him to buy me and he resented that.

We didn't get on — he didn't like people who stood up to him or who didn't agree with him, but I have never been one to hold my tongue. One of his best quotes was about players who argued with him: 'We talk about it for 20 minutes and then we decide I was right.' That was how it was, really.

But who am I to question his methods? He achieved an incredible amount of success and it was an honour to play for him and for Forest. I could have kept my mouth shut and played along, but that might not have worked any way.

Two of Ward's Forest teammates have differing views on why he wasn't able to establish himself in the first team. Gary Mills agrees with Ward's own assessment:

I got to know Pete well during our time at Seattle and he is his own man and liked his say. At Forest that could go against you, especially with Brian Clough. Pete was a confident man and wanted to voice his opinions.

Ian Wallace, however, saw Ward's plight as an indication of a wider problem with Clough and Taylor's approach:

Clough and Taylor were unique in the way that they could get the best out of players: they had perfected the good cop/bad cop routine. If I got a rollick-

*ing it would motivate me to do better but I think that Peter took it person-
ally and that it knocked his confidence.*

*I could see when Clough and Taylor's approach didn't help players and I
think Peter was an example of this. Clough and Taylor probably never saw
the best of him. There were many times when Peter would be shaking his
head, looking disgruntled after one of them had said something to him, and I
would be thinking 'Uh-oh, what have they said now?'*

*Personally, I think that Peter didn't have a fair crack of the whip at Forest
and at times I wouldn't agree with what was happening with the team...
but that wasn't my job. I would always put myself in the team before Peter
but if we were both in the team I was happy. Peter would come in and play
well and then next game he would be on the bench; it must have been very
frustrating for him.*

*Looking back, I think that if Peter Taylor and Brian Clough liked you then
you had a really good chance to thrive in the team but if one of them disliked
you then you struggled a bit. I think possibly Peter Taylor loved Peter, but
Brian had different ideas. Peter found it hard to please them both but all you
can do is your best. I think Peter took it personally that Brian Clough didn't
like him and thought that he was being picked upon.*

Ward's ex-Brighton colleague, Mark Lawrenson, had himself made a big
money move from Brighton and enjoyed a significantly more successful time
with his new club, Liverpool. He views Ward's difficult time at Forest as a result of bad timing:

*I think it was probably the wrong time for him to go to Forest but it was the
right time for him to leave Brighton. Brighton had run out of money and
the better players were going to be sold — Brian Horton went, I went and
Michael Robinson went too. At the same time, Forest had been so successful
but had peaked — they were in a slow decline.*

*Wardy and I had both signed ten-year contracts but there was an unwritten
rule that if a bigger club came in for us we'd be allowed to leave. Brighton
knew that they would get more money for us if we were on long term deals.*

*I felt sorry for him when he went to Forest: he was filling the shoes of Tony
Woodcock and Garry Birtles, who had been fantastic players for Forest, and
it appeared that Brian Clough didn't really want him.*

*He had been extremely comfortable in the Brighton team and he needed to
be loved; he didn't get that at Forest. That was something that it seemed
Clough and Taylor never did.*

*He didn't have the same success in the First Division, which is understand-
able, but you don't suddenly become a bad player. At Liverpool, I played
with Ian Rush and Kenny Dalglish, who were both totally world class*

— there was a big difference between them and virtually all of the other strikers in England. But in the Second and Third divisions there was nobody better than Wardy — he was unbelievable.

He had something that you hardly ever see apart from in the very best players: the ability to get you a goal out of nothing.

◇ ◇ ◇

With a line finally drawn under his Forest career, on 12th April, 1983, Ward signed a three-season contract with the Sounders, who agreed to pay Forest a reduced fee of £100,000 for his services. The new contract detailed a basic salary of $60,000 in the first year, which would rise to $70,000 in the final year. In addition, the Sounders would provide Peter and his family with a car, accommodation, flights and moving expenses. The deal was concluded on the same day that Alan Hinton's successor as Head Coach was announced: the new man in charge was Laurie Calloway, born in Birmingham but based in the US since 1974.

Ward remembers the new coach as "a nice fella and not a bad coach" but Calloway's appointment was not met with universal approval by his teammates; in his 1997 autobiography The Working Man's Ballet, Alan Hudson refers to Calloway and the new owner, Bruce Anderson, as "the two clowns who took over the great Seattle Sounders." He lays Seattle's problems during the season squarely at the feet of the new heads of the organisation.

Anderson, a former NFL player, had tasked Calloway with shedding what he saw as the Sounders' over-reliance on a British approach to soccer. Anderson assumed that playing more home-grown players and employing a pressing, direct, long-ball style of play would revitalise interest among the local fans. The new approach was given the marketing slogan 'Red, White, Black and Blue' and, along with a change of coach, the Sounders also introduced a new playing strip and a new club logo. Unfortunately, Anderson's assumptions proved to be way off and long-time Sounders fan David Falk was one of the supporters who voted with their feet:

1983 was a disaster in so many ways. I cancelled my season ticket during the off-season 'transition'. The whole 'Red, White, Black and Blue' campaign was ridiculous. We had fallen for the Sounders in part because they had a British tradition. To take that away, along with the club crest and colours, was quite a slap in the face to fans.

Laurie Calloway was not up to the task as gaffer. Crowds dropped off tremendously. Everyone could see that the end was coming, the ship was going down all the way. This wasn't just a season, but a club folding.

There was unrest among players who didn't understand all of the changes after a Finals appearance the year before. The off-pitch drama was too much to overcome.

Calloway's managerial credentials did not compare favourably to those of Hinton, the 1980 NASL Coach of the Year. The previous two management positions that Calloway had held had each ended with the clubs folding at the end of his single year in charge. His first team, the Southern Californian Lazers, were members of the American Soccer League but ceased to exist after just one year of operation. Coincidentally, Calloway's assistant at the Lazers was Brighton manager Jimmy Melia, who was revelling in the spotlight of the FA Cup run at the time of Calloway's appointment at Seattle. Calloway's second spell as manager was with the NASL's California Surf in 1981. Failing to make the play-offs, the Surf went the same way as the Lazers and disappeared at the end of the season.

Despite the dramatic off-pitch changes, the Sounders had maintained the majority of the squad which had reached Soccer Bowl the previous season. Three key players had left: Kenny Hibbitt, who returned to Wolves; Nicky Reid, who went back to Manchester City; and goalkeeper, Paul Hammond, who joined NASL rivals Team USA. New additions included three local players: Brian Schmetzer and Chance Fry, who had both come through from the Seattle reserve team; and defender Bill Crook.

Experience was added by the signing of midfielder John Bain, a former Scottish U21 international, who had been a star player for the Portland Timbers before they had folded after the previous season; and legendary goalkeeper Joe Corrigan, a £30,000 signing from Manchester City. Corrigan's career at City spanned 16 years, during which time he made 476 first team appearances. Just ten months earlier, he had earned the last of his nine England caps and he had also been part of England's World Cup squad during the previous summer.

Corrigan's signing was seen as a positive step from the Sounders by Ward:

Joe was brilliant and a great signing. I had played against him a number of times and had also played with him for England. He was huge — we used to call him 'Gwangi' after a great big, ugly monster from on old film. Steve Daley had told us that Manchester United fans used to call him that and he hated it!

I'm not sure that he really appreciated how strong he was and he used to tell this story about how, when he was at City, he had broken Martin O'Neill's ribs. Martin had just signed for City and as a joke some of the other City players told him that Big Joe liked being chipped in training, although in reality he hated it when players did that to him. So Martin had chipped a couple of shots over Joe's head and Joe got really annoyed. The next time that they were getting on the team coach, as payback, Joe jabbed Martin in his side (although he says that it was an accident) and broke one of Martin's ribs!

One time in Seattle, Sue and I were going out with Joe and his wife, Val. We were in the back and Joe and Val, who was driving, were in the front. We stopped at some traffic lights, chatting away, and Val hadn't realised that the lights had changed. The guy driving the car behind beeped his horn to tell Val to get a move on and Joe didn't like that much.

Despite Val shouting at him to stay in the car, Joe got out and walked up to the car behind. The other driver must have been a little worried, seeing this 6'5" giant walking towards him but I'm not sure he would have been expecting what happened next: rather than asking the guy to wind down his window or get out of the car, Joe just punched his hand through the windscreen glass and straight into this guy's face!

When he back got into the car Val gave him a real verbal battering. I'm not sure who came off worse, the guy with the broken windscreen or Big Joe.

Another time when we were in Toronto, a few of the players went to an English pub for lunch. We started playing drinking games with cards, and a couple came in who had tickets for a Billy Joel concert that night. They joined in with us and ended up getting drunk and missing the concert. Big Joe was with us but left early. When we were walking back to the hotel I noticed blood on a number of concrete lampposts. It was really weird but when we got back to the hotel, Corrigan was sitting in the bar with a bleeding forehead. As he had walked home he had been head-butting the lampposts — what a lunatic!

Both Ward and Corrigan expected their moves to Seattle to be long-term. The Wards put their house, near Derby, on the market; Corrigan sold his family home in Manchester and bought a $100,000 property in Seattle.

◇ ◇ ◇

Following the success of the previous year, Ward was hopeful that the Sounders could compete for the Western Division title again, but within two weeks of the start of the season the team had lost three of its best players:

When I got back, everything looked very positive: Big Joe had arrived, Gary Mills had signed again, and most of the other better players were still there. Then, after the first game, it was announced that Alan Hudson was leaving, which was a massive blow. There was obviously a big problem between him and Laurie Calloway because Alan had been stripped of the captaincy and was also no longer assistant coach.

A week later, Roger Davies left too and went to play for Fort Lauderdale. There were rumours in the papers that both Roger and Alan had gone because they were two of the best paid players and the club was short of money.

In the third game of the season, Gary Mills broke his leg against Vancouver. He went into a tackle with big Dave Watson and broke his leg in two places, which meant that he was out for the season.

We had started the season slowly again and lost six of the first eight games. Home crowds had dropped to about six thousand and we lost our first four home games, which didn't help.

On the day that the Sounders were suffering their second home defeat against Vancouver, a 1-0 win for Manchester City at the Goldstone Ground five thousand miles away, condemned Brighton to relegation and ended their First Division status.

Two weeks later, the Sounders were in the midst of an East Coast road trip when the Seagulls took to the pitch at Wembley to take on Manchester United in the FA Cup Final:

We were in Chicago and I watched it in the hotel with most of the Seattle players. I bet them all that Brighton would win and they came so close. It was hard to watch: I would have loved to have been part of that game.

◇ ◇ ◇

Poor results, low crowds and rumours of financial problems were far from an ideal start to Laurie Calloway's time at Seattle. In an attempt to improve results on the pitch, four new players were brought into the side. Ironically, all four new signings were English: midfielder David Bradford had enjoyed a long career in the NASL and was a former teammate of Trevor Francis at Detroit; David Kemp had been a high-scoring forward in the English lower leagues with Portsmouth and Plymouth; Neil Megson, brother of current Bolton manager, Gary; and Tony 'Knocker' Powell, who had played 275 times for Norwich City. Ward remembers Powell's off-pitch antics being somewhat unusual:

'Knocker' Powell certainly wasn't what you'd expect from someone who had a reputation as being a football 'hard man'. He used to hang around with this young black man and apparently, one day his wife found them in bed together. She was quite strange too and was, how shall we say, 'friendly' with quite a lot of the other players.

175

When they got divorced, she sold her story to a Sunday paper and named all of the players she had slept with. There were a few guys on the Seattle team who wished that they hadn't been so friendly with her when that came out!

The introduction of the new players sparked the Sounders, and three successive victories at the start of June renewed hope that the team may be able to emulate the form from the previous year. Seattle's resurgence coincided with Ward rediscovering his goalscoring touch: he scored once in a thrilling 4-3 victory at Tampa Bay and added two more as Montreal were beaten 5-1.

The following game saw Seattle travel to Vancouver to take on the Whitecaps in the very first game played at the new BC Place stadium. Over 60,000 fans packed into the arena, which is the largest air-supported dome stadium in the world, to see Vancouver's Peter Beardsley score twice in a 2-1 victory for the home side.

Seattle followed a victory at struggling San Diego with their biggest win of the season, 6-0 over the Tampa Bay Rowdies. Two goals for both Mark Peterson and Ward, his fifth and sixth of the season, helped Seattle to improve their record to seven wins and seven losses and put them in touching distance of Golden Bay, who were second-placed in the Division.

With the season seemingly on the brink of becoming a success, Seattle went on a disastrous run of six straight defeats in July. An overtime loss at Tulsa was followed by a shoot-out defeat to Golden Bay. A further defeat to Golden Bay, this time 5-2 at the King Dome, left Seattle floundering behind their Western Division rivals and struggling to muster a challenge for a play-off place.

Results were not going Sounders' way, but the players tried their best to keep spirits high, as Ward recalls:

After we had played Golden Bay in San Jose we all went to a big Mexican restaurant. Joe Corrigan was really going for it and was drinking vodka and orange out of a glass which was the size of a fish bowl. After a while he disappeared from the table and we thought that he had gone back to the hotel.

About half an hour later the manager of the restaurant came up to our table and pointing towards the door said: 'Excuse me, is he with you?'

We looked over and saw Big Joe hiding behind the restaurant door. Every time that someone came into the restaurant he would jump out in front of them, start to scream and wave his arms around to scare them away!

We apologised to the manager and bundled Joe into the back of a cab to take him back to the hotel.

When the rest of us went back after the meal, we saw someone lying face-down in the middle of the hotel lawn. Steve Daley, who I was rooming with, and I went over to see who it was and it was Corrigan! We thought that it was the perfect opportunity for us to take some revenge for the regular beat-

ings that Joe dished out during training, so we gave him a really good kicking and left him on the lawn.

The next morning Joe woke up with really painful ribs and somebody told him what Steve and I had done. We were still asleep in our room and were woken up when Joe started to bang on our door. We wouldn't answer and hoped that he would go away. All of a sudden he broke the door down and came charging in. He pulled both me and Steve out of bed - we only had our pants on - and dragged us into the corridor and gave us a hammering.

Two home victories at the end of July against Tulsa and Toronto, the two teams who would reach Soccer Bowl '83, put an end to the losing streak and the Sounders went into the Europac tournament looking to defend the title they had won in the previous season.

Victories over the Chinese national team (4-0) and Vancouver (2-1) were not enough for Seattle to retain the title, and a 2-1 defeat to Internacional saw the Brazilians win the tournament.

◇   ◇   ◇

Seattle returned to league action with a 5-2 victory over Chicago thanks to two goals each from Ward and Steve Daley. The visit of Vancouver on 13th August saw the Sounders first five-figure attendance since the opening month of the season. Unfortunately, the team failed to send the 13,000 crowd home happy and lost 3-2 in a shoot-out.

A 3-2 overtime defeat at Montreal and a 3-0 home victory over Fort Lauderdale left the Sounders with an outside chance of reaching the play-offs as they welcomed San Diego to the King Dome for the final home game of the regular season. Ward saved his most productive game of the season for what proved to be his last game in Seattle:

To try to encourage the crowds to come to the games, we tried lots of different publicity stunts. For the San Diego game all of the British players learned the American national anthem and sang it before kick-off. Then Benny Dargle, who was a really gritty defender, shaved off all his hair and his long shaggy beard in the middle of the pitch. It was all good fun and we didn't mind trying to help but it showed how much the team were struggling to get people into the stadium.

We beat San Diego 3-2 and I scored a hat-trick. I scored my third with a header just after half-time. The Sockers had a Polish striker called Kaz Deyna who had been at Man City with Joe (Corrigan). He got both their goals and was a very good player.

177

The win left Seattle tied with Montreal in the race for the final play-off spot but with the advantage of having three games left to play; Montreal had only two. Unfortunately, Seattle failed to take advantage of their game in hand and lost all three of their remaining matches. Missing out on the play-offs was a big disappointment for the players but it was clear that by the end of the season, there were more far-reaching problems within the organisation, as Ward recalls:

> *The owner, Bruce Anderson, had told us that the club was short of money but said that they were trying to enter a team in the NASL indoor league which would generate money to keep them going through the winter. That didn't happen and there were rumours that some of the players weren't being paid.*

> *Joe Corrigan was sold to Brighton, of all places, and apparently some of that money was used to pay the players' wages.*

Within a week of the final game of the season it was officially announced that the Sounders were closing down after ten years of NASL action. It was an unwelcome hat-trick of folding football teams for Seattle coach Laurie Calloway and left Ward in limbo just one season into a three-year contract.

CHAPTER 15

VANCOUVER AND THE END OF THE NASL

So, in the space of a week, we had beaten the North American champions, the Brazilian champions, and the West German champions — not bad, really.

– Peter Ward

The demise of the Sounders left Ward's immediate future unclear and, as he recalls, created confusion surrounding the status of his registration:

Although Seattle had signed me on a permanent deal they only paid Forest thirty percent of the money up front. When Seattle went bust, it left Forest without any chance of getting the rest of the money, so Forest told me that I had to go back there. I told them that there was absolutely no chance of that happening and that they couldn't make me go back, because they didn't hold my registration.

Then the Football League got involved because there was a rule that said that if a player was sold to an American team that they couldn't rejoin the same English team within twelve months. The League said that they were looking to see whether they could waive that rule so I could go back to Forest but the NASL said that they might not release my international registration papers because they wanted to me to stay in the US.

Further complication came when Derby manager Peter Taylor told the press that he was keen to sign Ward again. By this time, the relationship between Taylor and Clough had deteriorated to such an extent that neither spoke to the other again before Taylor died in 1990. The final straw for Clough was Derby's signing of Forest winger John Robertson in what Clough saw as an underhand manner. Ironically, after Taylor left Derby in 1984, Robertson returned to Forest to finish his career, once again playing for Clough.

Technically, Ward was a free agent but in response to Derby's interest, Forest announced that any English club wishing to sign Ward would have to pay them the outstanding amount still owed by Seattle - £70,000.

The Vancouver Whitecaps, having failed in their attempt to sign Ward a year earlier, renewed their interest and came to an agreement with Forest. Somewhat more complex than a usual player transfer, the deal resulted in a relieved Ward becoming a Vancouver Whitecaps player:

Johnny Giles spoke to me again and asked if I was interested in going to Vancouver. I told him that I was and that I really didn't want to go back to the UK.

The Whitecaps had acquired me in what they call a dispersal draft, which basically means that if a team goes bust, the other teams in the league get to pick over the bones and choose which players they would like from the defunct team. Vancouver chose me but Forest still wanted to recoup something for the money they had lost out on. Vancouver agreed to loan Frans Thijssen to Forest for a season as part payment for the missing Seattle money.

Vancouver paid me good money - $80,000 a year, which is more than I would have earned at Seattle. They also covered a car, house, medical insurance and all that sort of stuff plus I got appearance money for every game that I played, indoor or outdoor, so financially, moving to Vancouver worked out well.

Vancouver was the best city I ever lived in — it was a fantastic place. We lived just below Grouse Mountain and it was absolutely beautiful.

As Ward and his new teammates prepared to spend the winter months playing in the NASL indoor league, Thijssen, who had been the PFA Player of the Year in 1981, headed back to England and made his Forest debut in a dramatic match with local rivals Notts County.

County were now under the management of former Forest centre-half Larry Lloyd and featured ex-Forest flop Justin Fashanu in their starting line-up. Fashanu had been sold to County for just £150,000, having scored only 3 times for Forest after his £1 million pound move from Norwich. The Forest fans had little sympathy for Fashanu and subjected the striker to constant abuse about his disastrous time at the City Ground. The verbal battering from the terraces and the physical pummelling dished out by Forest defender Paul Hart proved too much for Fashanu and he was sent off in the second half for retaliation and dissent. For the record, Forest won 3-1 and eventually finished third in the table; Notts County were relegated.

◇ ◇ ◇

For the 1983-84 season, the NASL indoor league consisted of seven of the nine remaining NASL teams: only Minnesota and Toronto did not enter the winter league. The NASL's indoor offering had been set up as direct competition for the Major Indoor Soccer League (MISL) which had been in operation since 1978. In many ways, the MISL was the success story of soccer in the US during the 1980s and, by 1983, had become more popular with supporters than the NASL's outdoor league. In what appeared to be a statement conced-

180

ing defeat to the indoor game, the NASL announced that the 1984 outdoor season would be shortened to accommodate an extended indoor season the following winter. As it turned out, the NASL ran out of teams, and hope, before the 1984-85 season began.

The Vancouver Whitecaps were one of the NASL's most well-established and supported teams, but the Whitecaps fans found indoor soccer a turn-off and the 16,000 Pacific Coliseum Stadium was rarely more than a quarter full for an indoor game.

Most of the participating NASL teams, including Vancouver, used the same squad of players for their indoor team as they did for the main NASL outdoor season. However, a couple of the teams, including eventual champions San Diego Sockers, recruited indoor specialists such as high-scoring Julie Veee, whom Ward had first encountered five years earlier on Brighton's tour of the US.

Vancouver coach, Johnny Giles, was assisted by World Cup winner Nobby Stiles and former Millwall and Crystal Palace winger Derek Possee. Ward found working with the Whitecaps coaches to be an enjoyable experience:

> *Johnny Giles was very good — I liked him — he really knew his football. Nobby Stiles was there too, and he was hero of mine from Manchester United and England.*
>
> *Talking to Nobby, you would never have guessed that that he was a 'hit man' when he played.*

The team itself featured some familiar names, including Carl Valentine, whose time at the Whitecaps was sandwiched between spells at Oldham Athletic and West Bromwich Albion, and Ade Coker who had started his career at West Ham in the early seventies before establishing himself as a consistent goalscorer in the US.

◇　◇　◇

Ward's first experience of indoor soccer proved to be successful from a personal perspective, but somewhat mediocre in terms of the Whitecaps. He scored an impressive 42 goals in 28 games, a total only bettered by five other players in the league, but the Whitecaps struggled and won only 12 of 32 games. Finishing fifth in the seven-team league, Vancouver failed to make the end of season play-offs, although the season still provided some highlights for Ward:

> *I started really well and, on my debut, I got a hat-trick at Tampa Bay. We had a decent side but we struggled to achieve any sort of consistency. The top four teams in the league pulled away quite quickly, and it never looked like we would get into the play-offs.*

In the final two games of the season we beat two of the top four sides — Golden Bay and San Diego — so we knew that we could have done a lot better than we did. Against Golden Bay, we won 7-6 and I scored five goals. They had Steve Zungul, who was the top scorer in the league — he got 63 goals that season! We took an early lead but after that we were behind for the whole game. We pulled level near the end to force overtime and I got the winner after about ten minutes of the extra period.

Before the game, I had gone out for a meal with one of the other players — we didn't know what to have so we decided that we would go for fish and chips at an English pub in North Vancouver. It was only a few hours to go before the game and usually you wouldn't have anything too heavy to eat so close to kick-off, but it was at the end of the season and we couldn't get into the play-offs so we thought 'what the heck.' We got a little bit carried away in the restaurant and ordered a beer each… and then another… and then another. We both ended up having four or five pints plus a great big fish and chip meal. I could hardly stand up when I'd finished but we found our way to the stadium and I ended up scoring 5 goals!

In the game before, we beat San Diego 8-6 and Carl Valentine got four goals. San Diego went on to win the Championship and they had won the MISL the year before — they were a very good indoor side.

Carl had a great year and was Player of the Year for our team. He got 44 goals and between us we got nearly half of Vancouver's goals.

We both played in the All-Star game, which was an amazing match. As the league only had seven teams, they picked one All-Star team who played against Chicago Sting - one of the best teams in the league.

In the first period, Carl set me up and I scored to put us 3-1 up but Chicago came back and took the lead in the second period. Then I scored again, Carl got one and Steve Zungul got another, and we were 6-4 up going into the second half.

Normally, All-Star games were quite relaxed and not too competitive because players didn't want to get injured, but this one was really fierce. There was a fight in the third quarter and another in the fourth and Julie Veee was ejected for punching one of the Chicago players.

Chicago came back at us again and with ten minutes to go we were 7-8 down, but we equalised and, with a couple of minutes left, Gert Wieczorkowski, who had an enormous Viking-like moustache, got the winner for the All-Stars. What a game!

◇ ◇ ◇

Before the start of the outdoor season in May, the Whitecaps made the surprise announcement that manager Johnny Giles had left the club following a disagreement with majority owner Bob Carter. Carter had accused Giles of having a conflict of interest when he signed Pierce O'Leary, brother of ex-Arsenal star David, from Giles' former club Shamrock Rovers. In protest at the allegations, Giles, along with his assistant Nobby Stiles, resigned with immediate effect.

Ward was 'completely surprised' by Giles' departure, but relieved when his replacement was announced as Alan Hinton — 'I got on well with Alan, so I was happy that he was coming'.

Hinton was just as pleased to have his former Seattle star on-board:

> When I left the Sounders in January '83, I became a football agent for a while and I actually represented Peter and negotiated his contract with the Whitecaps. Of course, a few months later I got the head coach job and I was delighted to have Peter as part of the team.

In addition to a new manager, the Whitecaps welcomed back a number of experienced players for the outdoor season and a few faces that Ward knew well:

> The goalie at Vancouver was Paul Bradshaw, who had played at Wolves and who I'd put five goals past in one season when I was at Brighton. I had also played with him with the England Under-21 team so I knew him quite well.

> Colin Todd, who I used to watch play at Derby and had played with at Forest, joined too. He broke his leg really early in the season and missed most of it. Toddy lived on the same housing development as me, so we saw quite a lot of him.

> David Cross had joined the year before and been back to England to play for Oldham during the winter. He was a nice guy and very funny. He told one story that used to crack me up... 'There was an apprentice at West Ham who went for his driving test. The next day, he came into training and we asked him how he got on. The apprentice said, 'I did ok but when I was in the car the instructor asked me some real dead-hard questions. He asked if I was driving down a country lane what road signs I would expect to come across. So I thought about it for a little while and said 'Strawberries for sale.' He failed me.''

> David was a good player but didn't get on that well with Alan Hinton. He didn't score for a while so Alan dropped him and moved Carl Valentine up front with me.

> Frans Thijssen came back from Forest, where he hadn't played much, and he was brilliant. He was Dutch and had a really strong accent and, whenever we went for something to eat, if he was ordering he would say 'Err, cheese-

183

burger lager, cheeseburger lager.' We all used to do impressions of him, it was pretty funny.

I enjoyed it in Vancouver. I was 28, 29 years old and I suppose that, physically, I was at my peak. I had a coach who liked me which really helps, and I played pretty well that season.

I think that we had the strongest team in the league and it was disappointing not to get to Soccer Bowl again.

◇ ◇ ◇

The season started well with a 2-0 home victory over San Diego, who included Ward's ex-Seattle teammate Steve Daley in their line-up. Away defeats at Tampa Bay and New York, where Ward scored his first of the season, followed, but Vancouver got back to winning ways with a 5-3 home victory over the Golden Bay Earthquakes.

Vancouver seemed to be heading to their third straight defeat after two Golden Bay goals in the first fifteen minutes gave the visitors an early advantage. After half an hour, Ward gave Vancouver hope with a goal direct from a free-kick and, after Steve Zungul had missed a penalty for Golden Bay, Ward converted two spot-kicks to give the Whitecaps the lead. Two further goals from Vancouver's Fran O'Brien put the game beyond Golden Bay's reach despite a late second goal for Zungul.

The next two weeks saw the Whitecaps host three exhibition games against illustrious international opponents, plus a game against reigning NASL champions Tulsa Roughnecks. It was a busy but successful run of games for Ward:

We played Ajax from Holland on the Sunday and lost 2-1. They had some brilliant young players, including Marco Van Basten, Jesper Olsen and Frank Rijkaard.

The following weekend we beat Tulsa 3-2. We were 2-1 down with a few minutes to play and I played a one-two with Frans Thijssen: he scored. With less than a minute to go, we won a penalty when Fran O'Brien was fouled. I scored and we moved up to second in the table.

A few days later, we beat Fluminense, who were the Brazilian champions, 3-1 and I scored again. Two nights after that, we played VFB Stuttgart, who were the German champions, and I scored a hat-trick in a 3-1 win.

So, in the space of a week, we had beaten the North American champions, the Brazilian champions, and the West German champions — not bad, really.

184

With confidence sky-high, the Whitecaps returned to NASL action with another victory over Tulsa. Ward scored the only goal of the game, his sixth in six league games, with twenty minutes remaining.

Ward scored again in a 2-1 defeat at San Diego and he got an overtime winner; next, Vancouver sneaked past Minnesota 3-2 in front of 17,600 Whitecap fans, to bring his scoring run to six consecutive games.

Despite the team's production of encouraging results on the pitch, the club was struggling financially and a "Save the Whitecaps" campaign was started to raise money for the organisation. Fans and local businesses were encouraged to buy season tickets or to make donations and, although over $100,000 was collected, the amount fell below the target amount required to keep the team in business. Club owner, Bob Carter, called a press conference and Alan Hinton told the press that he wasn't sure whether the announcement would spell the end of the Whitecaps or a stay of execution.

To the relief of Hinton, his players and fans alike, Carter announced that he was investing a further $1.6 million in the club, which would guarantee the short-term future of the team.

The Whitecaps responded with three consecutive victories and moved to the top of the Western Division. On 11th July, Ward scored his ninth and tenth goals of the season in a 3-2 overtime loss to San Diego, and followed this with another in a 2-1 victory over Canadian rivals Toronto at BC Place Stadium.

An identical result three days later at Toronto gave Vancouver their ninth win in the last eleven games and kept them ahead of Minnesota and San Diego in the race for the Western Division title.

Consecutive narrow defeats to Minnesota, in a shootout, and Chicago, after overtime, stalled the title challenge but four goals from David Cross against Tampa Bay helped the Whitecaps to a 5-3 victory. A trip to California for a double-header with Golden Bay produced mixed results: the first game finished in a 3-2 victory for Vancouver, with Ward scoring twice; and the second game was a defeat by the same scoreline, with Ward notching his fifteenth goal of the campaign.

◇ ◇ ◇

A brief respite from soccer was provided with a meeting between Ward and singer Rod Stewart, one of the hottest pop stars of the time. Ward recalls the event:

"When I was at Brighton a local magazine had run a competition asking its readers to guess the weight of my Great Dane, Sumi. The prize was tickets to see Rod Stewart in Brighton and to go to a private party with Rod, me

and some of the other Albion players. It was a great night and Rod is a big football fan so he really enjoyed himself.

In 1984 he was due to play in Vancouver but his concerts clashed with one of our road trips. His manager arranged it so that we could meet at the airport and I could present Rod with a gold disc for his latest album. So I ended up making the presentation on the runway with the planes taking off and landing behind us."

◇   ◇   ◇

Ward scored his final goal as a Whitecap in a 3-0 victory over Tampa Bay, and with four games remaining of the regular season, Vancouver looked down on all their Western Division rivals. However, the final four games were all lost and San Diego took advantage of Vancouver's dip in form to clinch the Western Division crown. Vancouver finished with a record of 13 wins and 11 losses and the competitiveness of the league was demonstrated by the fact that 6 of the 9 teams finished the season with 13 or 14 victories.

Second position was enough to secure Vancouver a semi-final play-off encounter with the Eastern Division champions and Soccer Bowl holders Chicago Sting. The first game of the best-of-three series took place in Chicago but a rare injury threatened Peter Ward's participation in the game:

I had a sore groin and really shouldn't have played, but I was desperate to be involved. I hadn't missed a single outdoor game since I had been in the States, so I guess that I had been lucky with injuries up to that point.

I took some painkillers so that I could play in the first game in Chicago and I ended up creating the chance for Carl Valentine to score the only goal of the game.

We were confident that we could beat them in the second game back in Vancouver but my injury had worsened. I played again but was in real pain. We were well beaten, 3-1, and had to go back to Chicago for the deciding game.

I was in too much pain to play and it was incredibly frustrating. We lost 4-3 and that was it: our season was over. Actually, it was the Whitecaps' last game and the league folded at the end of the season.

Ward finished with 16 goals from 24 games, which made him the top scorer at the club and, for a second time in three years, he was voted onto the NASL All-Star First team along with Whitecaps teammate Frans Thijssen.

Vancouver's average attendance for the season had fallen to under 14,000, which, compared to the previous year's figure of 29,000, was a clear indication that interest in the league was at an all-time low. By the following March, only

Toronto and Minnesota expressed an interest in participating in the 1985 season and the NASL was finished.

◇   ◇   ◇

For the second year in a row, Ward found himself a victim of circumstances that left his career in limbo. While he had little control over the demise of the NASL, Ward's own actions were threatening to wreck his home life and to destroy his marriage:

> *I became friendly with a lady who worked for the Whitecaps organisation; one thing led to another and we ended up having an affair. They say you should never s*** on your own doorstep but I think I s*** on my own front lawn.*

> *I got home one night and Sue had found out from one of the other player's wives what I had been up to. She was justifiably mad and it was a horrible night. I didn't have any excuses.*

> *I stopped the affair after that; we moved away and I forgot about it, I suppose. It felt normal again for me — I just forget stuff like that [clicks fingers]. I'm not a bad person. You never think about it; it's just the life that I was in. Every city we went to, the same girls would be there. Everyone was doing it.*

CHAPTER 16

THE GREAT INDOORS – THREE YEARS IN CLEVELAND

The fans loved Peter's personality - his enthusiasm,
pace and obvious goal-threat. Every time he got the
ball he made something happen.

– Peter Millar, Cleveland Force

Although the demise of the NASL left North America without a recognised professional outdoor soccer league, it provided further momentum for the Major Indoor Soccer League. Four former NASL teams — Chicago, San Diego, Minnesota and the New York Cosmos - agreed to join the indoor league, and a new franchise in Dallas brought the number of participating teams to fourteen.

The collapse of the NASL left many players, and managers, in a similar position to Peter Ward — out of work and with a choice of jumping on the lucrative indoor bandwagon or leaving North America to find a team in Europe or even further afield:

After Vancouver folded, I had a few offers; I had spoken to Terry Venables at Queens Park Rangers who was keen on me going there but then he left for Barcelona. I also had a call from Terry Hennessey. He had been coaching at Tulsa but was moving out to Australia; he wanted to know whether we'd be interested in moving out there to play for a club that he was getting involved with.

I was 29 years old so I was far from finished. I knew that I could still play to a high standard, whether it was indoor or outdoor. I seriously considered going back to England but the money that the indoor teams were offering was good, probably better than I could have earned at home, and I loved the lifestyle in America.

In October 1984, Ward signed a four-year contract with the MISL's Cleveland Force to play indoor soccer (or what his mother refers to as 'five-a-side'). The Force had been one of the league's founding clubs and were well supported, with an average home crowd of over 13,500. They shared the Richfield Coliseum with the Cleveland Cavaliers of the NBA, and would often prove more popular with the Cleveland sport-watching public than the city's basketball team.

Back in the UK, Ward's Cleveland contract was incorrectly reported to be worth $500,000. In reality, his basic salary plus living allowance was $52,000 and, in addition, he received a signing-on bonus of $132,000 split over 4 years.

Another team in another city meant another change of school for Rachael and Rebekah. Rebekah was just six years old when the family moved to Cleveland and looks back on the frequent relocations as a blessing in disguise:

> *When I was little, we would move every two or three years and it was really hard. It was hard to make new friends: wherever we went, people would be in their cliques with friends they'd known for years.*

> *I remember that at one school, I had to have a 'special friend' eat lunch with me for two or three months because nobody else would talk to me and I didn't have any other friends.*

> *My parents were always very positive about moving and now I'm a bit like them: I'm keen to try new things and go to new places.*

Peter remembers picking Rebekah up from school in Cleveland on one occasion and being asked by one of the teachers for a quiet word:

> *Rebekah's teacher called me over to her and said that Rebekah had got into trouble. The teacher explained that the children had been asked if they knew any jokes and that Rebekah had stood up and told one that was a little inappropriate. I asked what it was and the teacher repeated the joke: 'What's the difference between snow men and snow women? Snow balls!' The teacher said that she thought it was funny, but maybe not suited to a room full of five year olds. It was hard not to laugh.*

◇ ◇ ◇

The MISL season consisted of 48 regular season games with the top five teams from each of the two conferences qualifying for the end of season play-offs. A match day squad would consist of 16 players with any six being on the pitch at any one time. Games tended to be fast, high-scoring affairs and, similar to basketball and ice hockey, teams could use multiple, rolling substitutions. Sides would often have two 'units' of 5 or 6 players who would play for a maximum of two minutes and then be replaced by the other. Much like the Masters football that is regularly shown on Sky Sports now, the playing surface was a carpet that would cover the arena floor and, in some cities, would sit on an ice rink.

In six years of MISL action, the Force had never finished higher than second in their conference and had progressed as far as the play-off semi-finals twice. The team were coached by Timo Liekoski, a native of Finland, who had

189

been with the Force since 1982 and who had previously coached Houston and Edmonton in the NASL. Ward's appraisal of his new manager was less than complimentary:

> *Timo, the manager, was a nice fella but he was f****** useless and didn't get respect from the players. He had never played the game and it was difficult to respect him. In fact, I think he'd played ice hockey, but he was clueless. He eventually got a job with the national team, too, which shows how bad the US soccer setup used to be.*

Ward's arrival in Cleveland added to an already well-stocked forward line, which included Finnish international Kai Haaskivi. Haaskivi had been the second leading scorer in the league during the previous season and had been an MISL All-Star for four consecutive years. Only one place behind Haaskivi in the league scoring table was another Force player, Craig Allen. Allen hailed from Guernsey and had scored over 100 goals in his two previous seasons with Cleveland. Force's other main offensive threat was Englishman Keith Furphy, who had hit 39 goals during 1983-84.

Peter Millar, one of Ward's new teammates, recalls that the introduction of yet another striker added a new dimension to the team:

> *Peter Ward came in and complemented the existing forwards and, because of the quick rotation of players during a game, it was easy to fit him into the system. When Wardy arrived, the main strikers were Keith Furphy and Craig Allen, and Kai Haaskivi scored a lot of goals too.*
>
> *Keith Furphy was a legend in his own mind - he thought himself to be better than the rest of us and wasn't very well liked off the field because of his arrogance. Give him the ball, though, and he would create something from nothing.*
>
> *Craig Allen was another prolific goalscorer but with a totally different style than Peter or Keith. Craig was very laid back in his approach to everything; training, games and life in general. He was slow and very one-paced, but give him the ball and he scored from all angles - sometimes impossible ones, where we all just shook our heads and said 'That's Craig for you'. He could hold the ball for an eternity and opponents just couldn't get it off him. He was a very likeable person, too, who lived the quiet life away from the game.*
>
> *Kai Haaskivi was God in Timo's eyes: he even allowed Kai to go over to England to play for Finland at Wembley when we had a crucial run of games. There is no doubt, though, that he was a great indoor player. A lot of the players regarded Kai to be more the coach than Timo; Kai was well respected by everyone.*
>
> *The fans loved Peter's personality - his enthusiasm, pace and obvious goal-threat. Every time he got the ball he made something happen, and if he wasn't scoring he was creating an assist. He was on the go every minute*

that he had playing time and this suited the indoor game, and, I must say, the indoor game suited Peter as well.

I can't speak highly enough of Peter: he conducted himself in a very professional manner on and off the field. He was a family man who cared deeply for his wife and kids; this was obvious to all the players.

When Wardy scored, he high-fived the fans and they took to him immediately.

Defensively, the Force were led by Ward's ex-Seattle teammate Benny Dargle as well as by Bernie James, who had spent three seasons with the Edmonton Drillers in the NASL. James has fond memories of the Force organisation and their avid fans:

Cleveland was about as professional as you could get. We travelled in suits, we were paid well and it was as professional, if not more, than any other team I played on in the MISL or NASL. They treated us very well.

It was a lot of fun. We were selling out the arena and were more popular in Cleveland than the NBA team and the baseball team. I guess it was more like playing in England — the Cleveland fans really loved soccer.

Dargle was delighted to be reunited with Ward:

He was one of the few forwards I knew who could buckle a defender's knees: you just didn't know which way he was going to go when he had the ball.

He's a great guy even though he is unusually cocky for someone so small. He had a real swagger about him and would walk into a room and say 'Hi, I'm Ward, Peter Ward' as if he was James Bond! He used to think he was really funny, and when we were on road trips travelling on the coach, if we drove past an old homeless guy with long hair and a beard, Peter would always point and say 'Look, there's Benny!'

It was great when he came to Cleveland, although it did mean that I had to put up with his driving again — he's the world's worst driver because he refuses to wear his glasses. His eyesight was so bad that once, in a hotel room, he said to me 'Look at the fantastic full moon' I said 'What the hell are you talking about?' He pointed towards the window and I said 'That's not the moon, that's a round lamp!' He said 'Oh, never mind.' It was a miracle that he scored so many goals with such awful vision.

◇   ◇   ◇

The Force started the season well and, by mid-December, had won seven of their first ten games. The first home game of the season had seen 19,360 fans pack the Coliseum to see the visit of the Cosmos. The crowd was a new record for the league and the fans were wowed by an impressive 6-1 victory for the Force.

A disastrous run of seven defeats in their next eight games included two losses to Eastern Conference rivals Chicago and an 8-5 reversal at home against local rivals and conference leaders, Baltimore Blast. By the halfway point of the season, at the end of January 1985, Cleveland had recovered to a record of twelve wins and twelve defeats and were battling Chicago, Minnesota and St. Louis for third spot in the division.

Ward had enjoyed a satisfactory, if not spectacular, start to his Cleveland career:

> *I was doing ok, but there had been a lot of expectation when I joined and the papers would always refer to me as 'high-scoring Peter Ward,' which added a bit of pressure. I had got a few goals and we were getting good crowds but I was still recovering from the injury I had at Vancouver and struggling to get fit.*

> *I was enjoying it and I liked the drama and excitement of the indoor game but I didn't see eye-to-eye with the coach, which made it more difficult. The standard was good, though, and because the NASL had folded, quite a few of the players from there had gone to the MISL, as I had.*

> *It was fast and furious and very skilful — the fans used to love it. There would be 5 for 5 substitutions and you would normally play with the same players. You were usually only on the field for a few minutes because you were sprinting all the time. It was a different sort of fitness and it took me a while to get used to it.*

> *It was just as professional as the outdoor league and we would train every day — each morning. During pre-season, it would be twice a day.*

> *We had moved to Cleveland but it wasn't as nice as Vancouver or Seattle and it was really cold. We weren't unhappy, though; I suppose that we had just been spoilt with Vancouver and Seattle.*

February started well for the Force, with four straight victories; unfortunately, three defeats on the spin followed. At the end of the month, the MISL was rocked by the news that the New York Cosmos were withdrawing from the league, having played only 33 of their 48 fixtures. The Cosmos, who were now owned by Georgio Chinaglia, were only averaging about 4,000 spectators at their home games - well below the number needed for the club to break even.

At the beginning of March, Force looked to step up their play-off push and signed Andy Chapman from Wichita Wings. Londoner Chapman had an impressive MISL scoring record and had hit the back of the net 220 times in six seasons with the Wings. Chapman's all-action approach and obvious love for

Back at Brighton... holding off Liverpool's Alan Kennedy in the FA Cup fifth round victory at Anfield in February 1983.

Celebrating a century of goals in English professional football. Ward salutes the North Stand after scoring the winner against Manchester United.

Picture: The Evening Argus

Presenting Rod Stewart with a Gold
Disc at Vancouver Airport.

Mickey, Minnie and Wardy.

Scoring a close range goal for the Tacoma Stars.

Leaving the pitch after a game for the Tampa Bay Rowdies.

Pulling a pint at The Scotland Yard.

Celebrating another Amateur Championship with the Kickers in 2001.

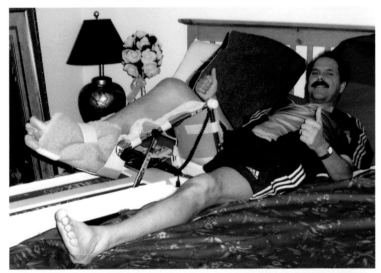

December 2006 - thumbs up for a new titanium knee.

With Man United and Republic of Ireland captain Roy Keane.

A proud dad with his daughters; Rebekah, Rachael and Louisa, in 2001.

Peter on a night out with his dad, sister and mum.

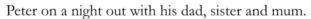

Peter and Jacqueline on their wedding day; 22nd June 2002.

Rebekah, Peter, Rachael and Louisa.

Mia and Xena.

Louisa's High School graduation in 2004.

Mr and Mrs Ward on
Brighton Beach

Peter signing autographs on a visit to Brighton's temporary home at Gillingham.

Friday afternoons... Al Mcleod, Peter Ward, Ray Hales and Steve 'the honorary Englishman' Deal

Sunday mornings... watching Chelsea v Manchester United at Beef 'o' Brady's in Tampa

The Robert Eaton Memorial Fund Game 2009

Picture by Roz South. www.allthingsbrightonbeautiful.com

the game was a big hit with the Force supporters and he soon developed a good camaraderie with Ward:

> *Andy was a good player and provided a real boost when he arrived. When-ever either of us scored, we would high-five each other in the middle of the pitch; the fans loved it, and the team used a picture of us doing that on the cover of their Media Guide for the following season.*

Teammate Peter Millar regarded the new signing as a bit of a Jekyll and Hyde character:

> *Andy Chapman was a similar type of player to Peter in many ways and played well, but where Peter was a clean living guy, Andy's lifestyle off the pitch saw him fall foul of the coaching staff on more than one occasion. This dropped him down the pecking order and restricted his opportunities.*

Four defeats at the start of March left the Force in danger of missing out on post-season action, but a great run of form over the last four weeks of the sea-son returned 9 wins from the last 11 games. Crucially, the run of victories in-cluded three morale-boosting wins over the Chicago Sting, who had finished one place above the Force, in second place. Ward found that playing against Chicago suited him:

> *We had lost twice to the Sting earlier in the season and we had been trying to catch them all year. At the end of March, they came to our place and we beat them 5-4; I got my first hat-trick of the season. It was the first time that we had beaten either Chicago or Baltimore, the two teams above us in the division, so it was good for our confidence. Chicago had a good team: they had Karl-Heinz Granitza, who was the second top scorer in NASL history; and Victor Moreland, who had played at Derby.*
>
> *A week later, we played them again and I scored another hat-trick! We won 4-2 and, for a long time, it looked like we might get a shut-out [keep-ing the opponents scoreless], which was really, really rare in the MISL. In fact, Cleveland had never had one, so it would have been quite something. Unfortunately, with about five minutes to go, Granitza had a shot and it bounced off my leg, sent our goalie the wrong way and went in the net.*

The final three regular season games saw Cleveland beat Wichita, Chicago again, and, for the first time in the season, Eastern Division champs Baltimore Blast. The Chicago victory was vital because it secured third place in the divi-sion and meant that Cleveland avoided the need to play a mini-series to secure their presence in the play-offs. For the third meeting in a row with Chicago, Ward made the telling contribution, scoring a goal that put Cleveland into a lead that they did not relinquish.

Ward's form in the second half of the season had been excellent and he finished the regular season with 34 goals in 47 games. Only Craig Allen and Keith Furphy scored more goals for the Force, who finished with 27 wins from

48 games. Unfortunately for Allen, he suffered a serious knee injury in the last game of the season against Baltimore, which kept him out of all the play-off games.

The Force's form had captured the interest of their home fans and the team averaged a league-leading 13,000 attendance for home games. Cleveland's reward for third place was a Quarter-Final play-off series with Chicago Sting - a team with which they had become very familiar over the preceding month.

Once again, the Sting suffered at the hands (or feet) of Ward:

> *It was a best-of-five series and we played the first two games in Chicago. In Game 1, we started well and I scored to put us 3-1 up just after half-time, but Chicago came back at us and went 4-3 in front. With about a minute to go in normal time, Keith Furphy equalised to take the game into overtime. Ten minutes into the extra period, I got the winner, a header from about two yards out, and we'd sneaked the win. My wife had brought the girls to come and watch, so I jumped into the crowd and gave them a big hug after scoring the winner.*

> *We stayed in Chicago for the second game and they hammered us, 8-4. Game 3 was back in Cleveland and we completely outplayed them and won 6-1 with Andy Chapman scoring a hat-trick.*

> *I opened the scoring in the fourth game and Andy got another hat-trick but it still took an overtime goal for us to win 5-4 again and go through to the Semi-Finals.*

Rachael Ward remembers the journey to Chicago for Game 1:

> *We were living in Cleveland and went with my mum's friend and her daughter. On the way our van broke down so we had to hitch-hike; all five of us, two women and three little girls! Luckily two men who were on their way to a bible convention stopped and gave us a lift all the way to the game.*

Waiting for the Force were the Baltimore Blast, who had disposed of the Los Angeles Lazers 3-0 in their quarter-final play-off series. Baltimore were the reigning MISL champions and had won the Eastern Conference for the previous three seasons. Their leading goalscorer was Serbian Stan Stamenkovic, who was MISL MVP for the 1983-84 season. He was joined by two MISL All-Stars: defender, Mike Stankovic; and goalkeeper, Scott Manning.

The champions proved to be too strong for Cleveland and, for the third consecutive year, the Force were knocked out at the semi-final stage by their bitterest rivals. Ward remembers the series as closely contested but, ultimately, won by the stronger team:

> *Baltimore were consistently good and they had won the Division by quite a long way. We played well in the play-off series and split the opening two*

games in Baltimore so we knew that if we won our two home games we would get through.

Game 3 was disappointing and they won 3-2, which meant that we had to win the final two games. We beat them 6-4 in the fourth game and had to travel back to Baltimore for the decider.

They used all of their experience to hold us off in the final game and we lost 7-4, so that was it: season over. I think we must have worn them out, though, because they lost 4-1 to San Diego in the Championship Series.

It was the third year in a row that Baltimore had knocked out Cleveland to get to the Finals. We got them back the next season.

◇ ◇ ◇

The summer of 1985 was full of good news for the MISL, the Cleveland Force and their number 8, Peter Ward: the league signed their first national TV contract with a 15-game schedule agreed with ESPN; the Force sold a record 5,000 season tickets; and Peter and his wife were delighted by the news that Sue was expecting their third child. Ward felt settled in Cleveland and had warmed to his new home:

We bought a house and it was in a nice area. We had grown to like Cleveland and it was nice to stay in the same city for more than a year. Sue was pregnant with Louisa; it was quite strange because there must have been seven or eight of the players on the team whose wives had babies within the space of two months... It was so cold that we had to keep warm somehow!

It was a good group of players and we had some fun nights out. We went to a fund-raiser for The Rock and Roll Hall of Fame which they wanted to build in the city. I was one of four players who put tuxedos on and went up onto the stage to mime to Twist and Shout by The Beatles. The music was really loud and we really went for it. I didn't know until I'd finished that my microphone had been left on so that everyone could hear my singing! We had a brilliant night and the atmosphere between the players was great.

Hoping to finally become the number one team in the Eastern Division, Cleveland made a few changes to their roster for the new season. The most significant departures were second top scorer Keith Furphy, who was traded to Kansas following a disagreement with Coach Liekoski; and Louie Nanchoff and keeper Krys Sobieski, who both joined Dallas. New faces included Canadians Chris Chueden, Pasquale DeLuca and Pat Ercoli. Ercoli, signed from rivals Baltimore, had scored 112 goals over the previous four seasons.

Carl Valentine, Ward's former Vancouver teammate, was the most high-profile addition. Ward was the instigator of his move to Cleveland:

195

Carl had gone back to the England after the NASL collapsed and played
for West Brom in the First Division. I still spoke to him fairly often and he
had said that it wasn't really working out in England. So I told him that
I would see if I could get him a spot at Cleveland. I told the coach, Timo,
about him and, after Keith Furphy had left, the club agreed to sign him.
Carl is a good guy; he did well and got plenty of goals with the Force.

In addition to becoming an integral part of Cleveland's offensive arsenal,
Valentine also became a big contributor to the Canadian national team and
helped them to qualify for the World Cup for the very first time. Making his
Canadian debut in the same month that he signed for Cleveland, Valentine set
up both goals in a 2-1 victory over Honduras that secured a place at Mexico '86
for his adopted country. He went on to play in all three of Canada's games in
the Finals, as they were knocked out in the first round.

◇　◇　◇

Peter Ward started the new season with a flourish and scored two goals
in each of Cleveland's first two games. Unfortunately, both games ended in
defeat for the Force, but an inspiring performance from Ward helped them
to romp to their first win of the season with a 10-6 pummelling of Tacoma. A
hat-trick against the Stars, who were coached by Ward's former Seattle and
Vancouver coach Alan Hinton, was followed by another goal for Ward in a 7-3
win over Los Angeles:

I had a great start to the season — 8 goals in the first 4 games — and we
started to play well as a team. The league had become stronger and there
were more ex-NASL players spread amongst the teams. Timo came out in
the papers saying that I was playing better now that I was working harder
and that people shouldn't get carried away, because goalscorers often go
through bad patches too. I had been working hard ever since I had joined; it
was just that I was now fully fit and had a bit more indoor experience. He
was right about 'bad patch,' mind you, and I only got one goal in the next
five games.

I started scoring again before the end of the year and got another hat-trick
against Chicago, who must have been sick of the sight of me. We beat them
three times in the first half of the season — 4-1, 8-2 and 9-3 — and their
coach came out after the third game and said that it would make more sense
for Chicago to forfeit games against Cleveland because it would save the
club money and the players from further embarrassment.

The third of the victories over Chicago left Cleveland with a record of 9
wins and 7 defeats and was witnessed by Ward's parents, who had made their
first trip to the US. The win lifted Cleveland to second place in a very close
Eastern Division. The Minnesota Strikers held first position with a 12-6 record

196

and included former Newcastle United player Ray Hudson and former Sunderland midfielder Stan Cummins in their team.

The battle to become Eastern Division champion continued throughout the first three months of 1986. In contrast to the Western Division, where reigning champions San Diego had built up a wide gap between themselves and the other teams, all six teams in the Eastern Division were in with a chance of securing top spot.

The highlight of early 1986 for Ward was another hat-trick, but this time it was girls rather than goals: his third daughter, Louisa, was born on 4th February.

February also saw the surprise transfer of the league's top scorer and MVP, Steve Zungul, from San Diego to Tacoma. Zungul's move was a proactive step by San Diego, who were looking to ensure that they would not fall foul to the salary cap ruling proposed by the league. At Tacoma, Zungul teamed up with the MISL's rising star, Preki, a young Serbian winger, who would go on to play for Everton and Portsmouth in the English league.

The All-Star Game provided a brief break to the MISL schedule in mid-February and Ward was rewarded for his impressive form with a place in the East All-Stars team.

In the week preceding the game, a routine examination by the Cleveland medical team resulted in some potentially devastating news for Ward:

> *They examined me to check that my knee was ok and they took quite a lot of x-rays. When they got the results they found a big dark lump near my groin and told me that they thought it might be a tumour, and that they would need to take a closer look. The doctor told me that if it was a tumour, the chances were that it would be the end of my career — just like that, finished - and that the All-Star game would be my last game.*

> *It was strange, because it obviously could have been incredibly bad news but I didn't feel worried or scared. They took an MRI scan and came back and said that it wasn't a tumour but a collection of blood that had been caused by getting kicked so many times. They removed it and it didn't cause me any long-term problems at all.*

The game ended in a 5-3 victory for the West, with San Diego's Branko Segota scoring twice for the winning team. The winners pocketed $800 for their success, whilst Ward and the other losing players each went home with a cheque for $600.

◇ ◇ ◇

Cleveland resumed league action with an important 6-3 victory over Dallas and went into the final five weeks of the season still fighting for their first-

197

ever divisional title. Ward remembers the tension of the title run-in and the response of the Cleveland fans:

> *With a handful of games left, it was still possible for any of the teams in the division to win it; also, two of the teams would end up missing out on the play-offs. They were saying that it was the closest divisional race ever and our fans were really getting behind us.*
>
> *None of the teams could put together a run of wins and I remember that we lost at Dallas and then a couple of games later, in our penultimate home game, absolutely battered them in front of a full house and won 9-3.*
>
> *It all went to the last game of the season, when we played Minnesota at home. We had both already qualified for the play-offs but whoever won this final game would be the winners of the division. Neither team had won the title before, so it was a hugely important game.*
>
> *The Coliseum was absolutely packed — it was the biggest crowd ever for an MISL game — and there were over 20,000 people there. It was a great game: we came out on top, 7-4, and won the division — fantastic!*

Cleveland's first-ever Eastern Division crown was a marvellous achievement, which set up yet another play-off encounter with arch-rivals Baltimore. The Blast had finished fourth in the division, their lowest-ever position, but were only 3 games behind Cleveland, having won 24 games compared to the Force's 27 victories.

The Force got off to a great start in the best-of-five series, winning the opening game 7-2. Baltimore bounced back and scored an equally impressive 8-3 victory in Game 2 at the Coliseum. After another Blast victory in Game 3, it looked as if Cleveland would succumb to their rivals for the fourth consecutive season, but a nerve-wrecking 4-3 overtime win in the fourth game took the series back to Ohio. With the home crowd spurring their favourites on, Cleveland finally laid the ghost to rest and, much to Ward's relief, secured an historic 5-1 victory and passage into the Semi-Finals:

> *It was an incredible series and to beat Baltimore at long last was tremendously satisfying. After we had won that series, we thought that we had a really good shot at winning it all but it went horribly wrong in the Semi-Finals.*
>
> *We were playing Minnesota, who we had just pipped to the league title and they were really ready for us. We won the first game but then lost the next one. We went to Minnesota knowing that we had to win at least one of the two games there, but we were shot; we had run out of energy. They beat us 5-4 in overtime in the first game and then 7-3 in Game 4 to knock us out.*

We'd made a lot of progress that season, winning the division and beating Baltimore in the play-offs, but it is always disappointing to get knocked out in the play-offs, so it was hard to label the season as a success.

I had a pretty good season, although I missed a few games [8] through injury. I still got 38 goals in 49 games, though, so I had done well.

The season over, Ward and his family took a much-needed holiday, as Sue remembers:

When Cleveland got knocked out of the play-offs, we decided that we'd take the girls on holiday. We came down to Florida and went to Disney World. Louisa was just a few months old, but Rachael and Rebekah were the perfect age for Disney and had a great time.

Pete and I were in sitting in the British Pub in the Epcot Centre and I remember us talking about how much we liked Florida and thought that it would be a great place to live. It was a few years before we got the opportunity to move to Tampa but we loved it. We've both been there ever since.

◇   ◇   ◇

Shortly after San Diego had secured their third consecutive MISL championship with a 4-3 series victory over Minnesota, the league announced that a salary cap would be imposed on all teams for the upcoming 1986-87 season. Each team were limited to spending a maximum of $1.2 million on players' wages for the season and this resulting in teams looking to cut back on their highest paid 'star' players and to look toward younger American players to make up a higher proportion of their rosters.

In Cleveland, the biggest departure was fourth top scorer, Andy Chapman, who signed for Eastern Division rivals Baltimore. New additions included draft pick John Stollmeyer, American defender Desmond Armstrong, and brothers Andy and Walter Schmetzer.

Following what was widely regarded to be the MISL's most successful season, the league announced an improved contract with ESPN that expanded the network's coverage to 18 games. Although the Pittsburgh Spirit folded during the off-season, they were replaced by a new franchise: the New York Express. The league were desperate to establish a successful presence in the nation's media capital, following the embarrassing mid-season demise of the Cosmos two seasons earlier and the collapse of the New York Arrows in 1984, but the Express were also destined to fail.

Peter Ward was entering the third season of his four-year contract with Cleveland and looked forward to the new campaign with a fair amount of confidence:

We still had a strong squad —out of the main players, only Andy Chap-man had left— and John Stollmeyer came in and did really well. We knew that the other teams in the division would be gunning for us because we had done so well during the previous season but we were confident that we could do even better than a year earlier.

My contract was halfway through and my relationship with Timo and his assistant was deteriorating. I suppose that I, as one of the senior players, had even more confidence to voice my opinions and I used to disagree with him a lot. He probably thought that he would rather spend my wages on someone who was less of a pain in the ass.

◇ ◇ ◇

Cleveland started the season with a defeat at Baltimore but bounced back with victories over Minnesota and Dallas. The Sidekicks' main threat still came from Brazilian hot-shot Tatu but they had lost the services of experienced Northern Ireland international, Billy Caskey. Caskey's exit from the league had been somewhat controversial, as Ward recalls:

Billy Caskey had come over to the US from Derby County with Victor Mo-reland, and they had both played at Tulsa in the NASL for a number of sea-sons. Billy went back to Ireland for a while and then came over and played indoor soccer for Dallas. He was a real loose cannon and used to go around kicking people. He spent a lot of time in the sin-bin and would get really frustrated by the referees.

In the play-off quarter-finals, Dallas were playing Minnesota, and Billy got a yellow card and had to go into the sin-bin for a two-minute penalty. He was still fuming when he came back on and when he got the ball he kicked it back towards his own goal so that he would have to run past one of the ref-erees. As he went past this ref, Billy clobbered him and knocked him to the ground. Then he started to run after the other ref and he chased them both off the pitch!

He ended up getting a three-year ban from the league for 'physically and vi-olently abusing an official,' although he was planning to go home anyway, so it didn't make much difference to him.

Six wins from nine games in December put the Force in second position in the Eastern Division behind Baltimore. The team were in good form but, behind the scenes, Ward's relationship with the coaching staff was close to breaking point:

I was getting increasingly frustrated with Timo and Jay Hoffman, his as-sistant.

Road trips could be really tiring, but as long as you got on the right plane and your bags were there when you arrived, there wasn't normally too much to get stressed about. However, we were at the airport, waiting to get a flight from Chicago to Minneapolis, and I was playing cards with Benny Dargle and four or five of the other players in a bar right across from the boarding gate.

Hoffman was keeping an eye on us and the time, to make sure that we didn't miss the flight. All of a sudden, Benny turned around and said, 'That's our plane pulling out!' He was right; our plane was heading to the runway with only half the team aboard. I went crazy at Hoffman and shouted at him 'You've only got two jobs to do — one is to open the gate and let us onto the pitch, and the other is to make sure we get on the bloody plane!'

We were late for the game and the league fined Timo and Hoffman. We still won the game 7-6 though!

Timo and I fell out for good after a game in Dallas. There was a break in play early in the game and we came in for a quick team-talk. Dallas were winning and Timo had a go at me and started to blame me for the fact we were losing. When the game restarted he left me off, out of the rotation.

At the end of the first quarter we had a shouting match; I lost my temper and threw a cup of water all over him.

At half-time, a couple of players heard Timo ask Hoffman what he should do about me. Hoffman told him to fine me $500. He ended up putting me back into the game in the third quarter and I scored a couple of goals and we won.

At the end of the game he came in and said that I would be fined $500. I said 'What for?' and he said that I'd thrown water at him. I said that I didn't throw the water at him and that I'd just thrown it at the bench because I was mad and it had splashed him - which was a complete lie. He didn't know what to say and told me that he would look at the game tape to see what had happened.

He didn't have the balls to say anything about it again and I ended up getting away with it.

Former Cleveland midfielder, Peter Millar, had witnessed the frosty relationship between Ward and his coach during the previous season:

Timo had his favourite players like Kai Haaskivi, Keith Furphy and Bernie James but Wardy would speak back to him when he didn't agree with some of his decisions regarding tactics and team selection. Of course Timo didn't like that, hence the reason for their strained relations.

Myself and another Scot, Vic Davidson, were more rebellious when it came to curfews and discipline, and Timo and his assistant, Jay Hoffman, were always on the lookout for us after every game on the road; more often than not, they found us in a bar somewhere. Timo didn't know how to handle this as he could not man-manage players, and as long as we were doing the business on the park he couldn't leave us out.

Wardy was in this category too and sort of got labelled with us as the drinkers in the team, though Wardy was more clever than we and did it where and when he knew Timo wouldn't see him.

Wardy was the star man, scoring goals by the barrow-load, and Timo couldn't leave him out of the starting line-up or the fans would have lynched him. Wardy knew this too, which gave him more confidence to voice his opinion at team talks.

◇   ◇   ◇

On 3rd January, 1987, the New York Express visited Richmond Coliseum for the first, and what proved to be the last, time. The New York team included ex-Arsenal and future-Leeds defender Chris Whyte and US national team captain Rick Davis but came to Ohio having lost all of their first thirteen games of the season. Ward returned to the team for the Express's visit after having been sidelined for a couple of weeks with a toe injury. The hapless visitors were an ideal opposition for Ward's comeback: he scored twice and contributed two assists as Cleveland secured a convincing 7-4 victory in front of thirteen thousand home fans.

The win kick-started a run of five consecutive victories for the Force — the fourth of which, a 5-3 success over Dallas, lifted Baltimore to the top of the division at the expense of the Sidekicks. Ward scored the goal which put Cleveland 4-3 ahead and the defeat broke a run of seven straight victories for the visitors.

The break for the All-Star game in early February coincided with the disappointing news that the New York Express were withdrawing from the league, having played just 25 games — of which just 3 were won. Two years after the Cosmos had done the exact same thing, the league was again left without a presence in the Big Apple.

Peter Ward was again voted to the East All-Star team and, along with teammates Carl Valentine and Kai Haaskivi, travelled to Los Angeles for the annual showcase event. At the team hotel, Ward received a surprise visit:

We had trained in the morning, had some lunch and then my roommate, Carl, and I went back to the hotel to get some rest. We were both sleeping when there was a knock on the door. I got up and opened it and standing in the corridor was Justin Fashanu! I was completely surprised and had no idea that he was in America.

He came in and we had a chat and it turned out that he was in LA for an operation on his knee. He had been playing at Brighton for a year but had been forced to retire the previous summer because of his knee injury — he was only 25. I think that was the last time I saw him, poor fella...

Before he signed for Brighton, Chris Cattlin the Brighton manager, had phoned me and asked what I thought about Justin. Chris explained how, when they had met, Fashanu had drawn a map to try to explain the choices in his personal life. He drew a fork in the road and said 'this road leads to bars and clubs and women', Chris interrupted him and said 'Wardy built that bloody bridge!' I thought that was really funny.

For only the second time in seven games, the Eastern Division team emerged victorious with a 6-5 overtime victory in front of a sell-out crowd at The Forum.

Cleveland resumed their MISL schedule with a 6-4 victory in Dallas: maintaining their 100% season record over the Sidekicks. Another win at St. Louis was followed by two Ward goals in a 6-3 victory over Los Angeles. San Diego's visit to the Coliseum on 21st February drew a season-high 18,600 spectators, but the visitors edged a close encounter: 6-5 after overtime. A win in Los Angeles was followed by three straight defeats which left Cleveland with a 21-12 record.

At the start of March, English-born defender Paul Kitson joined Cleveland from the Lazers in a swap deal which saw Chris Chueden head to California. Before joining the Force, Kitson had won championships with both the New York Arrows and Baltimore Blast, and it was hoped that his experience would help Cleveland reach their ultimate goal.

A run of four straight wins at the end of March kept the Force in the title hunt and their closest rivals were proving, once again, to be Baltimore. When the Force travelled to Baltimore on 24th April, they knew that victory would see them move within touching distance of the Blast and give them a great chance of retaining the Eastern Division crown. The game is one of the most memorable from Ward's time at Cleveland and broke the worst scoring drought of his indoor career:

We went to Baltimore with just five games left in the season. Our form had been a bit up and down for a few weeks, but so had Baltimore's and we were right behind them in the league. I had been having a bit of a nightmare and hadn't scored for thirteen games, so I was desperate for a goal.

The way that the pitch was set up at Baltimore meant that before the game, there would be fans walking along a walkway behind the goal as the teams warmed up. So they would be going to their seats with trays full of drinks, popcorn and hot dogs and when I was with Cleveland we would always take pot-shots at the Baltimore fans as they walked past to see if we could hit one of them and knock their refreshments flying — I'm sure that the home fans must have known what we were doing.

Before one game, by mistake, I accidently smashed a really sweet volley that hit a woman right in the face. What made it worse was that she was talking photos and had a camera up to her eye and she had to go to hospital. That didn't much help the relationship between our clubs!

We went out and absolutely destroyed them: I got the first goal after eight minutes and after twenty minutes we were 4-0 up! They got one goal back after half-time when Billy Ronson, who used to play at Blackpool, scored, but in the final period I got another. After I had scored I jumped on the boards at the side of the pitch and started to goad their fans... I was waving my arms around and shouting 'Come on, come on!' and they were booing and going nuts. They hated Cleveland and we were really sticking it to them. Carl Valentine got another goal right at the end of the game and we won 6-1 — Cleveland's biggest win over Baltimore since 1980.

After the game, one of their players was interviewed on TV and the reporter asked him about my goal celebrations. He said that 'you couldn't get enough mustard to cover that hot-dog': basically, he was calling me an asshole. It was quite funny; they hated losing to us.

Following the demolition of Baltimore, Cleveland beat Chicago 7-5 and then defeated Dallas 5-3 to move level with Baltimore at the top of the division. Ward's two goals against Dallas took his season total to 25 but, as Ward recalls, the most memorable goal of the evening came from Force goalkeeper Chris Vaccaro:

It was crazy because they allowed the goalies to throw the ball into the other team's net for a goal! It didn't happen very often because it was a long way from one end of the pitch to the other and there was normally a goalie or a defender guarding the goal; but Chris Vaccaro could throw for miles and against Dallas he had a chance — and scored!

A victory over bottom of the table Chicago set up a mouth-watering final game of the season for the Force — another trip to Baltimore. Both teams went into the match with a record of 33 wins and 18 defeats. The prize for the winner was considerable: the Eastern Division championship and home advantage for the play-offs.

Stunning the home crowd, ex-Baltimore player Paul Kitson hit the decisive goal against his former club as Cleveland triumphed 6-4, thus retaining the

Eastern Division title for the Force. Winning the title at the expense of their great rivals added to the sense of achievement for Ward:

> It was brilliant to win it in Baltimore - of course it would have been nice to have won it at home like the year before, but this was almost as good.

> After that game, we thought that we were going to win it all. In the first round of the play-offs, we struggled a little bit to beat Minnesota 3 games to 2, and then we had to play Dallas, who had knocked out Baltimore.

> We had played Dallas five times already that season and won four of the games and we were really confident that we would get through to the Finals. Looking back, we were too confident, especially after we won Game 1. They hammered us in Game 2 in Cleveland and then they beat us easily in both games in Dallas. So they were 3-1 up when we came back to Cleveland for the fifth game and we had to win. We didn't, though: we lost 4-3 and it was all over. We hadn't lost four games in a row all season up to that point, but they just outplayed us... it was hard to pinpoint why it had happened, but they were on a great run.

> Dallas played Tacoma in the Finals and Tacoma were overwhelming favourites. Tacoma won the first two games, but Dallas came back to tie it up. Tacoma went 3-2 up but Dallas won the final two games, both in overtime, to win 4-3. They were great games - I remember watching them on TV.

Ward's Cleveland contract ended after the Game 5 defeat against Dallas and, although his three years coincided with the most successful seasons in the club's history, Ward's contribution to the Force had lessened in each of the three years:

> I scored 32 goals in my final year at Cleveland which still made me one of the leading scorers on the team but was less than the previous season and the season before. I guess they thought that as I was almost 32 that I was over the hill.

> Timo clearly didn't want to offer me another contract and still hadn't forgiven me for throwing water over him. I bet he was glad to get rid of me.

> I spoke to my old coach, Alan Hinton, who was still in Seattle coaching Tacoma. He offered me a contract and it was a pretty easy decision. We had loved living in Seattle and I got on really well with Alan, so it didn't take us long to decide that we would go back.

> Instead of flying to Seattle, we decided to take the Amtrak train, which was a great experience. The journey took three days and it was really nice to be able to see lots of the country. The route took us through the mountains

and it was a super way to travel. We got a compartment with a toilet and shower and there was enough room for all of us to sleep.

The trains have two levels, and there is a big glass-walled viewing compartment where you can sit and have a drink and listen to an audio commentary that describes any interesting landmarks or historical events that occurred near the places we were travelling through. It made a refreshing change from flying and only seeing the airport.

CHAPTER 17

A STAR IN TACOMA

I met a girl who was a couple of years older than me
but we started to hang out and would go to watch Dad
together. The first time that I went back to her house, she
took me up to her bedroom and on her wall there was a
full-sized poster of my dad — it was really weird!

– Rachael Ward

The Tacoma Stars were coming off their best-ever season, having won the Western Division and having been within three minutes of beating Dallas in Game 7 of the MISL Championship. Their roster included the biggest star in the league, Yugoslav Steve Zungul, and his compatriot and rising star Preki (Predrag Radosavljević). The Stars forward line was further bolstered by two former Luton Town strikers - Gary Heale and Godfrey Ingram.

Tacoma coach, Alan Hinton, saw Ward as an ideal addition to his goalscoring options:

> Peter was very keen to come back to Seattle and was very well suited to indoor soccer — small, quick and with good control. He was a talent and a great addition to the team. I thought that he would be a great player for Tacoma and help us improve.

With the press reporting the signing of "Veteran Peter Ward" —rather than the "High-Scoring Peter Ward" who had joined Cleveland three years earlier— and a well-established forward rotation already in place, Ward knew that he would need to earn his playing time:

> Tacoma had some great players and they had four of the top twelve scorers in the league. Zungul was the best - he was a very good player and had scored hundreds of goals. They called him the 'Lord of all Indoors' and he had been by far the most successful player in the history of the MISL. I had played against him many times and it was great to be on his team at last.

> Preki was just a youngster, but he was a very good player. He only had a couple of tricks and defenders knew what he would do, but they still couldn't stop him. He eventually went to the Premier League in England and did the same tricks there!

> Neil Megson, with whom I had played at Seattle, was there, and he had been an All-Star the year before. Mark Davis, who was captain of the American national team, was at Tacoma and Bernie James had joined from Cleveland

207

at the same time as me. It was a strong team and the club were confident that they could go one step further than the previous season and win the Championship.

Because they had so many good forwards and because I was getting a little older, Alan Hinton had suggested that I would be used as more of a mid-fielder than a striker. That was fine with me and I just wanted to play, but, as it turned out, I scored a lot of goals and had a great season.

Tacoma had initially secured Ward's signing by agreeing a one-year contract worth $60,000 but, before the season started, he signed a two-year deal that paid $45,000 in the first year and $60,000 in the second:

Having the security of a two-year deal was good. The girls were getting a little bit older and it was becoming harder for them to keep moving schools. Alan Hinton looked after me and my contract guaranteed that I could not be cut in the first year, which gave even more security.

Rachael Ward, Peter's eldest daughter, was thrilled to be going back to Seattle, even if it did mean yet another change of schools:

I hated moving around so much. It was hard — you'd make friends and then you would have to leave. I went to ten different schools and I used to hate the first day. Looking back on it now, I'm glad that we saw so many places but at the time it wasn't fun.

I loved Seattle and was really pleased when we went back — it was one of my favourite places. We were there for three years and I loved everything about it.

We would go to the Stars games; I met a girl who was a couple of years older than me but we started to hang out and would go to watch Dad together. The first time that I went back to her house, she took me up to her bedroom and on her wall there was a full-sized poster of my dad — it was really weird!

⬦　⬦　⬦

Before pre-season training started, Hinton took his players for a three-day retreat on a small, isolated island south of the Tacoma Narrows. Hinton had warned his players that they would have to catch their own food and sleep in the woods, but the reality was a little more pampered, and the team enjoyed three days of Summer Camp activities and meals shipped in by the nearest Italian restaurant. At the end of the sojourn, each player shook the coach's hand and confirmed their commitment to securing the Stars' first championship.

Any team harmony developed during the island adventure soon disappeared, as a series of disputes between Hinton and his two high-scoring Yugoslavians threatened to overshadow preparation for the new season. The friction between the players and their coach came to a head when Hinton released another Yugoslavian forward, Cico, causing the two Tacoma stars to stage a one-day boycott of practice and Preki to request a transfer. The pair were temporarily placated after a team meeting, but the discontent bubbled under the surface all season and eventually cost Hinton his position.

Tacoma's season started with a visit from the MISL champions Dallas, but once again the Sidekicks prevailed with a 4-3 victory. Six wins from the next nine games put the Stars in a tie with San Diego at the top of the Western Division. Two defeats at the start of December, though, including a 7-3 defeat on Ward's first return to Cleveland, dropped the Stars to second place.

Against Cleveland, Ward was marked by his close friend Benny Dargle. Dargle remembers the rules of engagement:

> We agreed that if he didn't go past me I wouldn't kick the s*** out of him. We pretty much stayed away from each other because I knew that he could embarrass me and he knew that, if I caught him, I could give him a really good kick. We played against each other 7 or 8 times and it was the same thing every time — we didn't go near each other.

Before the next game, Tacoma made a surprise trade and sent forward Godfrey Ingram to St. Louis in return for Canadian international Charlie Falzon. Ingram had been the second-highest goalscorer in the league during the previous season — scoring 52 goals in 51 games — but demanded to be traded, complaining of a shortage of playing time. His lack of opportunities were in no small way brought about by Ward's early season form, which had seen him move ahead of Ingram in the rotation.

A 7-2 victory over the LA Lazers on 11th December, 1987, was more significant for Steve Zungul, scoring his 1000th career point, than for the result. It was a historic night for the MISL and Ward felt privileged to be part of it:

> Zungul had been stuck on 997 points [goals plus assists] for a few games and going into the fourth period against LA, he hadn't got any more. He created a goal for Preki, to put us 5-2 up, and then he made one for me, which gave him 999 points. With about three minutes to go he himself scored and had finally reached 1,000. The game stopped and the crowd went crazy. It was quite an achievement…

Defeat at the Tacoma Dome to San Diego brought to an end a run of three straight victories and, with it, a chance to replace the Sockers at the top of the table. A Boxing Day defeat at Minnesota was followed by victory over St. Louis in the final game of 1987, leaving the Stars with a 10-8 record going into the New Year.

◇ ◇ ◇

After five defeats in the first six games of 1988 Tacoma were trailing San Diego by seven games, and their chance of retaining the Western Division title appeared to be slipping away. An 8-3 victory over Baltimore sparked a mini-revival, with the Stars winning three of the next four games, but four straight defeats going into the All-Star break in mid-February left them with a disappointing 15-18 record.

Although Peter Ward was not selected for the West All-Star team, there was a significant Tacoma presence: Zungul, Preki, Neil Megson, Rick Davis and goalie Mike Dowler were all voted to represent the Western Conference in front of the Tacoma Dome fans, and Alan Hinton was selected as the team coach. The West won 9-3 and the victory appeared to improve the morale of the Stars, who returned to MISL action with a stunning 5-4 victory over the Chicago Sting. It was a memorable night for Ward, who was enjoying his best run of scoring since his move back to Seattle:

> I had scored a couple of goals in the previous three games but we had lost all of those. It looked like we were going to lose to Chicago as well: with four and a half minutes to go in the game we were 4-2 down and most of the fans had started to head for the exit. As teams would often do in that sort of situation, we took off our goalie and played with six attackers. It was the sort of tactic that would hardly ever work — a real desperation move.

> With just over a minute to go, we hadn't scored; but then Steve Zungul got one and, amazingly, just eleven seconds later I scored to tie the game at 4-4! With thirty seconds left to play, Gary Heale took a pot-shot, it hit the post and went in - we had scored three goals in 47 seconds and won the game 5-4!

Two nights later, Tacoma went to Wichita and defeated the Wings 5-4 in overtime:

> I scored twice and got the winner in overtime. After I scored, I jumped on the boards to celebrate and the Wichita fans went nuts — I got pelted with beer and anything else they could find.

On 22nd February, the day after the victory in Wichita, Alan Hinton was sacked sensationally from his role as coach, with the club citing unrest among the players as the key reason behind his departure. The decision left Hinton "shocked beyond belief", and initial rumours suggested that Steve Zungul, the player who had most publicly clashed with Hinton, was being lined up to take over as player/coach.

When the new coach was announced, although it was someone from within the Stars organisation, it was not Zungul. The new man was Jimmy McAlister, a former Tacoma player under Hinton, who had remained with the club as special events coordinator. Just 31 years old, McAlister was younger than a number of the team's star players and, with no previous coaching experience, his appointment was a risky move by the Stars.

The new coach's first game came with the visit of the Los Angeles Lazers, who sat in second place in the table, one place above Tacoma. Ward's first hat-trick for Tacoma gave McAlister a winning start to his coaching career and moved the Stars above their opponents. The best goal of the night was Ward's third, his twentieth of the season, a cheeky back-heel that hit the back of the net before the Lazers keeper could react.

Ward scored again, his eighth in five games, in a 4-3 success over St. Louis and for the next dozen games the Stars struggled in vain to make inroads into San Diego's lead at the top of the Division. Ward scored once against his previous employer as Cleveland were defeated 5-3, and hit two more as his old adversaries Baltimore were edged 7-6 at the Tacoma Dome.

Another brace, this time against San Diego, helped the Stars to defeat the Sockers for the first time in five attempts, in a bruising encounter. Tacoma's cause was helped when San Diego, who had already secured the Divisional title, lost their goalie, Zoltan Toth, early in the third quarter after he was sent off for throwing an elbow at Gary Heale.

The following game ended in a demoralising 8-1 defeat at Los Angeles, which virtually ended the Stars' hopes of finishing in second position. Two overtime victories over Wichita secured a play-off place for the Stars and a visit from Kansas City Comets completed Tacoma's regular season schedule. The Kansas City game was an emotional occasion for Ward:

> Sadly, Sue's dad had died that day and we spent most of the day in tears. I didn't know if I should play or not because I didn't want to leave Sue on her own, but she told me that I should and, as I was leaving, she said 'Play well, you know.'

> I scored four goals and had two assists, and we won 9-7.

> After the game we flew back to England for the funeral.

◇ ◇ ◇

With Ward back in the UK, the Stars started preparation for their first round play-off series with Western Division champions San Diego. Although San Diego had finished the season with an MISL record of 42 wins and 14 losses, their own play-off preparation had been somewhat sullied by news that the organisation had filed for bankruptcy. Sockers' coach Ron Newman (now a close neighbour of Ward in Tampa) rejected claims that the financial problems at the club would threaten their ability to play the remaining games, and insisted instead that the move would provide the team with enough time to seek new investors.

Tacoma's record of 27 victories and 29 defeats saw them limp into the play-offs with a fourth-placed finish; a far cry from the league-best 35-17 record and Western Division title twelve months earlier.

Tacoma succumbed to a 6-2 Game 1 defeat in San Diego but were boosted by Ward's return for Game 2:

> *I came back from the UK and headed straight to San Diego to meet up with the team. Steve Zungul had been injured in Game 1, so it was important that I make it back for the game. We hadn't won at San Diego all year. I scored early on but we were 3-1 down with about ten minutes to go, so it looked like another defeat. Preki got one back and then Ricky Davis equalised with twenty seconds to go, and sent the game into overtime. Five minutes in, I set up Preki and he scored again to win the game for us.*

> *Splitting the first two games in San Diego was ok and it gave us a chance. In Game 3, I scored an early goal again to put us ahead, and we went 2-0 up before the end of the first quarter. They came back in the second period and it was two each at half-time. We fell apart in the second half and they got five goals, beating us 7-2.*

> *We played better in the fourth game but, in the end, they were too good. I scored again but they won 7-6 and went on to beat my old team, Cleveland, in the Finals.*

◇ ◇ ◇

Ward's first season back in Seattle had, statistically, been his best indoor season yet, and his 42 goals made him Tacoma's third-highest goalscorer, behind Steve Zungul and Preki. Even with his recently acquired 'veteran' label, Ward once again demonstrated his durability - missing just two of 54 regular season games. In contrast, the health of the Tacoma Stars and the MISL was somewhat less encouraging...

A month after San Diego had secured their fourth MISL championship, the league announced that all teams who wished to participate in the following season had two weeks to pay $400,000 into the league pot. The Minnesota Strikers and St. Louis Steamers had already withdrawn from the league for financial reasons and, for Tacoma, finding $400,000 proved to be an impossible task. A week after the 1st July deadline had passed, the Stars announced that they were unable to find the money and would, therefore, have to fold. On the same day, the Chicago Sting made a similarly announcement, and a potential saviour for San Diego withdrew their offer after hearing of the fate of the Stars and the Sting.

With only six teams remaining, it looked like the MISL would follow the NASL into soccer oblivion but, by the end of July, the league had made an unlikely recovery, although it had to withstand one more hit. A renegotiated salary cap was agreed with the Players' Union and a new franchise was offered to a Tacoma-based consortium led by ex-Stars coach Alan Hinton. A rescue package was agreed for San Diego and it looked likely that the new season would start with eight teams.

Disappointing news came from a surprising source when the owner of the Cleveland Force, Bart Wolstein, announced that the Force, the league's best-supported club for the previous five seasons, was folding. Left with just seven clubs, half the number that there was when Ward joined the league four years earlier, the owners of the surviving teams agreed to do away with a two-conference set-up and play a single league format with each team playing 48 games.

On 9th August, Alan Hinton, who had been fired as coach some six months earlier, signed a three-year contract to coach the new Tacoma Stars and set about the task of building a team for the new season.

◇　◇　◇

Ward and his family returned to the UK for a holiday following the play-off defeat to San Diego. With the future of the Stars and the MISL in doubt, a number of his teammates made alternative arrangements for the upcoming season. Preki signed for a Portuguese team; Gary Heale kept his eggs in the MISL basket and signed for the LA Lazers; and captain Ricky Davis signed for the Seattle Storm, who played in a regional outdoor league. Fading superstar Steve Zungul publicly declared that he wouldn't play for the Stars again unless they showed ambition to match his own and, with the eventual appointment of Hinton as Head Coach, an opportunity for the temperamental striker to reject the club was never offered. Zungul eventually signed for one of his previous teams, the San Diego Sockers.

Hinton's key objective during the summer was to persuade Preki to join the re-born Stars. Despite the player having signed a three-year contract with Estrea De Amdadora of the Portuguese First Division, Hinton succeeded in recapturing his prize asset after spending a week in Lisbon negotiating with Preki and his new team. With Preki signed to a three-year deal with the Stars, Hinton turned his attention to Ward and travelled to England to discuss terms. With a one-year deal, worth $52,500, both Hinton and Ward returned to Seattle to prepare for the upcoming MISL campaign.

Including Preki and Ward, the new Stars re-signed ten of the players from the previous season and added reinforcements from the wreckage of the Cleveland Force. Goalkeeper PJ Johns, midfielder Ali Kazemaini, and brothers

Andy and Walter Schmetzer, all had their Cleveland contracts taken-up by the Stars, and with the addition of another Schmetzer brother, Brian, Tacoma had a solid, if not spectacular, squad.

To bolster the forward line, Hinton signed ex-Bolton attacking midfielder David Hoggan, who had scored 40 goals for Wichita during the previous season, and former Whitecap, Glaswegian Gerry Gray.

The new Stars were widely tipped to finish bottom of the seven-team league, which was no real surprise to Ward:

> We clearly weren't as strong as we had been the year before, but you could say that about most of the teams. The league had brought in a lower salary cap which meant that players either had to take a pay-cut or go to play else-where. We didn't have the strength in depth but we had some good young American players and, as Preki was coming back, we had one of the best players in the league.

◇ ◇ ◇

In the lead-up to the season opener with Dallas, Hinton suggested that he would use Ward as a midfielder and rely on Preki and new signing, Hoggan, to provide the scoring threat. His plans were thrown into turmoil before the first ball was kicked, as the league announced that Hoggan would be banned for the first 5 games of the season. The punishment was handed down in response to Hoggan being involved in a fight in the last game of the previous season while he was a Wichita player. Hoggan's ban meant that Ward's goals-coring services were once again in demand, and he didn't disappoint:

> In the first game of the season, we played Dallas and the game went to three overtimes. I scored a hat-trick and we came from 5-2 down in the final quarter to tie the game. I got the equaliser with a couple of minutes left, but neither team could score in the first two periods of overtime. In the third period, Dallas got the winner so we ended up losing 6-5.

Three further defeats gave the Stars a 0-4 record and it looked like those who had predicted a long, hard season for Tacoma would be right. A run of four straight wins restored confidence and a mixed December saw the Stars go into the New Year with a 7-9 record. Godfrey Ingram re-joined the club from Dallas and provided a welcome addition to the Stars' scoring options.

Two victories over league leaders Baltimore in January showed that, on their night, Tacoma could match any team in the league but the results were inconsistent. Between December and mid-March the Stars failed to win more than two consecutive games.

An exhibition match against Russian side Lokomotiv Moscow provided a break from MISL action, and Ward scored twice as Tacoma beat their guests 7-3.

By the middle of February, financial problems were once again plaguing the club. With crowds down to an average of 7,000, revenue was considerably lower than expected.

Consecutive overtime victories against Kansas City and Wichita were followed by two further wins and, going into the final month of the regular season, the Stars were still in with a chance of a play-off place. Ward remembers the regular season as having been a frustrating period:

> *We couldn't get a run going at all and we spent virtually the whole season in fourth or fifth position. We got as high as third a couple of times but not for long. It was frustrating because we beat every single team at least twice. We had quite a few injuries, which didn't help, but I only missed one game; Godfrey Ingram only missed a couple; and Preki didn't miss any.*
>
> *A good indication of how inconsistent we were was when we managed to achieve a shut-out, which was very unusual, beating Dallas 1-0; and then, the next game, we were shut out ourselves and beaten 4-0 by San Diego.*
>
> *With three games left, it was still touch and go whether we would make the play-offs. I got a couple of goals as we beat LA 6-3 and then we secured a play-off spot by defeating Dallas 5-2.*

By finishing fourth in the seven-team league, the Stars had to play fifth-placed Wichita in a Wild Card play-off series to determine who would progress to the semi-finals. Ward remembers anticipating a close, hard-fought series:

> *We won 8 of the last 11 games and were playing ok. Wichita had finished with an identical record and we were pretty well matched. We had fought some tough games with them during the season and there wasn't much love lost between the two sides so it should have been a really good series.*

In Game 1, a disappointing Tacoma Dome crowd of just over 4,000 watched Wichita remove the threat of league MVP Preki by marking him with two or three players, and, when that didn't work, fouling him as they rolled to a straightforward 4-1 victory.

The following night, things got worse for the Stars, even though they put up more of a fight as Wichita again emerged with a victory, this time 7 goals to 4.

With a view to seeing their team complete a three game sweep of the Stars, the majority of the 9,000 Wichita fans who turned up for Game 3 brought a broom with them. The over-confidence of the home fans spurred the Tacoma players on and Peter Ward scored the opening goal as the Stars produced a temporarily pride-saving 5-4 victory.

Two nights later, the Wichita fans (minus brooms) had the last laugh as the Wings secured a 6-2 victory and a three-games-to-one series victory.

Looking back at his second season in Tacoma, Ward has mixed memories:

As a team, we didn't really ever get going and by play-off time, there wasn't much belief. I had another good year and scored 43 goals in 53 games, which I think made me the fifth highest goalscorer in the league — not bad for a 33-year-old!

CHAPTER 18

TAMPA, WICHITA, BALTIMORE AND... HEDNESFORD

Mark [Lawrenson] said that Peter would be three things to the Rowdies: a quality performer on the pitch, a good influence in the dressing room and an excellent character to have at the club. All those things were true.

– Rodney Marsh, GM Tampa Bay Rowdies

While his Tacoma teammates looked forward to a holiday or a summer spent working in soccer camps, Ward packed his bags and headed to Florida:

A couple of weeks before the season ended I had a phone call, completely out of the blue, from Mark Lawrenson. I hadn't kept in touch him with him after I left Brighton but he had got my number from somewhere. He asked me if I wanted to join the Rowdies for the summer.

I didn't even know that he was down in Florida but he had joined as player-coach. The Rowdies played in the APSL [American Professional Soccer League], which was a new outdoor league. They were hoping to make it into another NASL but the standard was much lower.

My Tacoma contract was up but I was confident that I would get an indoor deal with someone, and I wasn't sure whether I wanted to go and play outdoor again. Mark said 'Come on, you'll be fine; I've got one player who has got a beer belly!'

I liked Florida, so I agreed to go and we all moved down to Tampa for the summer.

The Tampa Bay Rowdies had been one of the NASL's most glamorous and well-known clubs. Their best-known player had been Rodney Marsh who, after a four-year stint as General Manager for the Carolina Lightning, had returned to Tampa in 1983 as GM/Head Coach. Marsh remained part of the Rowdies organisation after the NASL collapsed, and by 1986 owned 24% of the club. Working closely with majority owner, Cornelia Corbett, he oversaw the Rowdies' entry into the American Soccer League in 1988 and, after a mediocre inaugural campaign, Marsh looked to the UK for a new Head Coach:

I was looking for the best possible people available — I wanted the late, great Bobby Moore to come but he wasn't very well by that time, and Mal-

217

colm Allison came for a little while but that didn't work out. I called Mark Lawrenson and, after a little persuasion, he agreed to come over for a year as player/coach.

The opportunity was an ideal fit for Lawrenson, who had retired from playing with Liverpool just a year earlier:

After I stopped playing, I had managed Oxford United but fallen out with the owner, Robert Maxwell. I was waiting to be paid off and knew that if I took a job in England, Maxwell wouldn't pay me what I was owed.

I was sitting at home and got a call from Rodney Marsh, who asked if I would play in a game in Tampa. I told him that I only had one leg because I had an Achilles injury, but he told me that I would be able to play over there standing on my head. I played and did OK, and Rodney asked if I would stay for six months as player/coach. I wasn't sure but decided that I would give it a go.

Marsh was keen to leave all player personnel decisions to his new Head Coach and, when Lawrenson approached him about signing Ward, arranged a meeting with Rowdies owner Cornelia Corbett to discuss the possible signing:

I knew of Peter Ward but it was Mark's suggestion that we sign him, so, in my role as GM, it was my responsibility to try to get a deal done.

Mark and I had a long conversation about Peter and we went out for lunch with Cornelia. It was a big move for us to go after Peter because he was a top-quality English player and was a big name in US football.

Mark said that Peter would be three things to the Rowdies: a quality performer on the pitch, a good influence in the dressing room and an excellent character to have at the club. All those things were true.

I knew that Peter had only played indoors for a few seasons but that didn't worry me because he is a 'box' player and, if anything, I thought that playing indoors would make him sharper. I was right, because when he arrived in Tampa, he was very sharp.

I think that if Peter hadn't been injured, he would have been the top goalscorer in the league.

◇　◇　◇

The ASL season started in April and, therefore, overlapped the MISL campaign by between one and two months. By the time Ward arrived in Tampa, following his play-off endeavours with Tacoma, the Rowdies had played 5 of their 20-game schedule.

218

The quality of the league was, in Marsh's words, 'similar to the old Third Division in England' and a team salary cap of $75,000 per season meant that the rewards on offer were way short of those available in the heyday of the NASL. To fit within the salary restrictions the majority of the players were part-time, and, for Lawrenson, this presented some unusual challenges:

It was so completely different from England — the players were part-time and we would train on Tuesday and Thursday nights.

We had three players who worked in a bank, and in those days, if you didn't balance your till at the end of the day you had to stay behind. So, most of the time, these lads would be late for training because they had been trying frantically to get their numbers right.

It was hard to get any professionalism into the team because the players were part-time. It wasn't their fault; it was just how the league was. We would be flying all over the East Coast and normally we would travel on the day of the game so that there were no hotel costs and people didn't miss work— it was unheard-of!

Rodney was great and the lady who owned the club, Cornelia Corbett, was fantastic: they did whatever they could to help.

Along with Ward, the Rowdies signed American international defender Steve Trittschuh and former Chelsea and Crystal Palace forward Tommy Langley. Langley's stay in Florida was over before Ward made his debut:

Tommy had arrived two weeks or so before me and played a couple of games. Then he went missing and it transpired that he had taken his family to Disney World for a couple of days. Rodney Marsh read him the riot act but in the next game, right at the start, Tommy ruptured a hamstring and his season was over. The club cancelled his contract and sent him home. I think they felt that if he had been training and had warmed up properly, he probably wouldn't have been injured.

Ward's first game, just two days after his arrival from Seattle, was a home match with Tampa's Floridian rivals, the Fort Lauderdale Strikers. A crowd of 5,624 at Tampa Stadium saw Ward set up Lawrenson for the first score of the game and then double the Rowdies lead with a debut goal. A third goal from Martin Hill completed a 3-0 victory for the Rowdies and capped a performance that Marsh hailed as "the best since I rejoined the Rowdies in 1983". Understandably weary, Ward was substituted after 70 minutes and received a standing ovation from the home supporters.

The following day, Tampa travelled to Orlando and lost 2-0 to the Lions with Ward, still getting used to the heat and exertion of the outdoor game, lasting just 60 minutes.

The Rowdies injury jinx struck again the following week, as Lawrenson tore the cartilage in his right knee. Marsh threatened to come out of retirement if any further players were forced to sit out.

Ward scored in victories over the Albany Capitals and the Boston Bolts, and got the only goal of the game as the Rowdies beat Miami in front of a bumper Independence Day crowd of 19,211: the largest in ASL history. The victory over Miami lifted Tampa Bay to the top of the Southern Division but was Ward's last appearance for a month:

> I was kicked on the side of the knee when we played Dallas and my leg started to stiffen up. It was still sore when we played Miami and after the game I couldn't straighten it at all.

> I saw the doctor and he told me that it was torn cartilage in my left knee. I had to have arthroscopic surgery and was out for 5 or 6 weeks. I had been playing professionally for 14 years and it was the most serious injury that I had.

Ward's injury kept him out of the final five regular season games but, without him, his teammates managed to secure the Southern Division title with a record of 12 wins and 8 defeats.

Ward returned for the semi-final play-off series with Boston, who had finished runners-up in the Northern Division. The two-game series started with a 2-0 victory for the Bolts in front of their own fans, leaving Tampa with the need to win Game 2 in order to force a deciding 30-minute mini-game.

Boston silenced the home crowd with an early goal, but a few minutes into the second half, Ward was fouled in the penalty area and Steve Wegerle scored the resulting spot-kick. With only four minutes remaining, Boston scored a decisive second goal and the season was over for Tampa Bay. Boston progressed to the Final but lost to Fort Lauderdale.

Ward's return to the outdoor game had produced a respectable four goals in eight starts and he finished as the Rowdies joint-second highest scorer, even though he played in less than half of the side's fixtures.

At the end of the summer, Mark Lawrenson called an end to his stay in Tampa:

> I'd had enough after six months. It was a great experience and I enjoyed it but it was very different — I needed to come home.

Ward returned to Seattle, hoping to agree another contract with the Tacoma Stars. Instead, he found himself in the middle of a feud between the Stars and their MISL rivals, the Wichita Wings.

◇ ◇ ◇

My contract had ended at Tacoma and I was a free agent. I could look for another team but if someone else offered me a contract, Tacoma would have first refusal on signing me if they could match the offer.

I had spoken to the LA Lazers at the end of the season and they had offered me really good money; I also received an offer from Wichita. Wichita weren't offering as much, but you could get a lot more for your money in Kansas than you could in California, so I decided to sign with the Wings. The Lazers went bust before the season started, so it was lucky that we hadn't all moved out there.

Tacoma had a chance to match Wichita's offer but they couldn't afford it - Alan Hinton told me that he was very sad that I was leaving and he wished me well. That was fine; there were no hard feelings and everything went quite smoothly.

That wasn't the case with Chris Vaccaro, though. He was a goalie who had played with Wichita the previous year but had signed for Tacoma at the same time that I went the other way. Wichita accused Tacoma of breaking the rules to sign him and there were lots of accusations flying around. Eventually, it went to arbitration and the league said that Tacoma hadn't done anything wrong so he joined with them.

I had played well against Wichita whilst I had been at Tacoma and scored quite a few game-winning goals against them. The papers in Wichita were calling me the 'Wings Killer.'

Ward's move to Wichita ended his five-year run of playing alongside Bernie James. James, a rugged defender, had been a teammate throughout Ward's spells at Cleveland and Tacoma and had become a very close friend:

Peter is one of my favourite guys — I can't say enough about him, a super guy. Everyone loved Pete: I didn't meet anyone who didn't like Peter Ward.

He was so quick and shifty, and could just turn you so easily and then you would never catch him — a tremendous player. He was very good at indoor but equally at good outdoor. I used to hate playing against him in the NASL.

I played against Georgie Best, Rodney Marsh, Johan Cruyff, and Pete was as good as any of them in the NASL: he was a really, really good player.

He was a pleasure to play with.

The Wings were coached by ex-English professional Terry Nicholl and their star player for the previous five seasons had been Erik Rasmussen - the team's all-time leading scorer. A couple of weeks after Ward signed for the Wings, Rasmussen announced that he was staying in Denmark to play in the Danish

First Division, which left the bulk of the goalscoring responsibility to Ward and his ex-Cleveland teammate Andy Chapman.

◇　◇　◇

In a mischievous twist of fate, the Wings opening game of the 1989-90 season was a visit from the team that they had spent most of the summer slinging mud at, the Tacoma Stars. The Stars bore little resemblance to the team of which Ward had been a major part during the previous season and included nine new faces in their line-up. League MVP Preki had re-signed for Tacoma but was injured and missed the first month of the season. One of Tacoma's new signings, goalkeeper Vaccaro, was given a far from friendly welcome from the Wichita fans, who roundly booed him every time he touched the ball.

It took Ward just fourteen minutes to put one over his old team and open the scoring. In an encouraging performance, Wichita controlled the game and were 3-1 up going into the final quarter. Two quick goals from Tacoma levelled the score and the game seemed destined for overtime, before Wichita's Chico Borja popped up with the winning goal with less than two minutes left on the clock.

Borja scored another game-winner four nights later against the Cleveland Crunch, who had entered the league to fill the gap left by the demise of the Cleveland Force. Apart from a change in name, the Crunch resembled their predecessors in many ways: playing out of the Richfield Coliseum, they were led by Kai Haaskivi in the role of player/coach and had also signed eight of his Force teammates.

The Wings' good start was undone by four defeats in the next five games but, as November made way for December, they went on a run of five consecutive victories — one short of a club record. The run took Wichita to the top of the Eastern Division but was ended by defeat in Tacoma.

On the morning of the Tacoma game, Ward was looking forward to a relaxing morning at the team hotel:

> The coach, Terry Nicholls, told us to meet in the hotel lobby at nine in the morning. I strolled down there a little bit early and got a coffee and a newspaper and took a seat. Terry came down at nine and said 'Right, let's go.' I asked him where he wanted to go and he said, 'For a run.' I thought he was joking - I had my flip-flops on and a hot cup of coffee so I stayed in the hotel while everyone else went for a run. He left me out of the first quarter of the game as a punishment.

> The Stars had just sacked Alan Hinton and it was the first match for the new coach, Keith Weller. They beat us quite easily, 6-3, and that started a bad run.

The loss to Tacoma was the first of six defeats in the next eight games as 1989 drew to a close. A couple of days before Christmas, the Wings players congregated for the team party. Surprisingly, Ward can still recall the night's events:

It was a big Christmas party and we had all been drinking since lunchtime. In the evening, all of the wives and girlfriends joined up with us and we had a shot-drinking contest. I came third with 24 shots!

Apparently, after the 21st, all hell had broken loose because, when I finished, I threw my glass at all the bottles behind the bar and the staff wanted to throw me out.

The morning after, Louisa came and woke me up —she was only four or five— and she said 'Daddy, Daddy, you didn't eat your pizza.' I didn't know what she was talking about but I looked down by the side of the bed and there was a perfectly round pile of vomit.

That morning, we had to go training: quite a few of the boys didn't make it and were fined. The coach said to me, 'Wardy, that's the most shots you've had all season.'

He was right too — I wasn't playing very well and didn't gel with some of the other players. I had picked up an infection in my elbow and that had kept me out of a couple of games too. Wichita were looking around to trade me and before the end of January they made a deal that sent me to Baltimore.

Ward and teammate Mike Stankovic joined division leaders Baltimore, while David Byrne and Keder went from the Blast to Wichita. There were mixed views on which team had got the better of the deal: San Diego coach, Ron Newman, suggested that because Ward, who was 34, and Stankovic, a battle weary 33, were nearing the end of their careers that Wichita had benefitted the most. Baltimore fans were delighted to see Stankovic back in Maryland. The Yugoslavian defender had been rewarded with five all-star selections during his first spell with the club and returned after two years in Wichita. As Ward remembers, the Blast supporters were a little more reluctant to give him such a warm welcome:

In my first game for Baltimore I got booed by my own fans when my name was read out over the PA system, because I had been a Cleveland player. They remembered me over-celebrating when I had scored against them a few years earlier. It took them a while to come 'round to me.

Baltimore were coached by Kenny Cooper, a Lancastrian who had played for ten seasons as Dallas Tornado's goalkeeper in the NASL. Cooper was keen to progress the trade once he had received a phone call from his Wichita counterpart suggesting the possibility of some sort of deal. The Blast coach was relieved to offload Byrne, who was rumoured to spend rather too much time at the horse racing track, and Keder, who had made little impact during the season. Stankovic's return gave the Blast a defensive enforcer and Ward would once again team up with good friend Carl Valentine, with whom he had played in both Vancouver and Cleveland.

◇ ◇ ◇

Leaving Wichita mid-season gave Ward and his family a dilemma; should they pack up en masse and move, or should Sue and the girls stay in Wichita while Peter found temporary accommodation in Baltimore? Sue recalls that not wishing to disrupt their daughters' schooling for the umpteenth time drove their decision:

> Wichita, Kansas was a little boring but we had just settled in and then Pete was traded to Baltimore. We decided that I would stay in Wichita because we didn't want to move the kids out of school again. Pete went to stay with Carl Valentine and his wife in Baltimore, which was over 1,200 miles away.

> The closest game to Wichita was Kansas City, which was still about a three hour drive. When Peter played against them, we all went to watch, although Louisa used to hate getting in her car seat, so it made the journeys quite a challenge.

> We didn't get to see much of him for the rest of that season and the girls did miss their dad. I would try to think of fun things to do to keep the girls busy, and to keep me busy, but it really could get lonely; sometimes he would be gone for four, five, six weeks.

Rachael Ward remembers her dad being gone for long periods:

> We hated it when Dad went away — we had a video of him playing and it had 'Eye of the Tiger' as a soundtrack and if he was away and we were sad, Mum would play that video so that we could see him. That song still reminds me of those days whenever I hear it.

◇ ◇ ◇

Four games into his Baltimore career, Ward welcomed the opportunity to face Wichita at the Baltimore Arena:

> I felt that I hadn't shown Wichita what I could do: it just wasn't the right place for me. They came to Baltimore and it was a very physical game. Stankovic gave David Byrne a real whack and also clobbered Andy Chap-

224

man — the crowd loved it. I scored a goal and had two assists and we won 7-4. It was an enjoyable game.

Ward scored again in the next game, a 7-1 victory at bottom of the division Cleveland, and was on target a week later in a 4-3 win at Dallas.

Six wins from ten games in March, including another victory over Wichita, put the Blast in pole position to claim the Eastern Division crown, going into the final month of the regular season. A victory over St. Louis on 13th April, which gave the Blast a 7-0 season sweep of the Storm, meant that victory over Wichita the following night would secure a second straight divisional championship for Baltimore. Ward remembers the trip to Kansas:

We travelled down to Wichita, knowing that we needed a win. I had been out for a few games because I needed more surgery on my knee but I was fit enough to play. It was a very close, low-scoring game but the 'Wings Killer' was back and I got the winning goal in our 2-1 victory. It was a sweet moment but I didn't feel any animosity towards the Wings. Their players and Terry Nicholl were very sporting afterwards.

Capturing the title afforded Baltimore the luxury of a bye in the first round of the play-offs. Their opponent in the semi-finals was Kansas City, who had been runners-up in the division and whose biggest threat came from Dutch striker Jan Goossens.

Although missing the injured Carl Valentine, Baltimore won the opening pair of home games. A 2-1 overtime victory in Kansas extended the Blast's lead and they looked to be cruising to the Finals. Games 4 and 5 both went to overtime and both ended in 3-2 victories for Kansas. Suddenly, Kansas were right back in the series and travelling to Baltimore for Game 6 with renewed hope.

That hope was soon squashed as Baltimore romped to a 7-2 victory and a second successive trip to the Finals where, once again, the San Diego Sockers stood between them and the MISL crown. While the majority of players from both sides had already experienced playing in the Finals, it had been a long time coming for Ward:

It was great to reach the Finals at last. We had got close when I was at Cleveland and, the year after I left, they managed to get to the Finals; the year before I joined Tacoma, they had reached the Finals, so it looked like I might always miss out.

San Diego had a great history of winning the Championship but we had finished with a better record than them and they were only runners-up in their division, so we thought we had a good chance.

Game 1 took place in Baltimore and, after a disastrous first half, the Blast recovered from 3-0 down to win 7-4. San Diego, the reigning champions, bounced back, winning the next three games; they were just one win away from their third straight MISL title. Ward and his teammates were well aware that another defeat would signal the end of their championship aspirations:

> *Winning Game 5 was vital and we played really well. We dominated the game, I scored a goal and we were 3-0 up with a few minutes to go. The Sockers got a couple of goals back at the end, and we were holding on, but we managed to see out the win which meant that the series was heading back to Baltimore.*

Unfortunately for Ward, Baltimore's Game 5 endeavours proved to be little more than a temporary hold-up in San Diego's march to the championship. A 6-4 win for the Sockers in Baltimore secured the series victory and San Diego's eighth indoor crown in nine years.

The defeat ended Ward's chance of securing the MISL title and also brought to an end his MISL career. Over six seasons, Ward had scored a staggering 212 goals at an average of over 35 per season, but he felt that the time was right to move on:

> *I had enjoyed a fantastic time playing in the MISL but the league was changing and it wasn't possible to make the same sort of money that you could a few years earlier.*

> *I had agreed to play for Tampa Bay Rowdies again during the summer but the league had ruled that each team could only have two players from the indoor league. Tampa had signed three and the other two — Perry Van der Beck and David Byrne — had played for teams which were knocked out of the indoor play-offs quite early on. Because Baltimore got through to the Finals, I was the last of the three to get back to Tampa, so I couldn't play.*

> *We decided that we would go back to England to see if I could get a club and, even though I was nearly 35, I was confident that I was still fit enough to play in the English league again. Kenny Hibbitt, with whom I had played at Seattle, had just become manager at Walsall in the Third Division and I trained with them for a few weeks and played a couple of games for their reserves.*

> *A couple of non-league teams made offers, and I needed to stay fit so I decided to join Hednesford Town who played in the Southern League. John Baldwin, who used to provide me with financial advice when I played in the States, was manager there and he set up the move. Cleveland still owned my registration and it was a real pain trying to get the paperwork through so that the FA would let me play in England again, but we got it sorted and I made by debut in October.*

Ward spent two months at Hednesford, starting six games and making a couple of substitute appearances. The stark contrast between playing Dudley Town away on a cold, wet Tuesday night in October and entertaining the Miami Freedom in 80 degrees of bright Florida sunshine proved too much for Ward:

> *I wasn't really enjoying it at Hednesford. They were good lads but the ball was up in the air all the time. I had got a couple of goals and they were having a good season — I think that they just missed out on promotion. They paid me decent money and I was grateful for the chance to play but after being back in England for a few months I was desperate to go back to America.*
>
> *I spoke to Rodney Marsh at Tampa again and he said that he'd like me back at the Rowdies for the 1991 season, which was to start in May. I couldn't wait to get back.*

Peter wasn't the only member of his family who was desperate to get on the plane back to Tampa, as Rachael explains:

> *It was really hard to come back to England. I went straight into the fourth year at school and everything was totally different. The TV show 90210 had just come out and because I had an American accent everyone thought I was one of these snotty Beverley Hills girls like on the show.*
>
> *I told my dad that I couldn't live there anymore and he said the same thing too. So we moved back to Tampa — Dad, Rebekah and me, and then, a few months later, after Louisa had finished school, she came back with my mum.*

◇ ◇ ◇

Back in Tampa, Ward signed a one-year deal that paid him $660 per game and also provided accommodation for him and his family. Since he had last played for the Rowdies, two years earlier, the American Soccer League had merged with its West coast equivalent, the Western Soccer League, to form the American Professional Soccer League. The Rowdies had finished second in the South Division with a record season —10 wins and 10 defeats— and then suffered a first round play-off defeat to Fort Lauderdale.

Following the end of the season, the Rowdies replaced head coach Ken Fogarty with Steve Wegerle, who had been a star player with the team during its heyday in the late 70s. Half a dozen players remained from Ward's previous spell and new faces included David Byrne, who had been part of the trade that took Ward from Wichita to Baltimore, ex-Manchester City forward Steve Kinsey and former Brentford defender Terry Rowe.

Two months before the season started, Rodney Marsh announced what he referred to at the time as "one of the most significant Rowdies signings ever": Peter Vermes, who was the US national team's captain and star striker. Unfortunately for both parties, the move was a disaster, as Marsh explains:

227

Peter Vermes came in and we thought he would be great. He turned out to be like a shop steward and didn't get on with the coach, Steve Wegerle, at all. He only played two or three games and then left by what they call 'mutual consent.'

With a number of new signings and a new head coach, who was the leading goalscorer in the history of the Rowdies, the signs were positive for the new season. Few, if any, observers would have anticipated the drought of goals that the team would suffer. Ward was not exempt from responsibility for the misfiring Rowdies:

We had a shocking season and just couldn't score. There were only five games where we scored more than once and we were shut out in eight games. I suffered along with everyone else — I scored in the second game of the season and then not again until the second-to-last match. The league had changed the rules too, so that if you won, you got more points for every goal you scored: that meant that scoring goals was even more important.

We only won three times in the first dozen games and we weren't playing badly, we were just missing our chances. I think our top scorer for the season ended up with four goals... terrible. We had some good players too; it was a really frustrating season.

With a late surge, the Rowdies managed to finish third in their five-team division but this was not enough for a place in the end-of-season play-offs.

Two weeks after the season ended, the team announced that Ward, Byrne and Kinsey were all being released. Ward wasn't surprised by the news:

About half a dozen games before the season ended, I had been substituted really early in the second half of a match and at that point, I got the feeling that my professional career was pretty much over.

You hope that you can go on forever but I was 36 years old and hadn't had a good season.

As your career draws to a close, you start to think about your future and it's not so easy once you stop being involved in the game.

Rodney Marsh was sorry to see Ward leave the Rowdies:

I thought that Peter was fantastic and that he was first class, all the way through. The decision not to renew Peter's contract would have been Steve Wegerle's — it was always down to the coaches. I wouldn't get involved in the personnel decisions.

CHAPTER 19

Peter Ward – ex-professional Footballer

*We struggled for three years and I would guess that I
lost around $100,000 in the pub. The other guys knew
less about running a bar than I did!*

— Peter Ward

Reflecting on her dad's playing days and the impact that his regular absence from the family home had on their relationship, Peter's daughter Rebekah is full of praise:

> *When I was young, he was the best dad ever, even though he would be away
> a lot. He would never be able to come to my plays or dance recitals because
> he would be playing or training — which sucked at the time, but we were
> still really close.*

> *Parents' Day and Career Day at school were cool, although I would get em-
> barrassed and asked my dad why he didn't have a normal job with a brief-
> case and suit. I would have to go in to school with his soccer kit on, which
> the other kids thought was cool.*

> *I think that when Dad stopped playing, he didn't know what to do with
> himself. For all of his life he had played soccer — that's all he did, all he
> talked about and all he got excited about.*

> *When he was in the real world he didn't really have any skills to fall back on
> and did lots of odd jobs. I think that changed him as a person: he wouldn't
> get the recognition, which must have been strange for him.*

◇　◇　◇

Unlike today's Bentley-collecting, diamond-encrusted Premier League players, very few professional footballers from the 70s and 80s managed to achieve financial security during their playing days. Stories of huge debts, financial ruin and bankruptcy are commonplace amongst the biographies of big name players from football's ironically named 'golden years'. Whilst Peter Ward fortunately did not reach the same financial depths as some of his co-

229

horts, attempting to carve out a living post-football proved to be an arduous challenge which, ultimately, had a cataclysmic effect on his family:

> If you look through my old contracts you would think that I should have money, but nearly everyone I played with still works. I earned good money but it isn't like it is now. We put the girls through private school and lived in nice houses but once you stop playing it gets a lot more difficult.

When Peter hung up his boots, his first wife, Sue, received some rather prophetic advice from the wife of another ex-player:

> A friend had told me that when it comes to the end of their playing days, your relationship can go either way: you will either have a great time or you'll split up. I think that I understand now. The adulation has gone, and the support has gone and you think 'Well, now what?'

For a few weeks after finishing with the Rowdies, Ward kicked his heels around the house - which he recalls as being 'very stressful for everyone' - before looking for something to occupy his time:

> I tried a few things. I was a salesman for a while, selling funeral plots to old folk, but they wanted me to be really aggressive to get a sale and I just couldn't do it. I also worked with a friend of mine, Jimmy Knowles, who ran a company that installed fountains and swimming pools. Jimmy was great and his dad, who unfortunately died a couple of years ago, was really funny. He used to tell me a story of how he boxed in the Army and that he was the first of the boxers to get sponsored: he said that because he got knocked out so many times, Coca-Cola used to pay him to put adverts on the bottom of his boots.

> Then I went and worked at Bern's Steak House, which is one of the premier steak restaurants in the US. A friend of mine who played for the Rowdies, Kokie [Refik Kozic], worked there and he said that some of the waiters were making $140,000 a year. They wouldn't get paid wages — instead, they got 12% of the bill — but people would spend a lot of money on their dinner and tip really heavily.

> So I went there and trained to become a waiter. Normally it takes 15 months but I completed the training in 10. Just as I was getting ready to start, though, I was offered an opportunity to buy into a pub.

Ward wasn't the first or the last ex-footballer to chance their arm at running a pub and, like many, fail. As Sue recalls, the choice to become involved in a pub, the Scotland Yard, created problems from day one:

> That is a bit of a sore point. Peter wanted to buy into the pub and I didn't. The kids were still young and it would mean long hours.

230

We had thought about buying an ice-cream shop in St. Petersburg that one of his teammates had owned, but we had already put down a deposit on a house in Tampa and getting the kids to and from school and working in St. Petersburg wouldn't really work.

I thought the pub would be our downfall, and it was.

Rebekah has similar memories:

Getting the pub turned our whole life upside down.

While Dad had been playing, money had never been an issue, although we weren't at all spoilt. They decided to go into business and I think Dad made the decision to go for the pub.

At first it was cool; I could take my friends, we could play pool, have as much soda as we wanted — it was a novelty.

But then things started to happen and I could see a shift in my parents' relationship.

Rebekah's older sister, Rachael concurs:

That's when everything started to go rocky. I was about 16 and still in high school. They had a choice between the pub and an ice cream store in St Petersburg.

My mum didn't want the pub but Dad decided to do it. Dad would be gone a lot and it wasn't a great situation. I wish he'd never got the pub, but maybe that was what was supposed to happen.

Ward looks back at the Scotland Yard years and wonders how things went so wrong:

I didn't have any idea about running a bar but I needed a job. I knew the guys who owned it and I bought a share in the business.

We struggled for three years and I would guess that I lost around $100,000 in the pub. The other guys knew less about running a bar than I did!

The pub is long gone: it's a drug store now.

By the time that Ward's involvement with the Scotland Yard came to an end, his marriage was over and his relationship with his children had disintegrated.

With her parents at loggerheads, Rebekah had decided to remove herself from the situation:

Rachael and I were going to private school and I thought that we wouldn't be able to carry on if Mum and Dad got divorced, so I went to my mum one day and said 'I'm moving to England' and three weeks later I did. I

231

went and lived with my nan and finished school in England. I came back to
Florida two years later, when I was 17.

Sue and youngest daughter, Louisa, soon followed Rebekah to England,
but Rachael stayed with her dad:

> I stayed in Tampa through the whole divorce; it was very hard. Bekah
> moved to England and then Mum moved over to England with Louisa. I
> was 18 and living my dad but we hardly ever saw each other. My sisters
> had gone and my mum had gone and in some ways it felt like my dad had
> gone too.

Reflecting on the break-up of his marriage, Ward regrets the turmoil that
resulted:

> It was hard but I had to leave. I was not in love and I'd had enough of the
> marriage. I moved out in '93 and we got divorced in '94.

> Rebekah, Louisa and Sue all went back to England. It was tough with the
> girls being so far away — it was difficult for everyone. After a year or so,
> they came back, which was great, but the older girls were both understand-
> ably angry with me. It has taken a while to rebuild my relationship with
> them.

> I had met Jackie [Ward's second wife] before I was divorced. The girls say
> that I left their mother for Jackie and in some ways that is true, but in other
> ways it isn't. They blame Jackie but it wasn't her fault; she wanted to get
> rid of me but I kept pursuing her.

> I had wanted out of the marriage for a while but I never did anything about
> it — typical me. I should have moved out sooner, before I had met someone
> else.

> I think I did the right thing — I had to get out. I'm sure that people thought
> that Jackie and I would just have a fling but we've been married for seven
> years now.

Although the Scotland Yard created many more problems than it solved,
one positive aspect for Ward was organising the pub's soccer team:

> We played in an amateur league and were one of the best teams. We had a
> few guys who had played for the Rowdies and although we were older than
> most of the other teams we would normally win. We also had an Over-30
> team and we won the State Finals every year for quite a few years.

There was a team from St. Petersburg, the Kickers, who were the only team that would always beat us in the league. They took it more seriously than we did and had some good players — they were generally a bit younger than we were. We would normally be in the game until the last 20 minutes and then our legs would go and they would get a goal and win.

One time, we decided to change our tactics and played with two sweepers, a back four, three midfielders and just me up front. They had most of the possession but couldn't break us down. We had a couple of chances but hit the bar and the post, and it was goalless with ten minutes to go. Just before the end I got the ball on the halfway line, went past three of their players and scored! It was brilliant: we won 1-0 — the first time that we had beaten them.

The Scotland Yard football team was a victim of the closure of the pub, but it didn't take Ward long to get set-up with another team:

When the pub folded I went and joined the Kickers. Their coach is a guy called Steve Gogas, who used to own a Greek restaurant. I knew him quite well and he'd always been niggling at me to try to get me to join his team.

With the Kickers, I won a couple of Amateur National Over-30 Championships. It would be quite funny because, although we wanted to win, we all knew how to enjoy ourselves, while a lot of the other teams were really serious. During the warm-up, a couple of our players would just stand on the touchline smoking a cigarette as the opposition were doing all their stretches and warm-up routines.

After the games, we would get these big beer coolers and sit around having a few beers, singing songs — it was great fun. The other teams would get really annoyed because they couldn't understand how we could drink so much and still go out and play really well, but some of us had spent the last 15 years doing that!

In 1995, I started to play in the Over-40 team and we got through to the National Finals again. We progressed to the Championship game and, the night before the match, we all went out for a few beers. We got back to the hotel just after midnight and a few of the players from the team we were up against were sitting in the hotel playing chess and drinking milk. They looked at us as if to say 'You've got to be kidding' but we went out the next day and beat them.

We had fun but we also had talent. Mark Lindsay, who had played at Crystal Palace and then in the NASL for a long time, played on our team and so did Mike Connell, who had spent 10 years with the Rowdies. When we went to the Nationals I would get Fran O'Brien, with whom I'd played at Vancouver, to play for us too. We could all play — if you can control and pass the ball you don't have to run around all over the place. Plus, if we needed a goal, I could get one.

It wasn't all laughs, mind you. We had played this team from St. Louis two years in a row in the semi-final of the Nationals; we'd both won our Regions and they beat us both times, although we were the better team and should really have beaten them. The third year we played them in the Final and it was the first time that we'd made the final for a few years. Just after half-time, the ball went out of play near the benches and I went to fetch it. Their coach, this old fella, stands up right in front of the ball so I just pushed him out of the way to get the ball and take the throw-in. The linesman starts flagging so I said 'What are you flagging for?' He said, 'I'm going to get you a card for that', I said 'For what?' and he replied 'for pushing their coach'. I told him to get lost and the ref came over and gave me a red card! I couldn't believe it.

We won after overtime and penalties. The organisers apologised at the end of the game, saying that I shouldn't have been sent off. I was the captain, so when I went up to get the trophy I went past the linesman and ref and told them where to go.

That was a great tournament, the first time we'd beaten them in three years, and it was in the Final so it was sweeter. That was in Portland, which was a six- or seven-hour flight. We would travel further than they do in the Premier League or the Champions League!

Ward's coach, Steve Gogas, regarded Ward as a hugely important member of the team:

Peter was fantastic. He was my coach on the field... a quarterback, a play-maker. I didn't have to say anything when Peter was on the pitch.

He gave us lots of great moments. One year in the Nationals, we had got through to the Finals but we had played three games during the weekend and Peter's knee was too sore for him to play in the Final. The game was tied and heading to penalties. I asked Peter if he would be able to take a penalty and he said that he could. So I made a substitution and bought Peter on. Two minutes into time added on, he got the ball, broke away and scored the winning goal. I couldn't believe it.

Off the pitch he was the funniest person: always joking, always making people happy.

◇ ◇ ◇

At the end of 1996, 41 years old, Ward made a surprise return to professional soccer. The National Professional Soccer League had emerged as the dominant professional indoor league in the aftermath of the MISL's collapse in 1992. Coached by Kenny Cooper, the Tampa Bay Terror had joined the league in 1995 and finished second from bottom in the seven-team American Division. Following a close season reshuffle, the league split onto four divisions with Tampa competing with Harrisburg, Baltimore and Philadelphia in the East Division.

The Terror's GM at the time was Steven Powell, who, ten years earlier, had been a keen admirer of Ward from the packed terraces of Brighton's Goldstone Ground. Powell recalls Ward's arrival at the Terror:

> At Tampa, we were chasing our second straight appearance in the play-offs, but lost a couple of key forwards to injuries. The club was very poorly funded and we were unable to purchase another player or to offer any other long-term contracts for new players through a trade. I proposed that we bring Peter Ward back out of retirement for the remainder of the season.

> Peter had been a tremendous indoor player at the end of his career and he didn't disappoint for us in Tampa. His legs didn't move as quickly, we had to limit his time on the pitch to avoid injury and assist with recovery, but his eye for goal, close ball control and vision was unequalled by any of his teammates, who were mostly 15-20 years his junior.

> Peter's influence on the side was huge. I was so impressed that I actually tried to talk the president of my next club, the Tampa Bay Mutiny of Major League Soccer, into hiring Peter as a coach for our forwards.

> I haven't seen Peter for many years since leaving that team and joining the MLS, but it was a joy for someone from East Sussex who spent many an afternoon on the terraces at the old Goldstone Ground to see the re-birth of a club legend.

For Ward, the chance for an unexpected return to the professional game was a real bonus:

> I had talked to the Terror the year before but we couldn't work out a deal, so it was a surprise when I got a call from Kenny Cooper, who had been my coach at Baltimore.

> They needed help, so we had a meeting and I agreed to sign.

> On the day of my debut, there was a warm-up exhibition game featuring an ex-Rowdies team, so loads of guys whom I knew were playing in that. They stayed behind to watch the Terror game and gave me a great big cheer when my name was announced.

> I scored twice in the first quarter and all the Rowdies boys were going crazy — it was quite funny. The goals were bigger than they used to be — which helped — and the scoring had changed so they gave more points for a goal outside of the box and even more for a really long-range goal.

I was 41, playing with all these young lads, and I was really enjoying it. I was still fit from playing amateur but training every day again was just great fun.

Part-way through the season, Kenny stopped coaching and started to work more on the business side of the club; Perry Van der Beck took over as coach and I helped him.

We went up to Cleveland to play the Crunch and I got a fantastic ovation when my name was announced before the game. The other Tampa players couldn't believe it — it was unbelievable.

Unfortunately, we didn't make the play-offs and, at the end of the season, the club hit financial problems. They were talking about relocating the team and I would have carried on if it was somewhere close but it didn't happen.

When the Terror folded, Ward looked to make a quick return to his amateur side, the Kickers. To Ward's frustration, the Amateur Soccer Association had a different idea:

I tried to register again for the Kickers but the league told me that I had to wait a year because I had been playing professionally again. It was ridiculous — the rule was there to stop people playing ringers in important games but I was 42 years old! I had to go and explain my situation and, luckily, common sense prevailed and they let me play. I've been playing with the Kickers ever since, although I only come on for a few minutes at a time now... time catches up with you.

In December 2006, it looked like Ward's playing days were finally drawing to a close; a long-overdue operation to replace his right knee with a titanium joint was looming. There was a chance that his final game before entering hospital would be his last and Louisa Ward made a three-and-a-half-hour trip to pay a surprise visit:

I was at college in Jacksonville but I knew that the game might be Dad's last so I wanted to come down to see him play. I drove to Tampa and he was really surprised to see me — it was a really nice evening.

In typical Ward fashion, a late cameo appearance was enough for a match-winning performance:

I was playing for the regular team, not the over-40s, and they were all young, fast and fit. I was sub and we were losing 1-0. I came on with 20 minutes to go and scored twice with my left foot. We won 2-1 — you wouldn't believe it, you couldn't write the script, unbelievable.

Kickers' coach, Steve Gogas, remembers the game well:

Peter called me and asked if he could play. He told me that he was going in for his operation and wanted to play one last game. I was worried that he would get hurt but he was adamant that he would be ok.

When he came on, he could hardly walk, yet within two minutes he had scored and a few minutes later he scored again. At the end of the game, we had to carry him off the pitch because his knee was so stiff.

A few months after from his operation, Ward was playing again and still turns out for the Kickers on the odd occasion. He also participates in an annual Rowdies alumni game:

Now I'm 54: I think that's about it.

There is a Rowdies alumni game every year and I play in that. Mike Connell and I are the only ones who ever score for us in that game. Mark Lindsay missed a penalty in last year's game but nobody else had the energy to take it! We play in the afternoon before a college game at USF [University of South Florida] and it's bloody hot.

I played in the Over-50 State this year and we got to the semi-final. I scored twice in the quarter-finals and we won 3-1, but near the end of the game I tweaked my hamstring. In the semi-final I could hardly run and we lost 2-1.

The most important and enjoyable thing is having a pint after the game.

CHAPTER 20

COACH WARD

> Dad made a speech at the team dinner in front of a
> roomful of people and it was very emotional. He was crying,
> I was crying — it was an awesome day. He told everyone
> how great I play and things that I wouldn't normally hear him
> say. It was a day that I'll never forget.
>
> – Louisa Ward

As Director of Training at Tarpon FC, Peter Ward spends every evening, from Monday to Thursday, coaching boys and girls from the age of 11 to 17. Ward first started coaching in 1992, when he had just finished with the Rowdies, and helped to run the Commitment to Excellence soccer camps with fellow Tampa Bay players Perry Van der Beck and Winston Dubose:

> The soccer camps were great fun — there would be kids aged from 6 right up to 18 and the course would last a week. The day would start at 9 and end at 4, and we'd have a couple of hours for lunch when we'd normally go for a swim in the pool. I loved coaching the kids; it's great to be out on the field and seeing them all learn different skills.

> I coached with West Pasco Thunder for a while and then went to Northdale Rangers with Adrian Bush, who is now head coach at the University of Tampa. Northdale merged with the Tampa Bay Kickers, where Perry Van der Beck was coaching. That was a great team and the same group of players won the Under-13, Under-14 and Under-15 State Championships in consecutive years.

> We took the kids to play against a team from Minnesota and their coach got really annoyed with me and called me an idiot. He came over and said that it was obvious that I had never played the game. I was sitting with Perry and I asked this coach if he had ever played; he was very pleased with himself and said 'Yeah, I played in the NASL', so Perry replied 'Actually, he (pointing at me) was MVP of the NASL'. The other coach went very quiet and walked away.

Whilst with Northdale, Peter and Jackie took four of his players on a trip to England for three weeks of training with the Brighton youth team:

> For the first two or three days of training it was hard for the boys, but after a while you wouldn't have known they were any different than the English lads.

While we were over, we went to see Man United against Arsenal in the Charity Shield at Wembley. We went up on the train from Brighton and it was packed with Man United supporters. I was recognised by some United fans and they took us to a United pub in Kilburn. They were singing all the time, the boys couldn't believe it, walking up Wembley Way when they were 16; they'll never forget that experience. Liam Brady had arranged the tickets for us and the only trouble was that we were in the Arsenal end!

United had just won the treble and Teddy Sheringham was waving his arms, conducting the Arsenal fans as they were singing 'Oh Teddy, Teddy! You went to Man United but you're still a c***! Oh Teddy, Teddy!'

One of the lads was Ricky Corbett, who is the son of the Rowdies owner Cornelia Corbett. He ended up breaking his cheek bone in a practice game on the last day; his mum flew over and they had to stay in Brighton to get it sorted out.

Apart from that, the trip was a real success and we did the same thing with some other lads the next year.

◇ ◇ ◇

In 2001, Ward started coaching at Tampa Catholic High School, a position which he held for the next seven years:

The official head coach was a teacher called Chris Meyer who was a really nice guy. He would do all of the admin and organising and I would take training and pick the team. It was actually the parents of the kids who paid for my position, so that I could give Chris a hand.

I remember that on my first day, I was trying really hard not to swear in front of the kids because it was a religious school and I wanted to make a good impression. After training, one of the players, who also played for me at Northdale, came up to me and said 'Coach, you're very quiet. It's alright, you can f*****g swear!'

Chris and I worked well together and in the first year we got to the State Finals. After that, the school started to pay me rather than the parents. I was incredibly busy because I had got a job at Continental Airlines and I was still coaching my club team. At Continental, I started off full-time but went to part-time when given the chance a couple of years later. I'm on COLA (company offered leave of absence) at the moment and hoping that I'll be offered a redundancy package over the next year or two.

When I was at Tampa Catholic, I would spend the mornings at work, then go to the school and then, in the evening, take training at the Kickers.

239

Sometimes, I would have to get games rearranged so that I didn't have a clash between the school and my club.

Eventually, Chris left and they invited me to be head coach but I just couldn't spend enough time there. It was strange, because I wasn't paid wages; they would just give me one cheque at the end of the year.

During his stint at Tampa Catholic, Ward changed club teams and left the Kickers for Hillsborough County United (HC United):

HC United were the biggest club in the region and had a lot of ex-pros involved with the coaching. I was one of the coaches of a girls' team and we won three State titles. It was an impressive club and parents would travel a long way so that their kids could play for us. We had one girl who would come from Miami and one who came down from Pensacola in a private jet every weekend!

Another of my Under-11 teams at HC United won the Regionals and we had a fullback who could take a free kick from inside his own half and put it in the top corner: he was incredible.

Parents pay from around $650 a year to $1500 for their kids to play and there is one team in Texas that charge parents $1,000 just to have their children try out. In the year in which we went to the Regional Finals with the Under-14 side it must have cost the parents about $10,000 because we won the Jefferson Cup in Washington, we won a cup in Raleigh, Durham and we went to Jacksonville too. The parents were paying for flights and hotels for themselves and their kids. We were ranked in the top 15 in the country: we had a fantastic team.

It is always difficult to balance between being competitive and making sure the kids are having fun. After we had got to the Regional Finals about eight of the team left because their parents thought we were too competitive and taking it too seriously. Two or three of the players went to a team that we'd twice beaten 9-0!

In 2007 I also started to do some coaching at another club, Tarpon. Mike Connell, with whom I'd played at the Rowdies, was involved with Tarpon and when he found out that they needed a new trainer, he arranged a meeting. I met the club organisers and that was it. Tarpon are one of the premier clubs on Florida's west coast and are the only club with which I am now involved. I train each one of their teams once a week and then coach two teams — one boys, one girls — on the weekends. I love it! The best part is watching the players develop.

◇ ◇ ◇

Peter's youngest daughter, Louisa, was a frequent companion for him at evening soccer training and soon started to display some skills of her own:

> *I first played soccer when I went back to England and I would join in with the boys at school. When we moved back to Tampa I played in high school and then I started to hang around at HC United when Dad took training.*
>
> *I started off as a forward but, when one of the seniors at High School was injured, I had a chance to play in defence and I loved it: I've played there ever since. At HC United, I joined the girls team and we were a strong side.*
>
> *I got a scholarship to go and play at Jacksonville University and had a fantastic time there. Dad would come to most home matches and I think that in my senior year, he made it to every home game. It meant a lot to me that he came.*
>
> *It takes about three and a half hours to drive from Tampa, so it was quite a trip. I played better when he was there — even though it did put a little more pressure on me. After games he would pick me up like a baby; that was like our trademark.*
>
> *When I was younger, Dad would take me to school and we would skip to the classroom — which I used to love. We would spend a lot of time together. Having soccer meant that we stayed very close and if I had any problems to do with soccer I would talk to him.*
>
> *For my final game at college, they have a Senior Day where they honour the players who are in their final year. Dad made a speech at the team dinner in front of a roomful of people and it was very emotional. He was crying, I was crying — it was an awesome day. He told everyone how great I play and things that I wouldn't normally hear him say. It was a day that I'll never forget.*

Peter had attempted to encourage Louisa's older sisters to play but neither was too keen on taking instructions from their dad, as Rachael recalls:

> *Bekah and I tried to play when we were younger. Dad was coaching us and I was in goal and he was saying 'do this and do that' and I was like 'Forget it!' and I walked off the field and never played again.*
>
> *Bekah was the same: she played a little bit and then thought it wasn't worth the hassle and quit too!*

Peter remembers Rachael's soccer career lasting a little longer but ending painfully:

> *I helped coach the team at Rachael's high school for the last two years she was there. She was sub on the boys' team and in one games she actually scored two goals — which was a miracle! In her last game she got squashed*

*between two boys from the other side and broke her leg — she didn't play
again after that.*

Peter was grateful that Louisa's soccer skills gave her an opportunity to at-
tend college ("We couldn't have afforded it otherwise") and enjoyed watching
his daughter play:

*When Louisa was playing, I used to sit away from the other players' parents
because they would drive me nuts. I normally wouldn't say anything when
she was playing — I wasn't one of these parents who spend the whole game
shouting instructions. Although when she was playing fullback, sometimes
I would sit close to the sidelines and, if she was marking someone, I would
say "Killlllllllllllll" in a low voice which would put a big smile on her face.*

*When she was playing in High School, she messed something up and I
shouted 'What was that?' She wasn't having it, though, and shouted back
'Shut up Dad!' which made everyone laugh.*

*In High School, they won their District to get to the Regional Finals. Lou-
isa's team were playing at home and they had to win; it went to penalties
and Louisa was taking the last one. I was more nervous for her than I ever
was when I played, but she slotted it in the corner and I ran over to her — it
was a great moment.*

*At her last High School game, her team were hanging on just before the end
of the match and one of the other team's players, who was a big girl, clobbered into Louisa when she was protecting the ball. When Louisa got up she
pushed this girl away and the ref thought that Louisa had punched her and
sent Louisa off. Louisa kept saying 'I didn't touch her' but we looked at the
video afterwards and you could see that Louisa had punched her right on
the chin - It was a great punch!*

Following her graduation in 2008, Louisa and Peter took part in a mixed
six-a-side tournament and proved to be quite a team:

*This was the first time that I had played with Dad on an actual team; we
scored nearly all the goals, it was great fun. We had a real connection and
he kept setting me up to score.*

Unfortunately, the tournament ended in an unsatisfactory manner for the
Wards, as Peter explains:

*The team was Louisa and me, Kokie and his daughter Marsha, another
friend, Johnny, and a couple of other guys. Johnny is 58, Kokie is 59 and
I'm 53 and we were playing against kids in their 20s.*

*We had to have two girls on the pitch at any time and we only had Louisa
and Marsha, who is about 30. The girls worked their butts off.*

*If a girl scored you got two goals and Louisa was doing really well. We got through to the semi-finals and we were winning 3-2. With about five minutes left, the ref made a bad call and Marsha shouted "You've got to be f****** kidding, ref!" and she got sent off. We were disqualified because we only had one girl. Marsha's sister-in-law was in the stands and she was originally on our roster to play but the ref wouldn't let her join in because she wasn't signed in at the start of the game.*

*Louisa was going nuts and telling some of the men to 'F*** off!' I went up to the ref after the game and said 'You know, I've played all over the world and you are the biggest twat I've ever had referee a game.' We've been banned from that tournament now.*

It was great playing together and Louisa really enjoys it. One of the goals she scored was a cracker: a volley right in the top corner — a real Wardy goal!

CHAPTER 21

HOME IN TAMPA

When I first went to England with Pete, I couldn't believe the
amount of recognition he would get... Seeing how much love
the Brighton fans have for him is wonderful.

— Jackie (Mrs Wardy) Ward

On 22nd June, 2002, Ward married Jacqueline (Jackie) Cagnina in Tampa.
Fifteen years Ward's junior, Jackie chose the date for its significance to her family:

> That day was picked because my grandparents were married on the same
> date, and my parents were also married on June 22nd.
>
> Pete and I had lived together for six years and he proposed to me on my
> 30th birthday. He had arranged a surprise party with our closest friends
> and family, at a restaurant nearby which was owned by his soccer coach,
> Steve Gogas. At the end of the night he had the waiter place the engagement
> ring inside my champagne glass.
>
> They were saying 'Come on Jackie, down it' and I remember I kept saying to
> them 'You don't down champagne, you sip champagne!' I didn't have a clue
> that it was there until one of our friends accidently knocked the glass out of
> my hand and the last of the champagne and the ring hit the floor.
>
> I saw the ring right before it landed on the floor and then my mouth
> dropped open... Pete kneeled down (on his good knee) and asked me to mar-
> ry him. That was one of the best moments of my life.

Before the big day, the soon-to-be-married pair visited the church to discuss
arrangements with the Monsignor. As Ward recalls, it look a little while to get
round to discussing the wedding:

> Monsignor Higgins was very well known in Tampa and was a huge sports
> fan. In his office, there were loads of photos on the walls of him with differ-
> ent sporting celebrities. He welcomed us in and then all he wanted to do
> was talk about soccer. We chatted about the Rowdies and my other teams for
> about twenty minutes before Jackie finally interrupted and reminded us that
> we had the small matter of the wedding to arrange!

Luckily for Peter, Jackie was already becoming used to the fact that football would often be the first, and frequently only, topic of conversation when Peter walked into a room:

I like sports and know how important they are to people. My Godfather, Mel, and my Aunt Virginia used to take me to see the Rowdies when I was little. I have a photo of me sitting on Rodney Marsh's knee when I was about five years old — Pete got Rodney to sign that for me a few years ago.

Before we were married, Pete got invited to play in a veteran's All-Star game. Pete, Louisa and I were flown to Cleveland, picked up in a limo and stayed at the wonderful Renaissance Hotel. They couldn't have done more for us. Pete loved meeting up with all his old friends and there was a private party at the Rock and Roll Hall of Fame on one night and a special ball on another — we had a great time.

When I first went to England with Pete, I couldn't believe the amount of recognition he would get. We would get stopped in the street by people who wanted his autograph or a photo, and it got to a stage that whenever I am in Brighton now I put a marker pen in my handbag so that Pete can use it to sign autographs.

It isn't a pain; we enjoy it and seeing how much love the Brighton fans have for Pete is wonderful. I also found out that being 'Peter Ward' also helps if you need a restaurant to stay open a little later or a free cab ride!

Peter's legacy at Brighton has continued to benefit him, though it's been over 25 years since he last played for the club. One example of this came when he received a message from his boss at Continental instructing him that he needed to travel to Philadelphia at short notice:

I thought that I was in trouble about something, but I couldn't work out what it could be. Instead I ended up having a really nice couple of days and then receiving the gift of a wonderful honeymoon - all paid for.

Philadelphia-based Brighton fan Michael Boult explains the story:

The Goldstone was my cathedral when I was younger — the Albion was a very big part of my life and Peter was my hero. I worked for British Caledonian and relocated to the States twenty or so years ago.

One of my friends over here is Eric Henderson, who worked at Continental Airlines, and whose dad had been the owner of the Cleveland Force. One day Eric and I were talking about who had been our heroes when we were younger and when I mentioned Peter Ward, Eric said 'Oh I know him, I've just hired him at Continental.' After commenting on what a strange set of coincidences that was, we ended the conversation.

Sometime later, Eric invited me out for dinner to celebrate my birthday. When I got there, there was a little guy standing with Eric at the bar: I didn't immediately recognise him but then I realised that it was Peter Ward — I couldn't believe it! Eric had flown him up from Tampa as a surprise for me. I was speechless. I had a fantastic night - we just talked and talked.

As a thank you to Peter for making the trip, and for putting up with me for a couple of days, Eric used his travel industry contacts to organise Peter and Jackie's honeymoon trip to Venice.

The honeymoon in Venice definitely had the wow factor for Jackie:

We stayed at the Hotel Gritti Place on the Grand Canal. It was absolutely amazing: more of a palace than a hotel. The hotel is often used by kings and queens, presidents and prime ministers, so it was a real privilege to stay there.

◇ ◇ ◇

With Tarpon FC occupying Ward's weekends and four evenings a week, Friday is his only day off and is usually spent on the golf course:

I have a great group of friends and usually three or four of us will go out and play a round of golf on a Friday afternoon. It is usually bright sunshine and we'll drive golf carts around the course and take a few cold beers with us. It's the only day on which I get to wind down and a great way to end the week.

I also watch the football in the pub with the same group of lads. There are three Englishmen: Big Al Mcleod, who is a United fan; Ray Hales, who supports Millwall; George Clamp, who is a Brummie; and one American guy, Steve Deal, who we call "the honorary Englishman" because he loves anything that is English.

They are a great bunch and we really enjoy each other's company.

Ward's coaching commitments, coupled with his reluctance to leave his beloved Great Danes, Mia and Xena, for too long, mean that trips to the UK are not as frequent as he, or Jackie, would like. Although Tampa is very much home for the Wards, Peter doesn't rule out a more long-term return to the UK at some point:

I love it in Florida and would find it hard to leave this weather behind, but Brighton still feels like home when I go back to the UK. At the end of 1993, I had a phone call from the Albion and they invited me to apply for the manager's job. I sent them my details but didn't hear anything back and then they appointed Liam Brady. That would have been interesting and I think that I would have added a few thousand to the gate again.

I went back for the opening game at Withdean in '99, and again for the Centenary Dinner in 2001. I also played in Kerry Mayo's testimonial game in 2007 and scored a penalty. Before that game, I met Steve Foster and Jimmy Case for a drink and was amazed that they could still run around after the number of beers they had between them — they are a really funny pair.

Being involved with the Robert Eaton fund is also rewarding and I hope to keep being part of that as long as I am invited.

When the new stadium opens at Falmer I would love to go back again and have thought about getting a job there as a hospitality host. I think that I would miss the sun too much but who knows…

◇ ◇ ◇

…Back to the Robert Eaton Memorial Fund match at Lewes, May 2009.

For the sixth year in a row, it's a victory for Brighton. And what of Peter Ward's penalty? Well, of course…

He Shot, He Scored.

INDEX